DEMOCRACY IN INDIA

DEMOCRACY IN INDIA

K.P. Karunakaran

INTELLECTUAL BOOK CORNER
NEW DELHI

Published by :
Intellectual Book Corner
23, Daryaganj, Pratap Gali,
New Delhi-110002

Printed at :
S.A. Composing Agency
W.P. 581 WAZIRPUR (*Ashok Vihar*)
Delhi-110052

PREFACE

The aim of the book is to examine the sources of strength of Indian democracy.

The first chapter deals with the legacy of the Indian nationalist movement. It is felt that the vitality of democracy in the country can, to some extent, be attributed to it.

The working of the political system of independent India is the theme of the second chapter. Here again the focus is on the roots democracy took in a soil which was not apparently very favourable to it.

The major challenges the system faced since India became free are dealt in the subsequent chapter. At first it was from the extremist right and then it came from extreme left. Indian democracy responded to them positively and gradually these political forces were brought to the national stream.

Then came the most formidable threat to Indian democracy. This was from the centre itself. Mrs. Indira Gandhi and the Congress government headed by her were its symbols. This is discussed at length in the chapter on Authoritananism. Unlike those who made the challenges to Indian democracy earlier, the Congress Party did not raise any ideological questions. But as its political base was strong, its challenge was the most formidable one. It was not, therefore, surprising that particularly after the Congress government's declaration of the Emergency observers of the Indian political scene expressed grave doubts about the staying power of Indian democracy.

When the Cnogress party and its leader were defeated in the general elections in March 1977, the whole atmosphere changed. Faith in the democracy was restored. This is noted in the next chapter.

The last chapter deals with the new directions of India's foreign policy. It is not directly connected with the democratic experiment. But as there is an interrelation between internal politics and foreign policy, it will not be out of place here.

Some significant documents wich are relevant to the study of Indian democracy are given in the next section.

The author is extremly grateful to Mr. V.K. Vijayagopalan for the valuable help he gave to him in the preparation of this book.

K.P. Karunakaran

CONTENTS

The Nationalist Movement's Legacy

The sources of strength of democracy in India can be traced to the nationalist movement. The movement's character also explains the nature of Indian nationalism. The politics and foreign policy of contemporary India can be understood only in the background of Indian nationalist movement and its rich legacy.

When Mrs Indira Gandhi declared "Emergency" in India in June 1975 and when she took many steps to impose authoritarian rule, she was bound to fail as she was going against the legacy of the Indian nationalist movement. She did not comprehend this fact. Nor did many political commentators who made the observation that the "Emergency" was the beginning of the end of democracy in India. Some of these observers did not rule out a development leading to the replacement of Mrs Indira Gandhi from the citadels of power. But they feared that she would be succeeded by a dictator—perhaps even a worse one. They pointed out to the parallel developments in Ghana, Indonesia and Bangla Desh. This did not happen in India. Mrs Indira Gandhi's exit was followed by the return of democracy to the country. What Mrs Indira Gandhi, her followers and these political commentators did not comprehend was that a large number of modern Indian leaders from Raja Rammohun Roy to Jayaprakash Narayan had not lived in vain. Their ideas and work had influenced not only the students of

modern Indian political thought and movements but a large
number of people. It was this legacy that asserted itself in the
elections of 1977.

While the Western impact in general and the British rule in
particular supplied the superstructure of institutions which
helped the transformation of Indian policy, the social and
economic changes that took place in modern India laid the
foundations on which that structure was built. In the political
field the outward expression of these changes was the nationalist movement, and its best known symbol was Mohandas
Karamchand Gandhi—often referred to as Mahatma Gandhi.
He emerged as the most important leader of the movement by
1920 and retained that position until 1948. The nationalist
movement itself began much earlier. It can be traced at least
to 1885 when the Indian National Congress—the organisation
which led the movement—was founded. Some of the socio-
religious reform movements which began earlier and which were
active towards the close of the nineteenth century and the
beginning of the twentieth century created the necessary social
outlook which were helpful to the nationalist movement. Some
of them also brought to the surface the social conflicts in India
which were based on religion. Later they were reflected in the
politics of the sub-continent also. These movements are a
background to the nationalist movement.

The Social and Religious Movements

Some of the most important social and religious movements
which influenced the Hindus were; the Brahmo Samaj, the Social
Reforms Conference, Arya Samaj, the Ramakrishna Mission
and the Theosophical Society. In the social sphere, they aimed
at caste reform and/or even caste abolition, equal rights for
women, a campaign against child marriage, a crusade against
social and legal inequalities. As far as religious beliefs and
practices were concerned, they tried to remove superstitions and
questioned the validity of idolatry, polytheism and hereditary
priesthood. Some of the principles they emphasised were

individual liberty and social equality. A few of these movements also propagated the idea of Indian nationalism. In the
social and religious fields the problems faced by Sikhs and the
Muslims were different from those of the Hindus. They had
separate movements aimed at reorganising the social order on
democratic lines.

It is, however, significant that the Muslim Social Reform
movements and Hindu Social Reform movements did not merge
into one stream because in India it was difficult to separate
social reforms from religious reforms.

Another aspect of these movements was that those who
were more effective in terms of their mass-base were revivalist
in form and sectarian in regard to some aspects of their
functioning.

The Brahmo Samaj, founded by Raja Rammohun Roy, in
1825 was frankly reformist. Its influence was primarily confined
to a small group of highly educated Hindus in Bengal. The
Prarthana Samaj, a similar organisation founded in Bombay in
1867, attracted a smaller group of people. The success of the
Social Reforms Conference, which was established in 1867 was
also limited. The importance of these organisations, lay in the
fact that they propagated ideas and ideologies which encouraged
educated Indians to re-examine their ancient civilization and
customs in the light of modern science and Western philosophy.

Another group or religious and social movements stood in
contrast with these because they did not acknowledge their
debt to the West. To take an instance. The Arya Samaj,
which was founded in Bombay in 1875 and which was reorganised in Lahore later, was revivalist in form. It insisted on the
infallibility of the Vedas. It often functioned as a purely Hindu
movement and ridiculed other religions. The Theosophical
Society, started in 1875, was another religious movement which
functioned as Hindu revivalist movement. Although it was

established at first in the US., it became primarily an Indian
movement and its headquarters was later transferred to Madras.
Like Arya Samaj, the Theosophical Society also contributed to
the growth of Indian nationalism by raising the pride of educated Indians in India's past and religious traditions.

These movements were not fully revivalist except in form.
The content of many of the reforms they suggested was conducive to the reconstruction of Indian society on modern lines.
The Arya Samaj, for instance, questioned the caste system, as it
was then practised, and opposed the idea of the hereditary
priest.   The Arya Samajists tried to raise the status of women
and popularise modern education.   It is, therefore, very difficult
to classify these movements as purely reformist or as purely
revivalist. Each of these movements has varying degrees of revivalist and reformist ideas.   But there is no doubt that a
movement such as Arya Smaj antagonized the non-Hindus in
general and the Muslims in particular.

The Ramakrishna Mission established by Swami Vivekananda
(1863-1902) stood in a class by itself.   It also wanted Indians
to be proud of the past and of the Hindu heritage but it did
not do anything to antagonise the non-Hindus.   The Mission
also helped the reorganisation of the Indian society on modern
lines. But its appeal in India was mostly confined to the Hindus.

Among the Indian Muslims also there were similar movements. Sir Syed Ahmed Khan (1817-1898) was the most outstanding of the Indian Muslims of the second half of the
nineteenth century. He wanted the Indian Muslims to accept
Western culture and to reconstruct Indian society in accordance
with it. Syed Ameer Ali (1849-1928) was another Indian
Muslim who wanted his community to modernise itself. The
Ahmadiya movement, founded by Ghulam Ahmad (1839-1908)
was a protest movement directed against Christianity and
Westernisation. All these movements among the Muslims had
varying degrees of revivalism and reform.

It is said that the "Hindu response to Christian challenge has now come full circle, from resistance, through defence by imitation, to proud self-confidence". A similar comment could be made on the Indian Muslims also. But as far as the Indian nationalist movement was concerned, these movements had some unfortunate repercussions arising from the fact that while Hindus went back to their religious and historical past to assert their self-confidence, the Muslims went back to early Islam and the past history of Arabia. Among many factors, this also contributes to the widening of the gulf between the Hindus and the Muslims, because the Hindu religious reform movements and the Muslim reform movements tried to rely on two separate sources of spiritual and intellectual sustenance.

Liberalism and the Origins of the Nationalist Movement

When we turn to the early phase of the political manifestation of the nationalist movement, we note the striking similarity between the religious movements and the political movements. The early phase of the Indian National Congress was led by the "moderates" (often referred to as the "liberals") who owed allegiance to Western political ideas. It was comparable to the Brahmo Samaj and the Prarthana Samaj which wanted the reconstruction of Indian society on modern and Western lines. This was followed by the political agitation led by the "extremists" which apparently stood for the rejection of Western ideas and prided itself in the Hindu past of the country. This resembled the religious movements like the Arya Samaj. The parallel continues in another respect; while the two movements—the reform movements and the political agitation of the moderates—though an advance in the realm of ideas placed before the Indian public, could not influence a large number of people because of their narrow social base; the revivalist religious movements and the extremist political movements became very effective in fulfilling their limited tasks of social reconstruction and political regeneration because of their wider social base. In practice, though not in theory, these revivalist movements fulfilled a progressive function because, with their roots in soil, they could mobilize the people to a great extent. This mobilisation of the masses and their participation in the social movements and political campaigns were, in the ultimate analysis the sources for the strength of the democratic forces in the country.

To examine in some detail the role of the impact of the Indian "liberals" first. They, with the support of some enlightened Englishman, founded the Indian National Congress in 1885. The educated Indians in this period were influenced by—almost indoctrinated in—the ideas of the Ages of Enlightenment, of Reason and Liberalism of Europe. These Indians accepted liberalism as their political doctrine and constitutional methods as the means of conducting political agitation.

Their first important contribution to the political awakening in modern India was that they spread the idea that India was a nation. This concept of Indian political unity, based on a nationalist feeling, was completely absent in India in an earlier period. Even before the founding of the Congress, Surrendra Nath Bannerjee who later became a prominent Congress leader, called upon the people of India to be united. In an address delivered in 1876, he focused the attention of his countrymen on the life of Mazzini and said : "Gentlemen, Mazzini lived and died for Italian unity. He rightly judged that Italy would never be great, unless the different Indian peoples were united together by the bonds of common nationality and common institutions... Is India's greatness possible unless we are thoroughly wedded together into a compact mass?"[1] Many leaders also spoke on the same lines. In 1905, Gokhale, one of the most prominent among them, rightly claimed that one of the achievements of the Congress under their leadership was this : "The minds of the people have been familiarised with the idea of a united India working for her salvation; a national public opinion was created;......the dignity of a consciousness of national existence has spread over

1. R.L. Pallit ed. *Surendranath Bennerjee's Speeches* (Calcutta, 1880) p. 21

the whole land".[1]

This group of leaders and their followers also demanded a modern state and the reconstruction of society and economy on modern lines. They opposed the idea of the racial superiority of the Englishmen. Some of their specific demands were : the Indianization of the services (by which they meant that Indians should be recruited to the civil service and the military), expansion of legislative bodies; civil and political liberty; freedom of speech and freedom of the press etc; and extension of the rule of law. Most of these demands were based on liberal political ideas. The fundamental principle was based on the concepts of the liberty of the individual and rights of the citizens. The ultimate objective of the leaders of the early phase of the nationalist movement was the achievement of freedom by the country. But they felt that this could be done only by stages. And their specific demands were aimed at giving Indians the necessary training for self-government.

It is significant that they departed from orthodox liberalism as far as their economic demands were concerned. The main economic issues with which they were concerned were (1) Industrialization of the country, (2) the role of the state in the economic developments, (3) creation of tarrrif walls for the protection of Indian industries and (4) the principles on which taxation and financial administration should be based. In regard to all these matters, they took an original line as they were aware that an underdeveloped country like India could compete with the industrially advanced countries only if its industries had state protection and even substantial state aid. They advocated economic nationalism and stood for the increasing role of the state in the economic development of the country. As the vast masses of the Indian people were poor, they also wanted an equitable system of taxation. Although these Indian leaders were by no means socialists, they were not orthodox liberals as far as their economic ideas were concerned. Their approach to economic questions was pragmatic rather than ideological.

1. Gopal Krishna Gokhale, *Speeches* (Madras, 1920), p. 697

The total effect of their political activities was to strengthen parliamentary democracy and rule of law in the country and to make Indian people conscious of their economic problems and their possible solutions.

Radicalism and Revivalism

Another group emerged in Indian politics towards the close of the nineteenth century. They were known as the extremists in contrast to the Moderates whose leadership and political ideas they challenged. Among the extremists there were two different groups; (1) the terrorists who organized conspiracies and planned the murder of the Britishers and their agents ; (2) those who were interested in mobilising the masses of the people for radical political agitation'. It is the latter group which made the greatest impact on the country.

The first group of the people also instilled courage in a small group of people and, in their opinion, raised the moral and prestige of the Indian people by avenging the inhuman treatment given to Indian nationalists by the British rulers. But the government could suppress them and crush their attempts at armed revolt. A small group of people in India continued to share their belief in violent revolt even when their organizations were annihilated. A few among them later became communists and contributed not a little to the building of their party and other organisations connected with them.

The following were the assumptions of the other group of the Extremists who made the greatest impact on Indian Nationalist Movement and who worked in open and who tried to capture the Indian National Congress : (1) nationalists must cease to have faith in the goodwill of the British rulers because the conflict between India and Britain was the conflict of the national interests of the two countries; (2) what were at stake in the nationalist movement was not the redress of specific grievances like the Indianization of the services; but the general issues of Indians getting a larger share in the administration of the country and of ending Britain's exploitation of India ; (3)

even if the withdrawal of British power was not demanded immediately the Indian nationalists had the right to declare that "freedom was their birth-right".

This group of leaders went further than the Moderates not only in their declared aims but in their methods of agitation also. One of their techniques was to glorify India's past and to organise festivals connected with a historical figure like Sivaji or Hindu gods and godesses like *Ganapathi* or *Kali*. They promoted what they characterized as 'national education'. Here, again, the aim was to give a nationalist orientation to the technical education which would help India's economy. In the economic field they made such a plea for the boycott of foreign, and particularly British, goods. In the political field they encouraged non-cooperation with the British rule and passive resistance to it. Another aspect of their programme was the development of Indian languages.

There were many reasons for the emergence of this kind of political radicalism as a major factor in Indian politics. One was the momentum of the earlier phase of the Indian nationalist movement itself. Another was the increasing authoritarianism of the British government in India. Many international events such as the defeat of Russia at the hands of Japan also strengthened political radicalism in India.

Unlike that of the "Moderates", the political agitation of the extremists brought a larger number of people to the political field. It also introduced a spirit of sacrifice for the nation. Referring to the role of B. G. Tilak,a prominent leader of the Extremists, Mohit Sen, an Indian communist, wrote later: "His (Tilak's) entire approach was one of rousing the masses and getting them to participate in the movement in as massive a manner as possible. He was a propagandist, agitator and organizer who believed in utilizing moreover all the avenues open to him to rouse the people. It was this approach that was more militant and revolutionary than the anarchist outlook of the undoubtedly brave souls who took to the revolver and tried to use it against particularly hated representatives of the

British raj. It had a far greater and far more lasting effect on the masses. gave them a sense of pride and participation and produced from them heroes on a mass scale, leaders to their spiritual emancipation even before their physical freedom had been won. Tilak did more for the Indian revolution than did the terrorists."[1]

Although Tilak was by no means a socialist or a leader of the working class, when he was arrested many labourers went on a strike. This was the first political strike in India. Another colleague of his, Lajpat Rai, presided over the general session of the All India Trade Union Congress. Many of the extremists also spoke of international issues and their relevance to India. These, as well as their interests in technical education, indicate their awareness of the problems of India and the world in the modern era.

But because they spoke in Hindu revivalist idioms they appealed primarily to the Hindus. Occasionally they spoke of a Hindu nation and the protection of Hindu interests on a political level. Their aim was to arouse enthusiasm for the nationalist movements among the Hindus who constituted the majority. But this antagonized the Muslims or at least made the Muslims, with a few exceptions, keep away from the political agitations they led.

While this was their negative contribution, they had many positive achievements to their credit. Some of them were ; (1) they made the concept of an Indian nation more precise ; (2) they instilled courage and self-confidence among the politically conscious people ; (3) they made the participation of the masses a major factor in Indian politics ; (4) their championing of the boycott of foreign goods helped the development of Indian industries; (5) by advocating uncompromising opposition to authoritarianism and by making sacrifices during the political struggle, they made the people of India militant. Thus they helped the cause of freedom and democracy in the country.

1. Mohit Sen, *The Indian Revolution* (New Delhi : 1970) 11-12

Gandhi and the Gandhian Era

Gandhi was one of the most complex personalities of modern India. Some of his political idioms gave the impression that his outlook was medieval. But no other individual has contributed to the modernization and democratization of Indian political life as much as Gandhi did.

In the Gandhian era there was other significant political leaders who carried forward the task of strengthening democratic forces in India. There were forces against democracy also. But they were not very influential and strong.

The period from 1920-1945 was the Gandhian era in Indian politics. By 1920 Gandhi emerged as the "Commander-in-Chief" of the Indian Nationalist Movement. And no one could successfully challenge his position as the supreme leader until 1945. There were, of course, many critics and opponents of Gandhi within the Indian National Congress itself. But he eclipsed almost all of them. Nehru very often criticized Gandhi, but during this period he accepted his leadership in the field of action. When other leaders refused to do so, Gandhi could easily make them leave the Congress, the organization which led the nationalist movement.

Outside the Congress, there were a few organizations, which expressed basic differences with Gandhi and the Congress leadership. The Muslim League, for instance, has its own distinctive views on the fundamental question of the political unity of the sub-continent and on the matter of the political structure with special reference to the place of Muslims in it.

Other major critics of Gandhi were the socialists and the Communists. The former, like Nehru, accepted Gandhi's leadership in the field of political action. The communists did not do so. The Hindu communalists were also uncompromising critics of Gandhi and he was assassinated by one of them. There were a few leaders of different minorities who also refused to accept Gandhi's leadership.

Although all these made their distinctive stamp on different areas on Indian politics, their influence on the majority of the people of India was limited.

In a short survey it is difficult to do justice to the various political compaigns and movements led or inspired by Gandhi. Only some of the most important ones, and that too which have a bearing on the democratic traditions, are noted here.

The non-co-operation movement of 1920-21 was one of the landmarks in the Gandhian era. Others were the Civil Disobedience Movement of 1930-31, the Individual Civil Disobedience of 1940 and the Quit India Movement of 1942-45. The character of one movement differed from another. Almost all of them were a combination of legal and extra-legal measures. Very often Gandhi and his followers frankly questioned the moral authority of the British government to rule India and courted arrest by openly violating the laws. But he also tried to negotiate with the representatives of the Government and to reach agreement with them in a spirit of conciliation.

One characteristic of the movements led by Gandhi was its stress on non-violence. Even those followers of Gandhi, who did not accept non-violence as a creed, accepted it as a politically expedient measure.

Gandhi was a unique leader in many respects. He tried to fulfil many different functions. He was a social reformer, a nationalist leader and a world prophet. This created a lot of confusion among those who could think only within established framework. Some of them accused him of revivalism and others of reckless revolutionary activities. And many contended that he was strengthening anarchy in the country.

The fact of the matter is this : like many creative leaders Gandhi was both a revivalist and a revolutionary. After accepting the framework of Hindu philosophical traditions, conceding the role of heredity in human life and using such idioms as Ram Rajya which made an appeal to the Hindu masses, Gandhi made an attack on the social behaviour of the Hindus based on the concepts of untouchability and of the superiority of one caste over another. No other Hindu leader fought as relentlessly and successfully against the intolerance of Hindus towards other religionists and particularly the Muslims. Although he had to pay for it by his life, its lasting effect was to strengthen liberalism and secularism in the country. As an Indian communist noted ; "The fact that India chose to remain a secular republic is in large measure due to him (Gandhi). The Hindu communalist (sectarian) felt at an enormous disadvantage in combating him since it was impossible to contest the Indianness or the "Hinduness" of the man or to dispute that. What he was telling the people sprang from the very depths of the traditions of India."[1]

Only the form of Gandhi's writings and speeches was typically Indian and, to some extent even Hindu. The content of his message was universal. And within India, he was the greatest force in favour of democracy and modernization.

When once Gandhi comprehended the evils of Indian society, he was bent upon removing them. One of the means of doing it, he realised, was by democratizing the Indian society. In the political field, he at first concentrated on the specific grievances to be redressed such as the Rowlatt Act. This was in 1920-21. Then the basic question was civil liberties. In 1931 it was the right of the Indian people to make salt without paying taxes. In 1940 he was concerned with the right of the people to make their own decision regarding the participation in the Second World War. By 1942 he came out with the basic question of Indian freedom and asked the British to quit India. After the achievement of freedom by India in 1947, he was involved in the battle against Hindu fanaticism. The sense of the direction of all political movements he led was in furtherance of democracy because he brought masses to political action. In other words, the important function he fulfilled was that the political socialization of the masses of the people

1. Mohit Sen, *The Indian Revolution*, New Delhi (1920) p. 20

of India.   In the ultimate analysis it is   this political socialzing
that makes a country democratic.

During the Gandhian era there were some liberals who were
criticizing Gandhi for this very act of political mobilization of
the masses because, according to them, by organizing civil
disobedience Gandhi was promoting anarchy and by using such
expressions as Ram Rajya and by organizing Ashrams and Prayer
meetings, he was spreading medieval ideas. They claimed that
they, themselves, owed allegiance to the most advanced political
thought of the times. They named themselves "Indian liberals".
In theory they were critics of some feudal aspects of Indian
society and its conservatism.   Once a year they met in the
annual conference of the "All India Liberal Federation" and
made some criticisms of some autocratic actions, of the British
government in India.   But their political radicalism ended there.
In the realm of action, they were very conservative.   They
were associated with the most reactionary forces in the country.
Many of them were the servants of the British imperial power;
some of them were employed by the princes in the native states
as Dewans (ministers).   Still others were primarily engaged in
making money under the then existing system as lawyers. They
occasionally left that jobs only to make speeches which were in
conflict with their day-to-day activities.

Gandhi, on the other hand, was leading a militant political
movement against a powerful government and social reform
movement against an equally powerful social system. He was an
open rebel.   His revolutionary activities were not the performances of an individual.   His allies were the masses of India
and he released the mass energy of India by putting before them
sepcific programmes of action to challenge the British authority
and Indian conservatism.

Gandhi's political campaigns strengthened democracy in
India because they brought the masses into action and successfully challanged authoritarian forces in Indian society and in the
political field.

It was wrong to conclude that Gandhi was a representative of the Indian bourgeoisie and that he strengthened democracy in India to the extent he did only because it was in the interests of that class. Many of the battles he and his followers conducted went beyond the interests of that class. His strict adherence to some basic ideals had also the same effect. Commenting on the gulf between Gandhi on the one hand and Nehru and Patel on the other which was evident between 1945-1948 : E.M.S. Namboodiripad, a foremost Communist leader of India writes: "It was this change in the position of the bourgeoisie as a class and its individual representatives that brought it into conflict with Gandhi, the man who still clung to the ideals which he has been preaching in the days of anti-imperialist struggle. The moral values which he had preached in the days of anti-imperialist struggle now became a hindrance to the politicians who came to power. Gandhi, on the other hand, remained true to them and could not reconcile himself to the sudden change which occured to his former colleagues and leiutenants...... We may conclude by saying that Gandhi became the Father of the Nation, precisely because his idealism to which he adhered to in the years of anti-imperialist struggle became practically useful political weapon in the hands of the bourgeoisie in the latter days of his life, because his idealism did in the post-independent years became a hindrance to the self-interest of the bourgeoisie."[1]

After 1945 Nehru did not always act in accordance with Gandhi's wishes. One can even say that after 1947—the year in which India achieved her freedom—Nehru and his colleagues acted in many fields against the spirit of Gandhi's thought. But it was not an accident that Gandhi had named Nehru as his political heir, because in regard to strengthening of democracy and liberalism, Nehru did carry forward the Gandhian traditions. The non-communal approach to politics was spread by Nehru in Western secular terms.

1. E.M.S. Namboodiripad, *The Mahatma and the Ism*, New Delhi (1959) p. 117

Nehru also further enriched the social and economic content of the nationalist movement by propagating socialism. Here again, he spoke in the language of the West.

Nehru's greatest contribution lay in giving a definite international outlook to the Indian nationalist movement. No other leader spoke as clearly as he did on international politics. He conceived the Indian nationalist movement as a part of the world-wide movement against imperialism. In fascism, he perceived the dangers to individual freedom and he was of the view that, under no circumstances, should Indian nationalism ally with fascism even if the fascist governments were also fighting the Western European imperial powers like Great Britain and France. Free India inherited his outlook and it influenced the foreign policy of the country.

Character of Indian Nationalism

Nationalism emphasises the political cohesion of one group of people and legitimizes the claims of one central authority within that group and asserts its independence from other groups. In this sense the concept of Indian nationalism began to take roots in the country towards the close of nineteenth century. The Indian National Congress, which later became the leading organ of the Indian nationalist movement was founded in 1885, and by the beginning of the twentieth century militant political movements began to take shape in India.

Like in many European countries, the origin of Indian nationalism was connected with the popularity of liberalism and the emergence of capitalism. Like in other countries in India also the middle class became a source of strength of nationalism. But unlike in the industrially advanced countries of the West, in India this middle class did not have solid social foundations arising from rapid industrialisation and economic transformation. But it was not as weak as the middle classes of many other African and Asian countries.

The Indian middle classes benefited from the British education and the extensive use of Indian personnel by the British government in such fields as civil service, the army, the judiciary and the expansion of universities, colleges, journalism and legal profession.

Moreover, when liberalism was popularized by the education the British introduced in India, it could take roots in India without much resistance because the intellectual legacy of ancient Indian civilization was favourable to it. It is this civilization transmittad from generation to generation through religious tradition folklore and epics which was one of the greatest sources of strength of democracy in India. Even when some of the educated elite was hesistant to defend democracy, the illiterate masses of the people of the country had done so. And the adult franchise given to the people by the Indian constitution gave them the power to exercise their democratic rights.

The action and interaction between the dominant Indian nationalist movement and other political movements of India between 1885-1947 gave Indian nationalism a unique character. The social and religious reform movements and the different phases of the nationalist movement had also made its impact on Indian nationalism. Modern India also witnessed a strong Muslim separatist movement which culminated in the demand and the establishment of Pakistan based on the theory that the Hindus and the Muslims were two separate nations. The leaders of the Indian nationalist movement never accepted this theory even when they yielded to the demand for the creation of Pakistan. The champions of Pakistan ideology could not fulfil all their demands and when both Bengal and Punjab were partitioned, they got, in their own words, only a moth-eaten Pakistan. And after the creation of Pakistan, Jinnah had to ask the citizens of Pakistan to forget that some of them were Muslims and others were Hindus. He was questioning his own theory. But the final repudiation of the "two-nation" theory took place when the "moth-eaten" Pakistan was further dismembered and the state of Bangla Desh was established in 1971.

The people of the territory which belonged to India in 1947 more or less accepted Indian nationalism based on territorial integrity and the unity of the people who lived in it. They also accepted political creeds connected with self-determination and legitimization of the authority of the central authority of the Indian nation.

Another aspect of Indian nationalism was that the political system it provided in 1947 and improved upon later had a high degree of popular sovereignty. There was a political consensus in the country. The forces strengthening secularism was gradually strengthened and there was a gradual weakening of communalism and feudal loyalties. The communication net work inside the country was improved and there was increasing urbanization. The plural nature of the society was accepted by the dominating elements in the Indian political life and necessary adjustments and compromises were made by them to satisfy the different sections of the people.

The Indian nationalist struggle was not just a struggle for the nation's liberation. It was also a struggle of the people to assert their civil liberties. Fascism was never a popular creed in modern India. And the country did not have the industrial-military complex to sustain a fascist ideology.

By the time the country became free, the Indian nationalist movement also developed an international outlook. This also strengthened the forces against fascism.

Another important feature of the movement was that there was a social and economic content in it. Various expressions such as Gandhism and socialism were used to indicate this aspect of the movement.

2

Democracy Takes Root

When India became free in 1947, the people of the country had first opportunity to frame a constitution in line with the legacy of the nationalist movement and work it out in true democratic spirit. Such a constitution was framed and on its basis the Indian Republic was established on 26 January, 1950. Broadly speaking, parliamentary democracy was worked out in India in accordance with the constitution. Not that it was not challenged at all by the political forces opposed to democracy. The last and most powerful challenge to it came from Mrs Indira Gandhi and her Congress Party during 1975-1977 when they were in power. But Indian democracy survived such challenges and has displayed a tremendous staying power.

Contrast with some Other Countries

India was not the only country among the newly independent countries of Asia and Africa in which a democratic experiment, based on the parliamentary system, was tried. But in many of them they did not take roots. Some striking failures of democracy were in some African countries. Many *coup de etats* took place in South and South East Asian countries also. The democratic political systems, which were at first established, in Indonesia, Burma, Bangla Desh, Nepal and Pakistan were subverted or destroyed by many political upheavals in these countries. In a country like Sri Lanka no dramatic structural change has taken place so for ; but the success of the parliamentary system was not very evident.

When the lamps of liberty were put off in these countries including India's neighbours, in India they continued to shine. Occasionally it was very dim in this country also. Many political commentators noted that between Japan and Israel, India was the only country where the democratic system of a Western variety was worked out successfully.

As we noted, one of the sources of power of Indian democracy was the legacy of the Indian nationalist movement. The Western impact and particularly, the educational, political and administrative institutions created by it were some others.

Some individual political leaders did play a great role in giving shape to the political culture of India. Nehru, India's first Prime Minister, was one of them. Jayaprakash Narain, who led the political movement against Mrs Gandhi's authoritarianism, was another. But in the ultimate analysis what counted most was the attitude of the people as a whole.

The Constitution—Some General Features

The Indian Constitution is very often referred to as the creation of some constitutional lawyers who were good scholars on Western political institutions, but who were not aware of the social realities of India. There is some element of truth in this view. But there is no doubt that the constitution has also the stamp of the political leaders of the country who tried to make it a political instrument which would fulfil India's needs. In the process of making it work, the political leaders had to make many amendments. The procedure to make the amendments was a bit cumbersome. Very often the ruling party at Centre had a clear majority in the Parliament and in most of the State Assemblies. So they could amend those provisions in the constitution which were a hindrance to social and economic reconstruction. In 1975, the ruling Congress, under Mrs Gandhi's leadership, made use of this procedure for strengthening authoritarianism in the country.

Federal Character—Strong Centre

Some other main features of the Constitution are as follows: India is a Union of States. In some respects it is federal in structure. There are at present twenty-two States and nine Union territories. To begin with ninety subjects were listed as union subjects and sixty-five as belonging to the States. The most important of the Union subjects are defence, foreign affairs, foreign trade, important communications such as railways and postal services, currency and inter-state commerce. The States are in charge of public order, the administration of justice, public health and education. There are many subjects in the concurrent list such as criminal law and procedure, civil procedure, marriage and divorce, newspapers, industrial and labour disputes, economic and social planning. Recently some subjects like education was added to the concurrent list.

In practice, the division between the State subjects and Union subjects are not clear-cut. There is an increasing encroachment on the powers of the State by the Central government. The tremendous economic resources at the hands of the Central Government and the nature of planning is mainly responsible for it.

Another is the extra-ordinary power given to the Central Government to dismiss a State government. The President of India—the Chief Executive of the Union Government—is given the power to assume to himself all or any of the functions of the government of the State. He has only to declare that he is satisfied that a situation has arisen in which the administration of the State cannot be carried out in accordance with the provisions of the Constitution. In such matters, the President is expected to act in accordance with the advice of the cabinet. While assuming the functions of the government of a State, the President's proclamation will also declare that the powers of the legislature of the State shall be exercised by or under the authority of the Parliament. It is this provision in the Constitution which has reduced the powers of the States considerably.

Other provisions in the constitution which has a direct bearing on Centre-State relations relate to the Governor of the State. The Governor is appointed by the Central Government. In ordinary circumstances the Governor is only a formal head of the state government, and the Chief Minister is virtually the chief executive. But in extraordinary circumstances, the Governor can exercise a lot of powers. Many of the political scientists are of the opinion that the governors in many Indian states are often used by the ruling party at the centre to weaken their political opponents in the states. As the Union Government itself is the final authority in deciding whether an extraordinary situation has arisen in the state or not, the political forces in the states cannot do anything to counteract the dictatorial tendencies of the Union Government in regard to these matters.

Political Vitality in the States

Although this has, to a limited extent, vitiated the political processes in some States, it is wrong to conclude that the people in the States have not generally succeeded in exercising their democratic rights.

When the government at the centre gives the picture of stability, the political situation in many states give an entirely different picture. There was no stability in many of the states and there was no stagnation also. New political forces emerged in the states and replaced from the seats of power elites which dominated them for a very long time. It is true that these new forces are not always led by the political parties which have clear-cut economic views.

Marxist party have some vague ideas on economic recons- truction but even their strength which was confined to such specific regions like West Bengal and Kerala, derived from the fact that they developed political strategies and tactics which made a tremendous appeal to the people of these states.

In Tamil Nadu, the state neighbouring Kerala, the D.M.K., which made an appeal to the people on the basis of language and race, had tremendous electoral successes in 1961 and in 1971. In 1977 when there was widespread impression that its leaders were corrupt and the D.M.K. failed miserably in securing votes, the A.D.M.K. captured power.

In Punjab, the Akali Dal is a major political force because it could appeal to the linguistic affinity of the Punjabis and to the religious affinity of the Sikhs.

In Gujaratand Maharashtra, the states which were carved out of former Bombay province and the neighbouring territories, language was a great factor in the politics until these states were formed on the basis of the linguistic affinity of the people. The situation was similar in Andhra Pradesh which was formed as a separate state for the Telegu speaking people.

In the Hindi speaking territories the champions of the lower classes also made language a major issue. Their objective, as the objective of those who wanted linguistic states, was to remove from power the elite which derived its pre-eminent position from the mastery of English language. In a limited way this aim was fulfilled in most of the states of India where power was no more monopolized by those whose claim to do so was the knowledge of English. As English was known only to limited few there was a wide gap between the ruling elite and the vast masses of the people who were ruled. A new elite replaced the old one and this new elite spoke in the language and idiom of the people. This was a healthy development as far as the strengthening of democracy in India was concerned.

The rural representation in the new elite is higher than the elite which is replaced by it. This, again, is particularly true of the situation in the states. Earlier, the political power and to a greater degree the power of the civil service were held by the urban classes. And in India this meant a small group of people because the majority of the people were concentrated in the villages.

Very often this is referred to as the political manifestation of a social revolution which is taking place in India. The word "revolution" is an exaggerated expression to describe the social change in India. There is, however, no doubt that there was rapid social change in the country. Even this change is not as much represented in the Central government as in the state governments.

Fundamental Rights—Theory and Practice

Another important feature of the Indian Constitution is the list of fundamental rights listed in it. They assure to all citizens equality before the law and guarantee that no citizen shall be discriminated against on grounds of religion, race, caste or sex. The Constitution also assures the citizens equality of opportunity on matters of employment under the state and the rights to freedom of speech and expression, to assemble peaceably and without arms and to form association and unions. Any citizen can move the Supreme Court for the enforcement of fundamental rights. As a rule, the judiciary in India displayed remarkable independence and integrity and it can safely be asserted that in normal times the Indian citizens enjoyed these rights fully.

But the Constitution gives extraordinary power to the executive in times of "emergency". And when the Chief Executive declares by a proclamation that there is an "emergency", that proclamation cannot be taken to a Court of law. The Indian President, who is nominally the Chief Executive and who is bound to accept the advice of the Prime Minister, has very sweeping powers when the country is threatened by war, external aggression or internal disturbances. One of the most striking instances of the use of extraordinary powers by the Executive was the proclamation of "emergency" by the Executive when the armed hostilities between India and China broke out in 1962. Although there was no regular war between the two countries and there was an uneasy peace in the border since 1962, the Indian government did not annul the proclamation of emergency for a very long time.

The political repercussions of the proclamation of emergency by the Indian President in June 1975, on the advice of Mrs Indira Gandhi's government, were disastrous. This is discussed in a subsequent chapter.

Parliamentary System—a Success

The most successful provisions of the Indian Constitution are those which deal with elections and the convening of the legislatures—both at New Delhi and in the states. In a limited way India has the experience of working out representative institution even before the country became free. Tracing the roots of India's democratic institution to 1892, one of the Indian political scientists observed : "The period from 1892 is best described as one which saw the growth and realization of self-government. The evolution of self-government in India has two aspects. On the one hand, it involves the demand by Indians for the government of the country by and for themselves—the nationalist idea; and, on the other, the demand for sharing of the political power by an increasing number of people—the democratic ideas. The Indian National Congress held its first meeting in 1885, and it demanded *inter alia* the presence of elected members in the Legislative Councils, the right to discuss the budget and ask questions, and the reference to a Standing Committee of the House of Commons of issues between the Councils and the Governments. Ultimately the maximum concession then deemed possible and wise by the Government took shape in an act of 1892, which recognized, though only indirectly, the principle of election to both the central and the local legislatures"[1]. The next step in the same direction was the Minto-Morley Reforms of 1909 which increased the representative elements in the Legislative Councils. But it was not based on a new policy because the Legislative Councils could only deliberate, but could not control the executive who were responsible only to the British Government. But "the Act of 1919 introduced several changes in the Constitution

1. A. Appodorai, *The Substance of Politics*, Oxford University Press, London : 1961—page 378.

of India, as regards both the Central and provincial governments. The central legislature was made bicameral ; in both the chambers, the Council of State and the Legislative Assembly, there was a majority of elected members. It also received additional powers to influence and criticize the government. The most important change in the government of the provinces was the introduction of the system known as dyarchy. Its essence is a division of the Executive into the Reserved Half, and the Transferred Half, the former responsible, through the Secretary of State for India, to the British Parliament and election for the administration of certain *other* subjects. Dyarchy was worked in different provinces until 1937, with varying degree of success."

The act of 1935, which followed and which was brought into operation in 1937, was an important landmark in India's march towards self-government. It gave autonomy to the provinces (the states) where even the executive was elected by the legislative assemblies and was responsible to it. The provisions relating to the Federal Government in the Act were not acceptable to India's leaders and they were not put into effect.

As these developments indicate, when India became free, she had considerable experience in parliamentary government. The most important innovations of the Indian Constitution relating to the Parliament and the legislative assemblies in the states were, firstly, that the Executive were made solely responsible to the elected bodies and secondly, the members were elected on adult franchise and not on the restricted franchise as before 1947.

One of the main challenges to Indian democracy was : How would the vast electorate, which constituted mostly of illiterate people, would function ? The experience of the six general elections clearly showed that the people had responded in a very encouraging manner. Elections were held in a peaceful atmosphere and the electorate exhibited a remarkable maturity in casting their votes. It must also be said to the credit of the Election Commissioner and his staff that they were capable of conducting the elections in a thoroughly impartial manner.

There was no interference by the Party in power at any stage. This applies even to the performance of Indira Gandhi Government in 1977.

Another related question is this : How did the members of the Parliament at the Centre and those in the state legislatures function after getting themselves elected ? In answer to this one can say that the performance on the whole was healthy. Like in any other legislature the members of the Indian Parliament also, particularly those who belong to the opposition, occasionally spoke in an irresponsible manner. In the beginning, the members of ruling party showed a tendency to be mechanically led by the Government on all matters. The situation gradually changed. And the government became aware of the fact that the Parliament was a power to reckon with. The state governments were aware of this fact from the very beginning itself. The exception was the performance of Mrs Indira Gandhi's government during 1975—1977 when it tried to ignore the Parliament. She had to pay a very high price for it. On the eve of the elections in 1977, many Congress members of the Parliament resigned from the Party and formed their own separate organization.

The following observation made by a keen foreign scholar on Indian politics a few years ago is still relevant; "How had the Constitution of India worked in the Indian environment ? Obviously this question cannot be definitely answered for less than a decade and half has passed since the Constitution went into effect. But on the whole the Indian experiment in democracy seems to be succeeding. The political leaders have been scrupulous in observing the Constitution and they have established certain convention which auger well for the future. The successful conduct of three general elections and several elections in the state, the economic progress of the country under Five Year Plans, tangible evidence that the government is trying to deal with ancient wrongs and to institute progress of economic and social reform—these achievements have given the people of India growing confidence that they will be able to cope with the many grievous problems that still confront them."[1]

The Indian National Congress, which was the organization which led the nationalist movement for freedom, retained its position as the majority party in the Parliament after each one of the three elections. The broad aims of the Congress—which can be termed as the centrist party—was declared to be the creation of a socialist pattern of society. But it had taken no important measure to usher in socialism. One can say that it was interested in modernizing the economy. In a country like India, as this would involve the state taking a leading part in economic life, the Congress Party would welcome it. After the elections of 1977 the Congress is no more in power.

During 1955—1962, the Communist Party was a significant opposition. It was by no means a close second to the Congress. After its split, the influence of the communist declined. Apart from the Communist Party, another party to the left of the Congress was the Socialists. These social democrats were never a force in India and now they are considerably weakened by splits among them also.

To the right of the Congress were the Swatanthra Party and the Jan Sangh—the first is a secular conservative opposition and the second derives its strength from Hindu revivalism.

Some of these parties have significant strength in the states; but none of them is a major political force on an all-India level. The Communists were in power in Kerala during 1957-1959 and again after 1967 they shared power with other parties in that state. For a short time after 1967, they shared power with others in West Bengal. Even now the Communists are significant forces in Kerala and West Bengal.

The parties, B.K.D, D.M.K. and the Akalis were powerful

---

1. Novman D. Palmer in the Section on India in the book, edited by G.M Kahin, *Major Governments of Asia*, Cornell University Press, Ithaca, New York : 1963. Page 322.

in some states.

In 1977 many of these parties were merged into one party—
the Janata. Then it became the ruling Party. This will be
discussed in the next chapter.

In many elections to the Parliament, many distinguished
individuals belonging to various parties, lost their seats. This
underlined the declining role of the factor of "personality" in
elections. In some constituencies the prestige of individuals
still counted more than the influence of political parties. In
many parts of the country caste and religion were important
factors.

After the third general election in 1962 one trend was obvious; gradually, the lower strata of the society could send representatives to the Parliament and the State Assemblies. The
number of women who were elected was also on the increase.
Another important feature is that the majority of the young
people showed a tendency to vote for the opposition. Many students of the Indian politics have also noted that the Parliament,
was increasingly moulded in the nation's image and it now con-
forms to the overall social structure of the country. The Parliament, after the sixth election, is more representative than before,
of such classes as the agriculturists, businessmen, social workers
and those who belong to various professions. In 1947 one saw a
domination of lawyers, journalists, educationists who were typical
products of Western culture and education in the Parliament.
Now they are eclipsed by businessmen, landlords and the landless agriculturists. A good number of them depend for their
livelihood on salaries they receive as member of the Parliament.

There was an optimistic note in many of the studies made by
various individuals on the emerging leadership of the country.
One of them wrote : "The political centre of gravity has long
last shifted from cities to the mofussil and the villages. There
is a lot of nauseating vulgarity in political exchange, because in
a way politics is moving closer to Indian earth...Does it mean
that the middle class had exhausted its role as builder and

moulder of parties in India ? I doubt whether the end of the
era would come that abruptly...The middle class, by its very
nature, is highly mobile in India and whoever comes to !eader-
ship would perhaps be absorbed by the Indian bourgeosie.   In
the process, however. politics will be increasingly 'plebianised'
which is of course something altogether different from being
proletarianised."

3

Authoritarian Challenges

During the short period since India became free, various kinds of authoritarianism challenged the democratic system. The first came from militant Hindu sectarianism. This was at the highest between 1947 and 1948. Then came the communist challenge which was very violently expressed from 1948—1951.

By 1952 it seemed that these extreme rightists and leftists could not subvert the democratic system and that it had a staying power.

Until 1971 this was the situation. Then the Congress Party in power in New Delhi, under Mrs Indira Gandhi's leadership, began to show some authoritarian tendencies. This reached its climax in June 1975 when an emergency was declared. Since then the Prime Minister did not show any subtlety. It was an open, and very often a crude, attempt to concentrate power on the Executive in New Delhi. This stopped only with the announcement of the decision to hold elections. The emergency itself was lifted only after the defeat of the Congress Party in the elections in March 1977. Democracy returned to India only after the assumption of the new government.

There was some basic differences between the earlier challenges to democracy and to the one posed by Mrs Indira Gandhi. One is this; while the Hindu sectarians and the communists were in the oppositon, Mrs Indira Gandhi was the

Prime Minister. And as such her capacity to subvert the system was much greater than that of others because she had the administrative apparatus and the state machinery at her disposal. Another was that the Hindu communalists and the communists were not all-India political forces. Their strength, though not their claims to strength, was always confined to some specific regions. The ruling Congress Party had an organizational strength and mass support in almost all parts of India. The threat it could give to Indian democracy was, therefore, very powerful.

There was another difference. The communists and the Communalists had some ideologues. The ruling Congress Party had none. Its leaders wanted power just for the sake of power.

The Hindu Sectarians Loose

As noted in an earlier chapter, one of the legacies of the nationalist movement was a non-communal and non-sectarian approach. Gandhi was the most widely known symbol of this. Occasionally it expressed itself as an adherence to secularism. And Nehru was its symbol. During the nationalist movement, various organizations were frankly communal and opposed to this dominant trend. Among the Muslims, there was the Muslim League which, expressed its adherence to the two-nation theory—the theory which maintained that the Hindus and the Muslims were two separate nations. The most well-known communal organization of the Hindus was the Hindu Mahasabha. In 1947 Muslim League had its major political victory when Pakistan was established and its leaders became its rulers. When India became free, the government was headed by the Congress leaders who were not communal. Among the Hindus, the communal forces were not the dominant before or after 1947.

But the Hindu communalists found that the climate created by the communal riots in 1946 and in 1947 was very favourable to them. Unlike the Muslims, the Hindus in India as a whole were not a minority. And as such they did not have the complex of the minority community—the complex based on the fear of the majority and on the ability to organize as a separate identity. But a well-organized section of the Hindus felt that during 1946 and 1947 their community lost everything and the Muslims gained everything. With the British help, the latter could establish Pakistan. According to the Hindu communalists, as the dominant leadership of the Congress wanted to appease the Muslims and Pakistan, they yielded to them on every vital issue. They also believed that Pakistan and the Muslims were given every concession by the Congress and Gandhi. And when communal riots led to widespread killing and murder, passions were aroused on a large scale. It was in this atmosphere that Gandhi was assassinated by a Hindu fanatic on 30 January, 1948.

Gandhi's martyrdom was a heavy blow on Hindu communalism from which it had not so far recovered.

Nehru made use of the administrative apparatus at his disposal to weaken the Hindu communalists in an atmosphere which was made favourable to him by Gandhi's martyrdom.

In the ultimate analysis, the final defeat of Hindu communalism was due to the fact that it had never taken deep roots in India.

As far as nationalism connected with territorial integrity and secularism was concerned, the defeat of Hindu sectarianism was significant. It was important to the strengthening of democratic forces also because the political ideology of the Hindu communalists was clearly one of repudiating parliamentary democracy and strengthening fascism. If they had won in 1947-48 in their major political battles, it is doubtful that the Muslims and other non-Hindus would have been treated as "full" citizens of the country.

After 1948, Hindu communalism did retain some influence in the Indian political field. These trends do not disappear on a particular day completely. But gradually they were drawn to the national stream and by participating in the political process of a democratic system, they are also becoming increasingly democratic and less communal. The election of 1977 is an important landmark in this respect. Many of the former Hindu communalists are now in the victorious Janata Party and some of them are the members of the Cabinet. And in north-western parts of India, the soil is still favourable to Hindu communalism. Now the basic questions are these : Will Hindu communalists be in a position to dominate the ruling Janata Party ? Alternatively, will they be modernized and democratized by their allies and by the very fact that they are working out a democratic system ? The answers are very clear : the first will not take place and the second will.

There were many reasons why a group of people who professed faith in a "militant Hinduism" could not organize a successful fascist party in India. Although the social behaviour of a large number of the Hindus for a very long time was influenced by exclusiveness and intolerance towards others, there was nothing in Hindu metaphysical tradition which can sanction intolerance and exclusiveness. On the other hand, Hinduism on that level was highly tolerant of others and cosmopolitan in outlook.

And the Hindus in India were in a majority. It is in their interest to work out a political system based on majority rule.

The minorities in India, unlike the Jews in Germany, were not privileged classes. They were socially and economically backward than the majority community. Those who belonged to the upper castes of the Hindus were in a minority. The lower castes, the Muslims, the Christians and others belonged to the majority. And in a plural society as that of India, any fascist group based upon the upper caste Hindus could only organize a party of a small group of people.

The experience also revealed that such a group has a limited territorial base. They were confined to north-western parts of India. In the South and in the coastal areas of India it could not take roots. The Sikhs in the Punjab were opposed to them.

When Mrs Indira Gandhi's government took strong action against them, their weakness was fully exposed. And they realized that they should work with other political groups to fight back against Mrs Gandhi and her supporters. This resulted their shedding their narrow social and political outlook and accepting Jayaprakash Narayan as their leader. And J.P. is as much non-communal and non-sectarian as Gandhi and Nehru were.

J. P. was the vigorous champion of the view that India should develop cordial relations with Pakistan and China. The Hindu communal groups were the severest critics of this view. When once they joined the government they also began to act in accordance with the opinion of Jayaprakash Narayan and others. This was because, as an opposition party, the Hindu communalists could afford to be the champions of national chauvinism, but as members of a broad-based government they had to function in a responsible manner and carry their allies with them. Moreover, they realized that India did not have the industrial and military complex to function as a fascist government. She has to pursue a foreign policy fully realizing her weakness and the strength of some other Powers. The fascist elements had no social, political, economic or military base in India.

The success of the administrative measures taken by Nehru's government against the Hindu communalists who had a fascist outlook was not a crossroad but a landmark. The next important landmark was the elections of 1977. In it the Hindu communal elements worked in close co-operation with the secular political forces in the country. And later, they participated in the national government of the Janata Party and openly gave up their communal and fascist outlook. Many of their political enemies think that this was only a tactical and expedient measure they had undertaken. Even some among them may be thinking on the same lines. But the fact of the matter is this : by participating in the political processes laid down in the Indian political system for a very long time, they had themselves become a part of the system. By coming to grip with political realities on the national and international scene, they have fully realized that fascism had no future and that democracy had a staying power in India.

Responding to the Communist Challenges

In many socially and economically backward countries, communists were a threat to the democratic system. In some they succeeded in capturing power. In some others they were one of the factors in creating a political crisis and anarchy which favoured the fascists or the rightist dictatorship to capture power. In India also the communists challenged the democratic system. But neither did they succeed in capturing power, nor was their challenge met by a fascist dictatorship. It was the centrists who defeated them. As the Hindu communalists, the Indian communists were also first tackled by administrative measures. Again, it was in the political field that they were finally beaten. They also were brought to th national stream by the political processes of the Indian democratic system.

It was in March 1948 that the Indian communists openly came out against the political system of free India. They thought that they should launch a violent revolution and capture power by force. The next item in their agenda was to establish the dictatorship of the Party which would represent the proletariat. Every detail was worked out neatly. And theoretical formulations were made in accordance with the classical writings of Lenin and other Russian leaders. During 1948-1950 Stalin himself did not oppose these programmes of the Indian communists.

Many of these programmes were framed in a bookish manner. They did not take into consideration the realities of the Indian situation. To take one instance, the urban proletariat was given a prominence which would have been justified in

Europe, but not in Asia. The peasants were not given an important role in the Indian "revolution". Another weakness arose from the fact that except in Andhra, Kerala and West Bengal there was no communist movement of any significance. In the vast parts of the Hindi-speaking areas, there were no communist party cells and in some of them not even a party member. A "revolution" was launched without taking into consideration any of these facts.

As the communists themselves admitted later, they also did not take into account the strength of the bourgeoisie. They had written at length about an economic crisis developing into a political crisis in India. Nothing of this kind happened except in their imagination.

The Indian State apparatus was also an efficient one. Combined with the communication system, it could suppress easily any armed rebellion in scattered parts of the country.

By 1950, the communists themselves realized some of their mistakes. But again in Telengana in Andhra, they organized armed rebellion. Unlike in the former rebellions of 1948-1949, in the latter ones of 1950 the peasants were given prominence. It was the Chinese and not the Soviet model. But India was neither Russia nor China. And the second set of armed rebellion failed miserably as the first one in achieving its objectives.

The Indian communists gradually realised that they made wrong assessments of the situation in the country, of their strength and strength of the political opponents. This realization was followed by an intensive debates among them. Simultaneously there was ideological and polemical debates among the communists of Russia, Western Europe and China. By the time the twentieth party of the Soviet Communist Party met, many communists all over the world had rejected the view that a bloody revolution was essential for the transition from capitalism to socialism. There was also a widespread rejection of the inevitability of establishing the dictatorship of the communist party after its capture of power. Although the Indian communists had not at that time, or for that matter later, examined these fundamental questions boldly and formulated their own ideas in regard to them, they moved away from the position of loyalty to such concepts as the dictatorship of the proletariat. They formulated many new political tactics in regard to making alliance with many non-communist groups and parties inside the country and in regards to the working of the Indian democratic system.

In 1956 the Communist Party of India captured power in the State of Kerala through parliamentary elections. This was their first experience in implementing the theory of "peaceful transition to socialism". Of course, it was impossible to establish socialism within one state of India when the rest of India has another system. But the importance of the Kerala experience lay in the fact that it indicated that a communist party could capture power through the elections in a parliamentary system. And within limits they could implement some of their programmes.

If this was an important event which "democratized" the Indian communists and drew them to the national stream. The dismissal of the communist government in Kerala in 1959 by the Central government was a step backward in regard to this matter. In the elections which followed the dismissal of the government, the communists could not capture power. But the votes they received were substantial and the elections were conducted in an impartial manner. Whether their representatives were sitting in the ministerial benches or not, the communists were always a part of the power structure of Kerala since 1956. And occasionally they were heading the Cabinet, or functioning as members of the Cabinet headed by others. In other words, they were a part of the political system. Even outside the government, they were fulfilling the important function as members of the opposition.

During 1952—1962, the communists were an important element in the political life of India.

What weakened them later was the dissensions among them. This is not the place to examine the causes of these dissensions and assess the responsibility of each group for that development. What we are concerned here is how these developments affected the action and interaction between the communists as a whole and the Indian democratic system.

Broadly speaking there were three groups among them. The first is the Communist Party of India which inherited the offices, the Press and journals of the undivided communist party. Some of the well-known leaders were inside the C.P.I. But they had practically no following in the country. When they began to support even the most unpopular actions of Mrs Indira Gandhi's government they were often referred to by their critics as the "tail" and the "appendage" of the Congress.

Another group—politically the most influential one—was the Communist Party of India (Marxist). The first is often referred to as the Moscow communists. This is unfair to them. The Marxists are named as the Peking communists. Nothing is farther from truth because Peking and the Chinese had practically no influence in the group. The Marxists are relatively strong in West Bengal and Kerala. But outside these two states, they are not a factor in politics.

Both of these groups—the C.P.I. and the Marxists—accept the Indian parliamentary system today. The later, of course, criticized it in their polemics; but they have not so far, even in theory, provided for an alternative system. There is an intellectual bankruptcy in them. This stands in glaring contrast with the recent records of the Italian, the French and the Spanish communists. On the fundamental question of working out a democratic system, the Indian Marxists had not so far given a theoretical lead to the nation and to their followers. In practice, they had shown great interest in participating in the political processes of the democratic system and in a region like Kerala, and West Bengal they had displayed remarkable ability also in working out the parliamentary system. But in West Bengal, there is a widespread impression that they were responsible for the anarchical conditions during 1968—69 and when some of their political opponents rigged the elections in 1972 and almost enforced a reign of terror against them, they could not assert themselves.

During the emergency, the Central government and various State governments imprisoned many Marxists and even tortured some of them. Many of their leaders were released after a short spell of imprisonment. The experiences during the emergency brought home to the members of the Marxist party the realization that they could not work as an isolated group in the Indian political field and it was in their vested interest to make democracy work in India. They grasped the fact that in any encounter between the totalitarians of the right and those of the left, the former was bound to win. As the result of this realization the Marxists worked in close co-operation with the Janata Party and against the Congress Party and the Communist Party of India. They said that the main issue in that electoral battle was democracy versus dictatorship and that they were on the side of democracy.

There is another significant group among the Indian communists known as the Naxalites. The word originated from Naxalbari—the region in which this group operated at first on a fairly large scale. Their political and social base is narrow. But during the past few years, they took many adventurous steps and, in scattered parts of India, committed a few isolated murders. Some of them characterized themselves as Maoists of India. A good number of them believed that the only way to organize revolution was by force and violence. According to them the preparation for imitating it was by organizing isolated murders and instilling a fear among the opponents. It is on this basis they acted. A large number of them were idealists. Some were inspired by adventurist spirit. The Central government and many State governments suppressed these activities of the Naxalites by great force. There were many instances of various atrocities committed by the police. Many Naxalites were tortured and even some of the innocent people were suspected as Naxalites and imprisoned. It was obvious that they were unable to match the force at the government's command with equal force. A good number met with death and a large number were imprisoned. Although some conspirators among them succeeded to continue some activities here and there, their political impact on the country as a whole was very negligible. There was great demoralization among the Naxalites inside and outside the jail. The government, which was formed after the elections of 1971, held negotiations with some representatives of the Naxalites. Some agreements were reached between them and a large number of the Naxalites were released on the basis of these agreements. There were specific charges of violence and terrorism against some of them. There would be some delay in releasing some of them. Many will have to undergo imprisonment and other punishments in accordance with the verdict of the court. An insignificant few among the few Naxalites may not be interested in coming to an agreement with the government. But the indications are that, barring them, the Naxalites will also be drawn to the national and democratic stream.

Mrs Gandhi's Authoritarianism

India's democratic system received the most powerful challenge from Mrs Indira Gandhi's authoritarianism. It is difficult to point out to a particular date as the beginning of this authoritarian trend in her. She became the Prime Minister of India on 24 January 1966 when the then Prime Minister, Lal Bahadur Shastri died. After the election in 1966 she was again elected as the leader of the ruling party and she continued as Prime Minister. In March 1972 there was another general election in which again she became victorious. It is after this year some authoritarian trends were visible in her administration. They reached the climax in June 1975 when her government declared emergency. From that day until her defeat at the polls in 1977 there was some kind of an authoritarian government in the country.

Although attempts were made by Mrs Indira Gandhi and

her supporters, including her son, to monopolize power, it will be wrong to conclude that there was a full-fledged dictatorship in the country. The attempt of the rulers was to monkey with the democratic system and alter it here and there by ordinances, administrative measures and constitutional amendments. In other words they wanted to work as dictators within a "democratic framework" and as far as possible give the impression that they were following all democratic norms and practices including the holding of impartial elections. This experiment was bound to fail. The authoritarian measures created a widespread resentment against those who were in power. And when the people were allowed to exercise their democratic rights in an impartially conducted elections, they threw out the ruling party from power.

But by the time this took place so much damage was done to the democratic processes in the country that it was feared that even if Mrs Indira Gandhi would be removed from power, another authoritarian regime would succeed her government.

As we are very close to this authoritarian phase of the Indian political experiment, it is difficult at this stage to objectively analyse it. It will not be easy to locate the force behind Indira Gandhi's government in its last phase. A cult was built around her. It was stated in various books and articles that she was an extraordinary leader with exceptional political sagacity. She herself occasionally spoke about her exceptional background and her qualities as a fighter. Certainly, she did not possess any of these qualities attributed to her and perhaps she might not have been the real centre of power.

Mrs Indira Gandhi once said that her son was a small fry and that he did not deserve the continuous attacks on him. Perhaps, she was also a small fry and the big fry might have been some invisible forces working behind her and which were not so far been located.

Anyway, there is no doubt that a cult was built around her. She was referred to as a modern and Indian version of Joan of

Arc and the successor to Mahatma Gandhi and Jawaharlal Nehru. "India is Indira" was one of the slogans used by the Congressmen.

Another development took place during the last phase. The Youth Congress and Sanjay Gandhi, Indira Gandhi's son, were built as great political factors. There was a systematic attempt to eclipse all the senior colleagues of Mrs Indira Gandhi in the Congress party and in the Cabinet. An enterprising author even wrote a book on Sanjay Gandhi with the title, "The World's Wisest Wizard". Many leaders stated that the Youth Congress was stealing the thunder from the Congress Party.

Under these circumstances it was difficult to explain the political motives of those in power and to determine the character of the political system they wanted to build up. There was, of course, concentration of power and the attempt to monopolize it in the hands of the few. These few individuals had no political ideology and no party with cadres. What they wanted was to hold on to power. And many observers even concluded that what was attempted in India was to establish a new type of dynasty, a monarchical system with the power always in the family of Mrs Indira Gandhi.

This may be an exaggeration. But there is no evidence to suggest that the ruling elite during the emergency had a clear picture in their mind of any political system which they wanted to build.

The increase in the authoritarian tendencies of the government was gradual. It was at first challenged politically by her opponents. Initially she won in many encounters with them.

When Mrs Indira Gandhi was challenged politically in Bihar and Gujarat, she almost lost her balance. In Bihar there was a popular political movement against the authoritarianism and the corruption of the Congress government. In Gujarat a political movement led by the students wanted the removal of the state government from power. In May 1974 there was the strike of the railwaymen, throughout India. The Congress governments in the States and at the Centre reacted very violently to all these developments.

Jayaprakash Narayan emerged as the Lok Nayak (leader of the people) and became the symbol of these protest movements in the couutry as a whole.

The leaders of the Akali Dal, the Bharatiya Lok Dal, the Dravida Munnetia Kazhagam, the Jana Sangh, the Organization Congress, the Revolutionary Socialist Party and the Socialist Party expressed great interest to work in co-operation among themselves and under the guidance of Jayaprakash Narayan for the protection of civil liberties in the country. The Communist Party of India (Marxist) also resisted the arbitrary and authoritarian actions of the Government.

Mrs Gandhi and her supporters decided to meet this opposition by force and repression on a large scale was used.

But occasionally the Central Government yielded. President's rule was imposed in Gujarat in January 1974. And again it became uncompromising. In Bihar there was greater support for the political movement against the government. But no concession was given to it.

Another development took place which gave another political challenge to the Prime Minister. To begin with, it was a legal battle. Mr. Raj Narayan, Mrs Gandhi's opponent in the 1971 election, had given a petition in the Allahabad High Court against Mrs Gandhi's election on the ground that she had employed corrupt practices. The court rejected fifty of the fifty-two charges, but set aside Mrs Gandhi's election on the ground that there were some corrupt practices in regard to the other two. This would have remained as a technical question if Mrs Gandhi had resigned and another leader of the Congress party had taken, at least temporarily, the post of the Prime Minister.

But she was not prepared to do so. And her son, Sanjay Gandhi, was one of the few who stood with her on this matter. There were many charges of corruption against him. Under the circumstances, another Prime Minister would have taken a view different from that of his mother on these charges. Whether this was or was not a reason for the support he gave to her, she said later that at time he was one of her few supporters. If she had stepped down, it was doubtful that the new incumbent would have left the seat for her later. Anyway she did not take that risk. She continued as the Prime Minister and her appeal was granted by the Supreme Court which set aside the judgment of the judge of the Allahabad Court.

A royal battle was fought outside the court and in the political field by Mrs Indira Gandhi's supporters and opponents.

Commenting on the Allahabad judgment Jayaprakash Narayan said that Mrs Indira Gandhi should resign. Barooah, the Congress president, said that she should not.

The representatives of the opposition parties met in New Delhi from 21 June to 25 June to plan united action to force the Prime Minister to resign.

Emergency and Total Power

It is in the background of these events that on the advice of the Prime Minister, the President declared the "State of Emergency in India". A large number of the political observers inside the country and outside concluded that the "Emergency" was declared to protect Mrs Indira Gandhi's personal interests and Mrs Indira Gandhi decided not to step down because she wanted to protect her son and her personal interests.

The clause (1) of Article 352 of the Constitution of India dealing with the Emergency says : "If the President is satisfied that a grave emergency exists whereby the security of India or any part of the territory thereof is threatened, whether by war or

external aggression or internal disturbance, he may by proclamation, make declaration to that effect." It was difficult to maintain that the security of India was threatened by the Allahabad
Judgment and by the events following it.

Other reasons were found by Mrs Gandhi's supporters.
According to them there was a conspiracy among Mr sIndira
Gandhi's political opponents to subvert Indian political system
and sabotage the "radical" economic programme of the
Congress. It was subtly and, often not that subtly, hinted that
these conspirators in India had foreign support. It was even
suggested that very powerful foreign governments, including
the U. S. government, was interested in undermining India's
freedom.

It is in the background of the hysteria created by this
propaganda that attempts were made to justify many of the
arbitrary action of the government.

The most important of these actions is the indiscriminate
arrests and imprisonment of a large number of political leaders
and workers. The present Prime Minister, Morarji Desai, and
Jayaprakash Narayan were some of the victims. Others were
the important leaders of the Congress Organization, the Jana
Sangh, the Socialist Party, the Marxist Party and a very large
number of their workers. Many of them were kept in solitary
confinement. The President issued an order on 27 June 1977
forbidding those detained under new Proclamation of Emergency
moving the courts for relief. Terrorism was let loose by the
government and never before in the history of modern India
were the political prisoners and suspects tortured on such a
large scale as they were tortured during the Emergency.

The Government of India banned on 4 July, 1975 the activities of twenty-six political organizations. Their offices were
sealed and their leaders were imprisoned.

A very strict Press censorship was imposed under the Emergency regulation. Even discussions and speeches made in the

Parliament, if they were not in the interest of the ruling Party, were not published in the Press. Those who were in power brought pressure on the Press by getting some editors removed from their posts.

Not satisfied by this stiff censorship, the government brought all news agencies under one management, "The Samachar" and it indirectly controlled it.

It was stated that the government wanted a committed civil service and a committed judiciary. The Samachar was a 'committed' news agency also—committed to the task of propagating the government's views. When Mrs Indira Gandhi criticized the Communist Party of India the Samachar circulated a background "research paper" explaining how the Indian communists had betrayed the Indian nationalist movement. The Government of India had complete monopoly of the Radio and the Television and they were unscruply used for the propaganda of the ruling Party and for projecting Sanjay Gandhi as a great political figure.

Sanjay Gandhi's emergence as a political factor was another significant development during the Emergency. He held no office either in the government or in the ruling Party. Very often he was referred to as the extra-Constitutional authority and the Super Prime Minister of India. It was stated that he terrorized the Cabinet Ministers, the Chief Ministers and the senior officials. At least once the Prime Minister defended him and said that any criticism of him was a criticism of her. Whatever might be the authenticity of the charges against him, there was no doubt that his emergence as a significant political power was not within the democratic structure.

An act referring to the publication of objectionable materials prevented the publication of any book or pamphlet which was not in the interest of the ruling Party.

Thus there was a complete reign of terror. There was widespread fear of the government. Psychophants and the opportunists wanted to please those in power and further their interests and made use of this opportunity. As the result of censorship, there was widespread ignorance in India of what was happening in this country and outside. The government and the ruling party were themselves ignorant of how the people in general resented them. The leaders of the ruling party were surprised when they were routed at the polls in 1977. This was because they had no idea of the feelings of the people.

One of the specific acts which made the ruling party extremely unpopular in northern parts of India was the forcible sterilization and other administrative measures the government took for birth-control. Later during the elections, the leaders of the ruling party apologized to the people for the administrative excesses in regard to this matter. But what they forgot was that this was not an administrative issue and that such excesses did not happen in a political vacuum. It was the situation created by the emergency that made these administrative excesses possible. In such a political atmosphere the people had no way of expressing their grievances. No letter to the Press could be published, no question would be raised in the Parliament with the purpose of giving publicity to the grievances, no processions could be organized and no public meetings could be held. In this background any act or irregular use of force on the part of one official is not an administrative excess, but only one of the many manifestations of authoritarian system which was dominating the country.

In the State of Kerala it was reported that a political prisoner was missing. Later it was revealed that he died of torture. Again it was not an atrocity of one official, but the product of authoritarianism.

The remedy to these was only the restoration of democracy. This was what the people of India achieved by their performances in the elections to the Parliament in 1977.

Looking from this viewpoint, Mrs Gandhi's authoritarianism was the greatest threat to the democratic system India faced since her independence. The significance of the fact that the political system survived is that the roots of democracy are very strongly entrenched in the country.

According to many political scientists, the last major act of Mrs Gandhi's ruling party to undermine the democratic base of Indian political system was to make some amendments to the Constitution.

Even under the emergency some of the acts of the government were challenged in the courts. In the Press also there was some criticism. Many periodicals, expressing the views of the opposition parties, were published in a clandestine manner. And even some of the organizations, which were not banned — like the Jana Sangh and the Marxist Party—did put forward some dissident views. The lawyers, some journals, some academicians and some other individuals did take a non-conformist view. Under the circumstances, the leaders of the government thought that they were loosing legitimacy in the eyes of the public, Moreover, they were faced with the problem that the "emergency", in the nature of it, could not be continued indefinitely, much less permanently. In identical circumstances in some other countries, there was a tendency to elect the president for life—to allow the incumbent of the post of the Chief Executive to hold his office until his death. In India this was not done that crudely. But some extensive amendments were made to the Constitution which would have made the Prime Minister and the government very powerful. It was as if the "Emergency Powers" were given permanency. And other centres of power and influence like courts, the Press and the President were reduced to non-entities.

The Law Minister introduced in the Lok Sabha on 1 September 1976 the Constitution Bill known as the forty-fourth Amendment Bill. It was rushed through the Parliament and the Assemblies and came into effect without much delay.

The Constitution (44th Amendment) Bill stated : "The democratic institutions provided in the Constitution are basically sound and the path of progress does not lie in denigrating any of its institutions. However, there could be no denial that these institutions have been subjected to considerable stresses and strains and that vested interests have been trying to promote their selfish ends to the great determinant of public good. It is, therefore, proposed to amend the Constitution to spell out expressly the high ideals of socialism, secularism and the integrity of the nation, to make the directive principles more comprehensive and give them precedence over those fundamental rights which have been allowed to be relied upon to frustrate socio-economic reforms for implementing the directive principles." These broadly stated aims cannot be objected to by any one.

But their expression in concrete provisions had dangerous implications because of the curtailment of the rights of the individual and the increase of the powers of the Executive.

To take one instance. One of the provisions stated: "Notwithstanding anything contained in Article 13, no law providing for (a) the promotion or prohibition of anti-national activities; or the promotion or formation of, or prohibition of, anti-national associations, shall be deemed to be void on the ground that it is inconsistent with, or takes away or abridges any of the rights conferred by Article 19 or Article 31." This gave sweeping powers to the executive and an individual or group of individuals could not question any part of them in a court of law.

It was the convention that the President would act in accordance with the advice of the Prime Minister. But the amendment specifically stated : "There shall be a Council of Ministers with the Prime Minister as the head to aid and advise the President who shall, in the exercise of his functions, act in accordance with such advice". The purpose of this clause was to make the president a non-entity and to make the Prime Minister all-powerful.

The power of the courts were reduced. The objects and reasons given for this are as follows : "Parliament and the State Legislature embody the will of the people and the essence of democracy is that the will of the people should prevail...... It is proposed to strengthen the presumption in favour of the Constitutionality of the legislation enacted by Parliament and State Legislature by providing for a requirement as to the minimum number of judges for determining question as to the Constitutionality of laws and for a special majority of not less than two-thirds for declaring any law to be Constitutionally valid. It is also proposed to take away the jurisdiction of High Courts with regard to the Constitutional validity of Central laws and confer exclusive jurisdiction in this behalf on the Supreme Court as to avoid multiplicity of proceedings with regard to validity of the same Central law being valid in one State and invalid in another States". All these meant a curtailment of the power of the courts. And with the power of the Chief Executive to pack the courts with the judges of his persuasion, this could result in an increase in the power of the Executive. The courts were denied the right to question the validity of the Constitutional amendments also except upon the ground that it has not been made in accordance with the regular procedure.

The spirit of all these provisions were clear. It was to legitimatize the increase of the powers of the Executive and curtail the rights and liberty of the citizens.

Weakness of Authoritarianism

In spite of the sweeping Constitutional amendments and various steps taken to concentrate power in the hands of the Executive, authoritarianism collapsed in India like a house of cards when the elections were held to the Parliament in 1977. The reason for this was the basic strength of Indian democracy. The authoritarian system which the Congress government was trying to impose on the country had also many inherent weaknesses.

The clique around Mrs Indira Gandhi did not have any ideology. They had no party cadre or any closely-knit organization to stand firmly behind her and the party at the time of a crisis. As Walter Lippman observes, "The totalitarian revolution generally liquidate the elite of the old regime, and then recruit their own elite of specially trained and specially dedicated and highly disciplined men...... In their different ways—which ideologically may be at the opposite end of the world—the post-democratic rulers are men set apart from the masses of the people. They are apart not only because they have the power to arrest others and shoot them. They have also an aura of majesty which causes them to be obeyed. That aura emanates from the popular belief that they have subjected themselves to a code and are under a discipline by which they are dedicated to ends that transcend their ends and their own private lives".[1] In this sense Mrs Gandhi did not have an aura of majesty. There was even a widespread belief that she was interested in protecting her corrupt son, even if she herself was not personally corrupt. In fact some of her political opponents had this aura. The failure of Mrs Gandhi's attempt to impose an authoritarian regime arises from the fact that she was not a political dictator with a political ideology and political party committed to support an authoritarian system. She did not liquidate the elite of the old regime. At best she was trying to function as a dictatorial administrative officer. She was not leading a revolution or a counter-revolution. That is why her dictatorship was half-hearted and inefficient.

The political culture under her regime remained the same as the one before she came to power. Loyalty to parliamentary democracy and the rule of law was a part of it.

The political and administrative institutions were also not changed. The Civil Service, the judiciary, the educational institutions and the Press were not committed to support her. Not even the armed forces and the President. The majority of those, who held high positions in these fields, were against any kind of authoritarianism. When Mrs Gandhi and some of her colleagues realized this, they did not dispute this fact. Some of them, of course, said that they wanted a committed judiciary and

1. Lippman, Walters, Essays, in Public Philosophy, Little Brown and Company, Boston (1955), 60-61.

a committed Civil Service without explicitly making clear the meaning of the word "commitment". Another aspect of their political campaign was to say that these institutions and the elite were not major factors and what counted was the masses of the people. According to them these masses supported her and ultimately what counted in any political encounter was the support of the masses. There was no evidence to support this claim. Mrs Gandhi and her supporters were much more alienated from the masses than their political opponents. Moreover, her government had undermined the political processes of the democratic system and concentrated power on the bureaucrats around her. The ruling clique in New Delhi did not know that there was a wide gap between them and the masses. This was to prove very damaging to them in the elections of 1977 which restored democracy in this country.

4

Political System's Response

The elections to the Indian Parliament in March 1977 inaugurated a new era in Indian politics. One of its features is that democracy asserted itself in the country after a brief interlude of authoritarianism. Earlier there was the fear that if at all Mrs Indira Gandhi was thrown out of power, another authoritarian regime would replace hers in some respects and it would be worse than that. The elections and subsequent events proved that this fear was unfounded. Now it is also hoped that in the near future there will not be any such powerful threat to Indian democratic system. And even if such a threat occurs, it is again widely believed that the system has the inherent strength to face it successfully.

It is too early to say that the defeat of the Congress Party and its allies and the success of the Janata and its allies will inaugurate a new era of social and economic change in the country. Although the elections is occasionally referred to as the "revolution by ballot" and the beginning of a "total revolution", the new government formed after it, had not so far done anything drastic or put forward any programme which is fundamentally new in the economic field. The new Planning Commission and the plans they will formulate will have some departures from the earlier ones. There will be some direction in foreign policy also. The degree of continuity and change in these fields will be debatable because, at least in the near future, the emphasis will be on caution. But there is one field where definite steps are already taken and there will be further action. And that is in regard to the restoration of democracy.

The new governments cannot escape from taking these actions because in the elections the people had given a clear verdict against dictatorship and authoritarianism and for the restoration of democracy. And the leaders of the new government, with all their faults, are sincere democrats also. If the restoration of democracy after a brief interlude of authoritarianism is a revolution, in this limited sense, one can say that there is already a revolution by ballots in the country. The new government's useful function can at best be to create a favourable soil for the free action and interaction of different political forces in the country. This will no doubt lead to some confusion, if not chaos, in the near future. It would be in contrast with the stability and peace which existed during the Emergency and which the Congress party claimed would exist after the elections if it would be returned to power.

The Election and the Political Processes

Very often a question is asked : Why did Mrs Gandhi go to polls in 1977. She announced on 19 January that an election to the Parliament would be held in March. Speculations vary on the motives of Indira Gandhi. The most popular explanation was that she thought she would win the elections because the opposition was not united and, in a short time, they would not be in a position to create a machinery which would fight elections. Whether she thought on these lines or not, this is not what happened.

Another view was that there was foreign and internal pressure on her to hold elections. It is very difficult to substantiate this.

It was also contended that she was loosing the control of the Congress Party and that the delay in holding elections would have resulted in her loosing this control further. There is some evidence to support this view. Mrs Gandhi and her group did replace one Chief Minister from power—in the State of Orissa— and some among them tried to do so in West Bengal, but did not succeed. After the announcement to hold election, one senior colleague of Mrs Gandhi resigned from the party and the government. It was obvious that he had differences of opinion with her for a very long time. Rumours were afloat that Mrs Indira Gandhi and her followers would try to replace many Congressmen from positions of power and influence and that they would give Congress tickets to Sanjay Gandhi and members of Youth Congress to fight the elections as Congress candidates. It is not easy to assess precisely the impact of each one of these factors on the making of the decision to hold the elections. The announcement to hold the elections was followed by a series of dramatic developments.

A large number of political leaders were released and censorship and some other stringent measures of the "Emergency" were partially released. Suddenly, the fear in the minds of the people were gone and the resentment against the government was openly expressed. The released leaders and the large number of their supporters began to function as if India was again an open society. The circulation of many newspapers and journals which were supporting the government went down and that of those in the opposition went up. The released leaders were given welcome given to heroes in great battles and the popular enthusiasm in the meetings they addressed were reminiscent of that which were visible in the meetings addressed by great nationalist leaders during India's struggle for freedom. Jayaprakash Narayan became the symbol of the aspirations of the people.

On the other hand, the meetings addressed by the Ministers including the Prime Minister, were thinly attended, and very often audiences were hostile to them. It became usual for a Minister to request the people to forgive him and his colleagues for their mistakes and excesses. Very soon it was obvious that they were on the defensive and that the opposition leaders were in a self-confident mood.

Another spectacular and dramatic event took place on 2 February 1977. Jagjivan Ram, who was a senior colleague of Mrs Gandhi, and a very prominent Congress leader, tendered his resignation as a member of the Cabinet. He resigned from the Congress Party and formed a new organization, the "Congress for Democracy". He appealed to all Congressmen to join the new Party and to seek an end of the Emergency and other totalitarian and authoritarian trends that had of late crept into the nation's politics. Very many prominent Congress leaders who were influential in national politics and the politics of some states joined Jagjivan Ram. This gave the impression that the Congress was a leaking boat. It thoroughly demoralized the Congressmen and boosted the morale of the opposition. The 'Congress for Democracy' decided to work in co-operation with the opposition.

Jayaprakash Narayan, in spite of his old age and illness, became the symbol of fearlessness and courage. And he worked outside the party and beyond any ideology. His repeated pleas for co-ordinated action among the parties had the desired effect. Morarji Desai, who later became the Prime Minister, also displayed an indomitable will. He was a prominent leader of the Congress Organization. Fearlessness was his main theme also. And both showed no malice towards those who imprisoned them. They were very balanced and calm in their utterances.

A remarkable spirit of accomodation and adjustment were shown by the leaders of the two extremist parties—the Jana Sangh and the Communist Party of India (Marxist). Both had a great tradition of sectarianism and ideological dogmatism. But their leaders decided to work in close co-operation with other parties. So did the Socialist Party leaders. Among them George Fernandes had a great halo around him because of his underground activities and the cruel treatment he was subjected to in jail. The Swatantra Party leaders also decided to work in close co-operation with other opposition parties. So did the Akali Dal, B.L.D. and the D.M.K. which were regional parties. The degree of co-operation given by each one of them to the united effort of the opposition was different from that given by another. For instance, the Jana Sangh, the Congress Organization, the B.L.D. and the Socialist Party themselves merged into one Party—the Janata. It was formed on 20 January, 1977. Later the Swatantra joined it also. This was possible partly because of the lead given by Jayaprakash Narayan who had tremendous prestige by this time. Another reason was the pressure exerted on the leaders by the rank and file members of the different parties. They had undergone an experience during the Emergency which brought home to them the reality that their ideologies were obsolete and in the new situation that was developing in India, each one of them should give up part of their ideology and work in close co-operation with other parties of different ideological persuasions at least for the limited purpose of defending democracy.

The degree of co-operation between the Janata and the Congress Party was not made clear. The C.F.D. wanted to attract to itself further defectors from the Congress, while the Janata Party was not interested in promoting defections. But both had electoral adjustments and gave united opposition to the Congress Party at the polls. A few weeks after the elections the C.F.D. merged into the Janata Party.

The Marxists were prepared to reach electoral agreements with the Janata Party and others. The Akalis and the D.M.K. were prepared to go further and work as units within the Janata Parliamentary Party.

When the campaign was launched in this atmosphere, the Congress was demoralized and the opposition gathered great strength.

But when the results of the elections were announced, even the most optimistic of the opposition party members and the most pessimistic of the Congress members were surprised. The Janata had a clear majority and the Congress was almost routed at the polls. Many Cabinet Ministers including the Prime Minister, were defeated. The controversial Sanjay Gandhi was also defeated. The party position in the new Parliament was as follows :—

Janata: 271 and the Congress : 152. The Congress for Democracy got 28 and the Marxist Party got 22 and the C.F.D. later joined the Janata Party and the Marxist Party offered its co-operation. Other parties received less than twenty seats each and they were not significant. The Akalis got eight seats and they joined the Janata Parliamentary Party.

Consolidating the Victory of Democracy

These elections have many wide repercussions. We already referred to the fact that the ordinary members of different parties almost compelled the leaders to give up the separate identity of their parties and formed a united front against the Congress. After the elections when three prominent leaders like Jagjivan Ram, George Fernandes and Raj Narain refused to accept the offer of Cabinet posts to them, their followers almost compelled them to accept it. This was one of the many situations which revealed that the people were ahead of the leaders and the party machines.

Although the administrative excesses during the emergency was a factor in the defeat of the Congress, it is wrong to conclude that what had happened was just a protest against these and only an expression of resentment against the arrogance of Mrs Gandhi and the idiosyncrasies of Sanjay Gandhi.

In this election the issue was primarily democracy versus dictatorship. No party or any of its leaders had called for a radical reorientation of the policies of the government. The manifesto of the Janata Party, which was drafted in a hurry by technocrats but not by any leader with great political vision, had not touched upon them in detail. Vague references to new programmes were there. They were evident in many of the statements of Jayaprakash Narayan who often spoke of a total revolution.

The present Prime Minister, Morarji Desai is not a symbol of any great revolution. His assets are his austerity, administrative ability and incorruptibility. Such a man can fulfil a positive funcion of consolidating the victory of democratic forces against authoritarianism.

Under his leadership, the democratic processes will be fully revived and the rule of law will again be established. Freedom of the Press and all other civil and political rights will be returned to the people. Commissions of enquiry will be established to investigate corruption and administrative excesses and those guilty will be punished. It is in this field that concrete actions are already taken and will further be taken by the government. Those, who lived under the suffocating atmosphere of the emergency, are already having a sigh of relief.

There is no fear in the political atmosphere now. The emergency was the reign of informers and opportunists. This is all over. There is a restoration of intellectual activity also. Like in other dictatorships, during the emergency in India, the pursuit of knowledge was also a casualty.

These will by no means be insignificant achievements. They should be welcomed for their own sake and also because they are the necessary prelude to other desirable actions.

Towards the Future

The mass awakening which was evident during the elections and which was, to some extent, the culmination of the political processes in India during the past sixty years, will not be satisfied with only correctives. Even the consolidation of the success of the democratic forces against authoritarian trends demands further battles for economic and social reconstruction.

If the vast majority of the electorate were interested only in correctives, Jagjivan Ram would have been the right symbol of the new regime. He displayed considerble tact and political skill and tremendous powers of manoeuvre. As noted earlier, these had a significant role to play in the electoral battles. But, because the Congress defeat wa s total, Jagjivan Ram's share of influence in the new set-up was not very much.

This was not expected. If Janata and the Congress were equally balanced or if Janata had not received this clear-cut majority, the Congress for Democracy would have been the decisive factor in Indian politics. And further defections from the Congress to C.F.D. would also have been important. All these did not happen because the electorate went beyond a situation in which these manoeuvres had any relevance.

The fact that, under the circumstances, they had to work through these experienced politicians does not make a difference to the fact that their rebellion against the establishment was on basic issues.

To take some specific issues. The elite in power had a narrow base. In a limited sense, the elite which replaced the earlier one, had a wider base. It is true that the utterances of the Congressmen were more radical than those of the Janata leaders. But these were the rhetoric of those who had no social foundations.

At the beginning of the twentieth Century the Extremists, represented by Tilak, B.C. Pal and Lajpat Rai, were less modern than the Indian moderates represented by Gokhale and others. Again, when Gandhi entered the Indian political scene and moved to the position of the most prominent leader of the nationalist leaders, he was referred to as a man with modieval views. But the critics of the extremists and Gandhi were modern only in their words. And they forgot that the democratic function which a leader could fulfil in their situations was by making the masses participate in political activities. This was realized and accomplished by only the Extremists and Gandhi. And it is in this sense that Jayaprakash took a lead over the Congressmen and the masses of the people who voted the Congress out of power, went ahead of the Party organization and its leaders.

What took place in India in the 1977 elections was a radical mass action outside the parties and beyond ideologies. This does not mean that ideologies and parties are unnecessary. But it does mean that some of the prevalent ideologies are obsolete in Indian situation and that the existing parties are inadequate to fulfil the tasks assigned to them.

It is not an accident that the Marxists were compelled to co-operate with the Jana Sangh which became constituents of the Janata Party. The Jana Sangh leaders tried to get, with some success, the Muslim voters and their leader, when he become the Foreign Minister, spoke in conciliatory terms in regard to India's relations with Pakistan. Jayaprakash Narayan has became receptive to many new ideas and he is giving a lead in giving expression to them. Morarji Desai is considerably mellowed and he is no more his former 'rigid' self. No doubt some of these developments are due to political expediency. But they also indicate a capacity of these leaders to react to a new situation in a realistic manner.

A series of *ad hoc* decisions the new government took will lead to some departure from traditions. But very soon they will have to take deliberate steps based on new policies which are consciously formulated. In other words, the situation calls for an intellectual activity connected with political and social movements. This is not the first time that such an activity follows the movements.

Very often it is stated that as this election was not fought on foreign policy issues, the foreign policy of India will not change now. It is tactically wise to make such statement because the new government must not suddenly give a feeling of uncertainty to the foreign governments in regard to India's relations with them.

But one must add here that the basic approach of the political leadership is a major factor in the making of the foreign policy of any country. And when that has changed, one need not be ashamed to admit that the foreign policy will change.

Is the present Indian government interested in asserting its independence from the Super Powers more than the earlier government was ? Is it in a position to do so ? The answers to these questions are in the positive. And, therefore, there cannot but be a change in Indian foreign policy. To take one instance. During the past few years India's powers of manoeuvre in the international field was limited because of her dependence on the Soviet Union. This is bound to change. And there will be innumerable other changes also.

When we turn to the domestic front, are there some of the matters which will demand immediate interest. What will be the priority to be given to rural development ? In the industrial field, will light industries replace heavy industries as the first priority of the government ? Will India turn to the most advanced technology or devolop its own intermediate technology ? What are the steps to be taken for solving unemployment ? In the educational field, will the government give more attention to the spread of literacy to the masses or will it be concerned primarily with advanced research ? What will be the cultural policy of the government ? Will that be connected with austerity and importance to Indian language ? There are innumerable questions demanding a departure from traditions. Naturally the opposition represented by the Congress Party will not bring pressure on the government to follow a new line of development. This will have to spring from the masses who voted for the ruling Party.

For a New Politics

There is a basic difference between political activity, which is a spontaneous outburst, and one which is consciously led. The only positive achievement of the first can be to put an end to stagnation. Today's India needed it. And as such what happened is healthy. But chaos and crisis are to be stopped and the reconstruction is to begin, political activity is to be moved with a sense of direction. If the existing parties are to be found wanting in this field, it is because the ideologies of most of them are obsolete and their pattern of organization have no relation to the existing realities. The splits which the various parties in this country have undergone during the recent period are due to these factors.

Although Jayaprakash Narain often spoke of a total revolution, no political movement with that objective had so far arisen in the country. There were some powerful movements in some regions making such specific demands as the dissolution of the Assembly or stopping the price rise and corruption. There was isolated action like a railway strike. There was no total approach which could co-ordinate these scattered movements. That can only emerge gradually. In the short run it is possible for different political groups to work together on the basis of an alliance or understanding. This has taken place to the extent. This understanding or alliance among them took the shape of a movement during the elections. This was partly because they were in opposition at the time and they were faced with the challenge of an authoritarian government. Now that they are in the government, it will be difficult for the political activities of these groups to continue to take the shape of a movement. On the other hand, the tendency will be to fight for spoils among them.

Another defect from which the political parties in India suffer from is their regional approach. The Janata Party does not have any significant strength in the South. The B.L.D. wing has a U.P. approach and the Jana Sangh wing is mostly confined to north-western parts of India. The present leaders of the trade unions, student organisations and present movements are not capable of looking beyond their limited horizons. What India needs now is a total approach and vision which can see the inter-relation between various groups and interests. Such a political approach must worry about the ends and limits of state activity. Of course, it should also have the understanding of the power of the government and the willingness to use it as an instrument.

If the tragedy of the earlier situations in the country was that on those occasions the blue-prints of the revolutions were made by those who had not grasped the Indian realities and who were mechanically trying to apply to this country the ideologies which evolved in the social and cultural contexts which were different from those of India, today we are faced with "revolutions" without any ideology and any systematically worked out strategy of action. If the "former" revolution failed because it had no roots, the latter would reach nowhere because they have no capacity for growth. Only with proper roots some trees can survive the winds, but only when they are exposed to fresh air and light from all parts can they grow. This is true of political movements also.

The solution of many of India's problems lie in healthy political life. The term "political" is not used here in its narrow meaning—that is, capturing power and controlling the state. It is not an accident that the most creative political thinkers were also philosophers and that political leaders were connected with social reforms and cultural renaissance. In this broad sense, Gandhi was the only creative political thinker and leader India had produced. If the Indian political system and society were highly stabilized, we do not need any such Gandhi now. Anyway one connot aspire to have continuous streams of Gandhis, Lenins and Maos in one country. At best what we can aspire for is a creative interpretation of Gandhism and its applications. The new rulers of the country are always swearing by Gandhi. Before they took oath as Members of Parliament they went to Rajghat where Gandhi was cremated and expressed their allegiance to his ideals.

Towards a Scientific Gandhism

Has Gandhi returned to India after an eclipse of more than thirty years ? It is an irony if he has done so under the present circumstances. Gandhi was assassinated by a Hindu sectarian. The R.S.S. was known for its militant Hinduism. This organization had blessed, if not supported, the Janata Party during the elections. Now that Party is in power and Gandhi's programme is taken seriously by the ruling Party. Such ironies occur in history. In this particuler case, the Janata's primary source of power is not R.S.S. It is one of the many organizations which had supported it.

Even if such an irony exists, it is a minor matter. The major problem is this : How to develop Gandhism creatively ? So far there were two opposite schools of thought of Gandhi ; one accepting him totally and the other rejecting him completely. What we need now is a fresh and critical look at Gandhi by those who comprehended Gandhi's thought, but are not bound to accept his sayings literally.

To begin with, one has to accept the fact that many of Gandhi's sayings were relevent only to the period in which he lived and some only to the people around him. But some of his ideas were of permanent value and of universal application even when they were couched in a language and idiom capable of making profound appeal to the Indians—and among the Indians particularly to the Hindus—of his times. And if these ideas were to be translated into practice today and in different parts of the world, they must be expressed in a different style. In view of the new problems in the contemporary world, which Gandhi could not envisage, there is also the need for creatively developing and enriching some aspects of Gandhi's thought.

Marx and Engels, although connected with active politics in a limited manner, were primarily the intellectuals of the nineteenth century. Lenin and Mao, although they were intellectuals of a fairly high order, were primarily the politicians of the twentieth century. Noting this gap between the Marxist theoreticians of the nineteenth century and the twentieth century politicians, C. Wright Mills observes : "Marx wrote in a world situation in which there were no post-capitalist societies; these politicians are in the middle of a 'socialist reconstruction' about which Marx had very little or nothing to say. So it is little wonder that these politicians are more tightly ideological and less freely theoretical; that they are less abstract and more practical; that their theoretical or 'verbocratic' work has to do, first of all, with policy, with decisions, with justifications." Focusing attention on the need for the creative development of Marxism, Khruschev said in 1960 : "We live at a time when we have neither Marx nor Engels nor Lenin with us. If we act like children who, studying the alphabet, compile words from letters, we shall not go very far. Based on the Marxist-Leninist teaching we must think for ourselves, we must thoroughly study life, analyse the present situation and draw conclusions that are useful to the common causes of communism."

This approach is as much necessary towards Gandhism as towards communism. Of course, Gandhi was by no means a theoretician. But there is a theoretical, almost dogmatic orientation in some of his utterances. Jawaharlal Nehru once observed : "(but) from time to time he pulls himself up, as if he were afraid that he had gone too far in his compromising and returns to his moorings. In the midst of action, he seems to be in tune with man's mind, responsive to his capacity and therefore, adapting itself to it to some extent; at other times he becomes more theoretical and apparently less adaptable. There is also the difference observable in action and writings."

In spite of an occasional bent towards abstract theories in his writings, Gandhi never stood for a sect or a dogma. It was not an accident that he named his autobiography, "My Experiments with Truth." His total approach towards his actions was that they were experiments to be tested for acceptance or rejection later...

Gandhi's writings are full of such declarations : "I claim no infallibility. I am conscious of having made Himalayan blunders. I have never made a fetish of consistency. I am a votary of truth and must say what I feel and think at a given moment on the question, without regard to what I said before on it. My vision gets clearer with daily practice." He had also said that if there was inconsistency between one utterance of his and another, the last should be accepted. But the evolution of the Gandhian school of thought should not stop with his death. Others have as much a duty and right to enrich it as he himself continuously did. For that purpose we should be beyond his last utterance.

If the view is put forward in this manner, no one will disagree with it. Differences of opinion will arise when in the field of action and in the realm of ideas, the relevance of some aspects of Gandhi's ideas are questioned. This is partly because the line of resistance is to accept him totally and not to pick and choose some of Gandhi's ideas and reject others. We have, therefore, the interesting spectacle of a large number of people owing verbal allegiance to Gandhi—accepting him totally in theory and rejecting him almost with the same totality in practice on the ground that it is practically impossible to adhere to Gandhi's ideas in real life.

The essential aspects of Gandhi are broadly divided into two parts : the aims and the instruments.

Gandhi would not have liked to make his separation because, according to him they were inter-related and his choice of words were the "end and means". He asserted, "As the means, so the ends...There is no wall of separation between means and ends." What he meant was substantially correct in the long run. In the short run he himself used the means, which was not always ethical or moral, for good ends. But he never accepted the theoretical position that "ends justify the means".

Gandhi's aims were always sound and the search for justice was his paramount concern. And he realised more than any other Indian leader of his times that this search could be undertaken only with a spirit of rebellion. He, therefore, set in motion many revolutionary movements in the country.

One of the most important movements he initiated was concerned with the question of the *Harijans*—those who were referred to as untouchables—and to ensure that they are treated as equals to the high castes. But in a sense, the situaton of today is vastly different from the India of the period when Gandhi started the movement for the uplift of the "low castes". One basic difference is that the country is politically free and now on such matters the major responsibility rests with the government. Another is that in regard to such matters neither metaphysics nor a reinterpretation of religious texts is now called for. A secular approach to socio-cultural issues which can interrelate science, technology, politics and economics is relevant now. When the so-called low caste gets equal opportunities in the political, administrative and economic fields no one will be in a position to deny them rights which are enjoyed by others. The under-privileged non-Brahmins of Madras had proved this. So did the "low caste" of Kerala who worked through the communist movement of the State. It is significant that neither the D.M.K. in Madras nor the Kerala communist movement used Gandhi's idioms. And yet no other political group in India has continued the unfinished Gandhian task, with success in this particular field. Even the word "Harijan" has lost its significance now. Why bring Hari—Lord Vishnu—if at all he exists, to these worldly encounters ?

To take the case of national independence. Now that the country has technically achieved its independence, the relevant questions today are : How to defend and extend the hard-won freedom ? How to secure our frontiers from a possible penetration from a super power ? Although self-reliance, as Gandhi and Mao conceived it, should be fully taken into account even now, the tasks of defending the freedom could be fulfilled only by looking beyond our borders. Gandhi was not concerned with India making alliances in the international field, but the leaders of contemporary India cannot ignore them even from the narrow standpoint of promoting the national interests of this country.

Gandhi's ideas on the economic reconstruction of the country are by no means completely irrelevant to contemporary India. But one has to pick and choose from them even if one agrees with his total philosophy. Mechines can now be extensively used much more than was envisaged by Gandhi without harming the economy of the country. And, perhaps, India does not have much choice in this matter. This country is a part of the world community and the sense of direction of economic forces in the world in general is towards making use of more and more sophisticated technology.

The importance of Khadi during India's freedom struggle was that it provided a political uniform. Cottage industries, including the production of Khadi, will still have some limited functions. For aesthetic and other reasons there will be a demand for their products. But it must be fully understood that they are no solution to India's complex socio-economic and technological problems.

It is also doubtful that any government in India will ever be in a position to accept the total economic philosophy of Gandhi. Because it is connected with other aspects of his thought intrinsically related to non-violence as a creed. The head of any government has to accept the fact that the game of national and international politics is played on the basis of the rules of the power struggle and that the State, with which he is connected, should also acquire some power on the basis of military strength and economic growth.

Gandhi's contribution to India and the world is the doctrine of fearlessness (abhayata)—that he made a large section of the people of India and the world fearless and uncompromising fighters for what they considered to be just. No one can improve upon this aspect of Gandhi. This is an area where total acceptance of Gandhi's philosophy in life is not only desirable, but commendable. But even here those who follow Gandhi now will have to discover for themselves what are the just causes they should fight for.

Gandhi was not concerned with social questions alone. He also dwelled upon the problems of the individual. Diet, modern medicines, drinking liquor and sexual life also attracted his attention. It is doubtful that many people today will accept his ideas totally in these fields. Although he himself made extensive use of modern medicines, he occasionally said that the invention, in relation to the cure of venereal diseases, would promote immorality. He should have known that prostitution and diseases connected with it existed much before the medicines were discovered by modern men. Even if he was right in regard to observations on the promotion of loose morals by these medicines, we should have to make use of all modern medicines in the context in which we are living.

Gandhi's opposition to birth control measures and family planning devices and his insistence on self-control as the exclusive method of brith-control is, to say the least, impractical and unrealistic. One cannot also accept his view that the purpose of sexual activity is only the perpetuation of the race.

Perhaps, his advice against the inhuman application of machinery, indiscriminate use of drugs and again loose sexual life is relevent. But one need not accept his total philosophy in these matters. On the other hand, one should reject some of his suggestions and accept others with modifications and additions. A few may be accepetd totally.

The question of relevance of Gandhism today should be approached in a rational manner. Aldous Huxley wrote an article entitled "New Fashions in Love" in which he contended that under the new circumstances, an appeal based on reason might convince a modern man of the morality, but not one based on religion and metaphysics. Much of Gandhism will have to be reinterpreted in this spirit.

Much more complicated is the attempt at creative interpretations of Gandhi's methods with the aim of making them effective in the contemporary period. He never used the word tactics, though, after his death, many wrote on "Gandhian Tactics". Gandhi was, however, supremely aware of the importance of strategy and tactics of any struggle he led. He, of course, took a theoretical stand that the means one employs must always be just and right. One may even get an impression from his writings that, unlike Marx, he was less interested in the ultimate result than in the methods. He emphasised non-violent methods because they were the only feasible form of mass action open to the people of the country in the nineteen-twenties and thirties. By 1942, he was not as much concerned with violence and non-violence. For the violence that took place during the "Quit India" movement, he only said that the British Government was responsible for it.

After 1947, Gandhi occasionally even sanctioned the use of force to stop the communal riots in the country.

This is not to say that throughout this period, as earlier, he did not emphasise the fundamental importance of non-violence. In this period when also he spoke as a prophet, he focused attention on it. But when he worked out the strategy and tactics of a struggle he was as much concerned with their effectiveness as with the "ethics" involved in them.

A view was often expressed that Gandhi was a typical Hindu and Indian. This is far from the truth. As V.S. Naipaul, the well known novelist of the West Indies, notes : "He (Gandhi) looked at India as no Indian was able to, his vision was direct, and his directness was, and is, revolutionary. He sees exactly what the visitor sees, he does not ignore the obvious ... No Indian attitude escapes him, no Indian problem; he looks down to the roots of the static, decayed society." The same view, in different words, was expressed by Rajni Kothari, an Indian political scientist: "unalienated from the people of India, as is the general presumption about him, Gandhi represented a nega- tion of much that is Indian. The very freshness and originality of approach that he brought to Indian affairs, the rapport that he could establish with the masses of India or the ease with which he could understand the inner striving of all classes of Indians—all this was possible because, in a very basic sense, Gandhi was an outsider, a prophet from somewhere else, a messiah with a totally new mission." He was more universal than any other leader of modern India. It is not an accident that his spiritual Guru was a Russian—Tolstoy. And the only creative disciple he has had so far was Martin Luther King—an American citizen of African origin. Gandhi was thus linking Russia, the U.S. and Africa and Asia. Some of the best books on Gandhi and his teachings were written outside India. A few of them came from Italy and France and their authors never met Gandhi. But they comprehended him because he was in line with their thinking and unlike Gandhi's followers in India, they were in a position to critically examine Gandhi without any sentimental nonsense. To put it in other words : It is in inverse proportion to one's blind allegiance to any system of ideas, one understands the person who originated them and one is in a position to interpret them.

The questions raised and some of the suggestions made here are only the beginning of discussion on creative Gandhism. The new politics of India call for further discussions on them. And it could go on only with the implementation of some of the Gandhian programmes. There should be action and interaction between thought and action in this field.

5

New Directions of Foreign Policy

When the Congress Party was removed from power for the first time by the 1977 elections, a question is naturally raised : Will India's foreign policy change ? No dramatic announcement by the spokesmen of the ruling party has suggested that it will. On the other hand, the new foreign minister has emphasised continuity in this field. In spite of it, there is a widespread feeling in India and abroad that the Indian foreign policy will gradually take new directions.

This is evident from the fact that the Western Press which was very critical of Mrs Indira Gandhi has welcomed the new government and showered considerable praise on its leaders. There were some apprehensions in West Asia about India's policy in their region. Some non-alignment governments had a sense of relief when the new government assured them of its loyalty to non-alignment. The Soviet press and scholars were praising Mrs Gandhi and supporting the "Emergency" in India. As the Indian voters had rejected both, there can be an impression that India-Soviet Union relations will take a new shape. The most of the matter is this : the recent Indian elections have led to a turning point in Indian politics--a turning point which cannot be confined to the internal field.

The Basis of Continuity

There will, of course, be a certain degree of continuity. Some aspects of geo-politics may change as the result of technical revolutions and a new political leadership viewing the country's external problems in a new light. But geography itself does not change. And if what Chanakya said centuries ago on this matter has any sense, it applies to a changing situation also : according to him a country's neighbour is its enemy and the neighbour's neighbour is its friend. To be specific, India will have some hostile relations with Pakistan and China and cordial relations with Afghanistan and U.S.S.R. But these maxims are not self-evident truth and the experience of many countries has shown their weakness. The recent relations between the United Kingdom and France and West Germany and Canada and the U.S. tell a different story. But the limited validity of some of these ideas will stress the continuity in foreign policy.

There are other areas in which continuity will not be broken suddenly. For instance, no government, not even one which has come to power after a bloody revolution, will like to give up the advantages of a treaty signed by an earlier government. For instance, the Soviet Government after 1917, the Chinese Government after 1949 and the French Government after the revolution, tried to retain some of the international rights which the earlier governments have acquired. Free India's government quoted the sanctity of the McMohan Line which it inherited from the British Government of India.

But, here again, there are exceptions. The Soviet Government after 1917 did give up some of its extra-territorial rights. This may be partly true because it was unable to retain them unless it could work in close co-operation with the capitalist states. And it is also true because it wanted to acquire a new tower as the centre of world revolution and anti-imperialist sentiments.

When a new government wanted continuity in relation to its rights, it may have to display its interest in fulfilling its international obligations also. A treaty is not easily repudiated by any single party.

The continuity will be maintained in the external economic relations of a country also. This will be particularly evident when the new government does not have a new radical economic programme at home. There will be change—though a gradual one—if a new group of people even within the same class acquires power or when a government decides as a matter of policy to depend less upon foreign help than its predecessor.

There are three other factors in favour of continuity. The civil service in the foreign ministry, the army and the defence ministry, and the public opinion resist radical changes in foreign policy. Even such prominent leaders with some vision as Kennedy and Khruschev could not very often overrule the recommendations of senior civil servants. Kennedy had to continue the previous regime's polcies in Vietnam and in Cuba—and that too with disastrous results. Khruschev spoke eloquently on de-Stalinization but pursued systematically, and in the long run unwisely, Stalin's policies in regard to Eastern Europe. It was not an accident that Gallbraith told a recent American Ambassador in India that the latter could be success-ful in New Delhi only if he would disregard all the instructions of the State Department. In India also the tendency of some senior civil servants will be to take a conservative view and to resist any radical change on substantial matters.

The perspective planning of India's foreign policy has taken into account India's defence needs. And in some branches of the ammunitions and defence industries, the Indian government was depending upon the Soviet Union. China and the U.A.R. disentangled themselves from the dependence on the Soviet Union. Can the new government of India afford to do it ? Or is it interested in doing so ? The answers to these questions will partly depend upon the Soviet attitude towards the new government also.

The Public Opinion

Very often the general public, or that section of the people who take interest in foreign policy, accept some traditions in foreign policy. The Americans cannot ignore the terms such as "free world", the Russians "Socialism", the Chinese "anti-imperialism" and many countries like India, "non-alignment". And if the government has to make changes, it has to give new formulations which are acceptable to the people or new interpretations to the current concepts.

Some Changes Inevitable

In spite of all these factors in favour of continuity, some changes are inevitable in Indian foreign policy. For one thing, international politics is dynamic and in a changing world, every country has to readjust its policy to the new situation. And for anoher, there is a qualitative change in the Indian political situation which cannot but be reflected in its foreign policy. There can be difference of opinions on the manner and speed in which these changes have to take place, but not on the fact that changes are inevitable.

Pandit Nehru was the architect of India's foreign policy. He was its ideologue also. But then he was working on a clean slate. And he himself had not a little to do in giving an international outlook to the Indian nationalist movement. He had no experienced foreign ministry to help him. And the relatively weak India was not involved in power politics—except in relation to a still weaker Pakistan. Nehru had a historical sense and a vision. It is in this context that the ideas expounding and explaining the mojor factors in Indian foreign policy were formulated by him. Some of his ideas were similar to those of the leaders of the newly independent countries of Asia and Africa.

Moreover, he led the rest of Indian leaders by a wide margin as far as the interest in, and understanding of, international politics were concerned. So he could easily lead the Indian public opinion on foreign policy.

The following were theoretically put forward by Nehru as the Indian government's aspirations : (1) Development of an independent foreign policy—not joining any power bloc. Later this is referred to as non-alignment; (2) Pursuit of peace ; not only because peace is desirable but because weak countries like India could not afford war and the preparation for wars ; (3) Opposition to racialism ; (4) Opposition to colonialism and (5) Acceptance of foreign aid without any strings.

It is often said that the leadership of the country, which had undergone a revolution forty years ago, will not have a revolutionary outlook. One has only to look at the Soviet leaders and the Chinese of today to realise this fact. They resemble civil servants aud technocrats and not revolutionaries. This is true of the emerging leaders of India including the present Foreign Minister. They do not have the exeprience of Nehru. They are expected to fulfil different functions today. We have a relatively stabilized political set-up in the country. Defending and extending the freedom of the country are not the problems facing the country. Whether we like it or not, we are a part of power politics in the international field. And in a limited sense, India is a centre of power though at present it could make itself felt only in South Asia.

India's acquiring nuclear capability is also not without significance.

There are no crystallised power blocs now. This is no more a bi-polar world. Whatever may be the technical position, it is wrong to conclude that China and France, which are not non-aligned, have less initiative and powers of manoeuvre in the international fields. The relations between the two Super Powers have gone beyond detente. The expressions such as "independent foreign policy", "pursuit of peace" and "non-alignment" do not have the same relevance today. If these terms have to be used, it must be done with the understanding that they have lost their original meaning and that they should be given a new interpretation in the new context. And also it should de realised that they would sound hollow, if they are mechanically repeated now. Vajpayee is not a Nehru, nor will the audiences in Asian-African conferences in the Non-Aligned Conferences and in the U.N. General Assembly which the former will address be the same as those addressed by Nehru. Even the political mood of the young people of India is very different from that of the time when Nehru began to formulate his ideas on foreign policy.

In other words the present and future Foreign Ministers will have to do their own original thinking and give expression to them. One of the factors which Vajpayee has to take into account is that power politics is an aspect of international politics and that India is involved in it.

One of the questions facing those who are interested in foreign policy making in India should be this : how to formulate fresh ideas and concepts and to what extent they should owe allegiance to them. To take an illustraon : Can we not frankly say that we are gradually manufacturing nuclear weapons and developing a delivery system because they are in our national interest and that whether or not we will use them in any armed conflict will depend upon the then existing circumstances ?

Colonialism is not a major factor in world affairs today and the conflicts connected with racialism will also not assume the same proportion because no major power or group of powers is any more in a position to support frankly racialism and colonialism.

Naturally the emphasis on these matters will have to be reduced.

Third World Neighbours, Super Powers

This is in the realm of ideas. Concretely, the foreign policy makers will have to be concerned with India's relations with the Third World, her neighbours and Super Powers.

Apart from the political aspects of colonialism and racialism, there is the economic aspects of the relations with the Third World and the economically advanced countries. This has assumed new proportions now. What will be India's international role in regard to this matter.

Two of India's neighbours—Pakistan and China—are members of the third world. In the new context what will be India's relations with each one of them.

Relatively speaking, the party in power in New Delhi now is a conservative one. The members of this party when they were in the opposition or when they were the dissidents of the Congress Party were critical of what they characterized as Nehru's policy of appeasement of Pakistan and China. Occasionally Nehru became the critic of his political opponents and followed very rigid and uncompromising policies towards these countries. Some of them had disastrous results. Internally, the present government will not be faced with such opposition if it follows a policy of conciliation with China and Pakistan. Externally, they will not be faced with the support of any Super Power to any one of them. It may, therefore, look ironic but a reality that an apparently rightist party with the traditions of miliant national chuavinism, is in a position to deal realistically and rationally with India's neighbours than Nehru and the Congress Party with its leftist and cosmopolitan image were. There is no irony in this. Nixon, connected with the investigations on "un-Americans" and McCarthyism, was in a position to initiate a policy of friendship with China.

One of the problems to be tackled is this : What should be the changing character of India's relations with Pakistan and China ?

This takes us to another important matter : India's relations with the Super Power. Whatever the official spokesmen say, there is no doubt that there will be a departure from the traditional approach. India will be less dependent upon the U.S.S.R. than she was before. There will be close relations between India and the U.S. As noted earlier the degree and speed of changes in this field will be a matter of debate.

The new trends in this area will definitely affect India's

relations with her neighbours and her position in South Asia.

India's relations with the countries of West Asia (Middle East) are connected with her policies related with the Super Powers and her neighbours, particularly Pakistan. But they also have an autonomy of their own. For instance, the oil is a factor. So is India's continuous need of the market in this area for her goods. This is another singificant aspect of India's external relations calling for a fresh look.

In many of these areas there will be some continuity in India's foreign policy. But there is also a change in many areas.

DOCUMENTS

DOCUMENTS

1

Liberalism and Democracy[*]

Gopal Krishna Gokhale

Gentlemen, this is the twenty-first session of the Indian National Congress. Year after year, since 1885, we have been assembling in these gatherings to give voice to eur aspirations and to formulate our wants. The Congress movement was the direct and immediate outcome of this realization. It was started to focus and organize the patriotic forces that were working independently of one another in different parts of the country so as to invest their work with a national character and to increase their general effectiveness. Hope at that time was warm and faith shone bright, largely as a result of Lord Ripon's Viceroyalty, and those who started the Congress believed that, by offering their criticism and urging their demands from a national platform where they could speak in the name of all India, they would be able to secure a continuous improvement of the administration and a steady advance in the direction of the political emancipation of the people. Twenty years have since elapsed, and during the time much has happened to chill that hope and dim that faith, but there can be no doubt that work of great value in our national life has already been accomplished. The minds of the people have been familiarised with the idea of a united India working for her salvation; a national public opinion has been created ; close bonds of sympathy now knit together the different provinces ; caste and creed separa-

[*]Extracts from the President's address delivered at the annual session of the Indian National Congress held at Benares in 1905.

tions hamper less and less the pursuit of common aims ; the dignity of a consciousness of national existence has spread overt he whole land. Our record of political concessions won is, no doubt, very meagre, but those that have been secured are of considerable value ; some retrogression has been prevented ; and if latterly we have been unable to stem the tide of reaction, the resistances we have offered, though it has failed of its avowed purpose, has substantially strengthened our public life. Our deliberations have extended over a very wide range of problems ; public opinion in the country is, in consequence, better informed and the Press is steadily growing in authority and usefulness. About all, there is general perception now of the goal towards which we have to strive and a wide recognition of the arduous character of the struggle and the immense sacrifices it requires.

The goal of the Congress is that India should be governed in the interests of the Indians themselves, and that, in course of time, a form of governmant should be attained in this country similar to what exists in the self governing colonies of the British Empire. For better, for worse, our destinies are now linked with those of England, and the Congress freely recognises that whatever advance we seek must be within the Empire itself. That advance, moreover, can only be gradual, as at each stage of the progress it may be necessary for us to pass through a brief course of apprenticeship before we are enabled to go to the next one ; for it is a reasonable proposition that the sense of responsibility, required for the proper exercise of the political institutions of the West, can be acquired by an Eastern people through practical training and experiment only. To admit this is not to express any agreement with those who usually oppose all attempts at reform on the plea that the people are not ready for it. "It is liberty alone," says Mr. Gladstone in words of profound wisdom, "which fits men for liberty. This proposition like every other in politics, has its bound ; but it is far safer than the counter doctrine, wait till they are fit."

The Spread of Education

While, therefore, we are prepared to allow that an advance towards our goal may be made only by reasonably cautious steps, what we emphatically insist on is that the resources of the country should be primarily devoted to the work of qualifying the people by means of education and in other ways for such advance. Even the most bigoted champion of the existing system of administration will not pretend that this is in any degree the case at present. Our net revenue is about 44 millions sterling. Of this very nearly one-half is now eaten up by the Army. The Home Charges, exclusive of their military portion, absorb nearly one-third. The two, between them, account for about 35 millions out of 44. Then over 3 millions are paid to European officials in civil employ. This leaves about 7 millions at the disposal of the Government to be applied to other purposes. Can any one, who realises what this means, wonder that the Government spends only a miserable three-quarters of a million out of State funds on the education of the people—primary, secondary and higher, all put together ! Japan came under the influence of Western ideas only forty years ago, and yet already she is in line with the most advanced nations of the West in matters of mass education, the State finding funds for the education of every child of schoolgoing age. We have now been a hundred years under England's rule, and yet today four villages out of every five are without a school-house and seven children out of eight are allowed to grow up in ignorance and in darkness. Militarism, service interests and the interests of English capitalists—all take precedence to-day of the true interests of Indian people in the administration of the country. Things cannot be otherwise, for it is the government of the people of one country by the people of another and this, as Mill points out, is bound to produce great evils. Now the Congress wants that all this should be governed, first and foremost, in the interests of the Indians themselves. This result will be achieved only in proportion as we obtain more and more voice in the government of our country.

Our whole future, it is needless to say, is bound up with this question of the relative position of the two races in this country. The domination of one race over another—especially when there is no great disparity between the intellectual endowments of their general civilization—inflicts great injury on the subject race in thousand insidious ways. On the moral side, the present situation it steadily destroying our capacity for initiative and dwarfing us as men of action. On the material side, it has resulted in a fearful impoverishment of the people. For a hundred years and more now India has been for members of the dominant race a country where fortunes were to be made to be taken out and spent elsewhere. As in Ireland, the evil of absentee landlordism has in the past aggravated the racial domination of the English over the Irish, so in India what may be called absentee capitalism has been added to the racial ascendancy of Englishmen. A great and ruinous drain of wealth from the country has gone on for many years, the net excess of exports over imports (including treasure) during the last forty years amounting to no less than a thousand millions sterling. The steady rise in the death-rate of the country—from 24 per thousand, the average for 1882-84, to 30 per thousand, the average for 1892-94, and 34 per thousand, the present average—is a terrible and conclusive proof of this continuous impoverishment of the mass of our people. India's best interests—material and moral—no less than the honour of England, demand that policy of equality for the two races promised by the Sovereign and by Parliament should be faithfully and courageously carried out.

Political Rights for the Educated Minority

We have now in this country about 15 million people who can read and about a million of these have come under the influence of some kind of English education. Moreover, what we ask for at present is a voice in the government of the country, not for the whole population, but for such portion of it as has been qualified by education to discharge properly the responsibilities of such association. Another argument brought forward in favour of maintaining the present bureaucratic monopoly of power is that though the educated classes make a grievance of it, the mass of the people are quite indifferent in the matter. Now, in the first place, this is not true. However, it may suit the interests of the officials to dany the fact, the educated classes are, in the present circumstances of India, the natural leaders of the people. Theirs is the vernacular Press, the contents of which do not fail to reach the mass of our population; in a hundred ways they have access to the minds of the latter; and what the educated Indians think today the rest of India thinks tomorrow. Moreover, do the officials realise how their contention condemns their rule out of their own mouths ? For it means that only so long as the people of India were kept in ignorance and their faculties are forced to lie dormant, that they do not raise any objection to the present system of administration. The moment education quickens those faculties and clears their vision, they range themselves against a continuance of the system !

Our Immediate Demands

Speaking broadly, most of the reforms that we have been advocating may be grouped under heads :

(1) Those which aim at securing for our people a larger and larger share in the administration and control of our affairs; these include a reform of our legislative councils, the appointment of Indians to the Secretary of State's Council and the Executive Councils in India, and a steady substitution of the Indian for the European agency in the public service of the country;

(2) those which seek to improve the methods of administration, such as the separation of judicial from executive fuuctions, police reforms, and similar proposals ;

(3) those which propose a readjustment of financial arrangements with the object of securing a reduction of the burdens of the taxpayers and a more efficient application of our resources ; under this head come a reduction of military charges, the moderating of land assessments and so forth; and

(4) those which urge the adoption of measures calculated to improve the condition of the mass of the people; those include a vigorous extension of primary education, facilities for industrial and technical instruction, grants for improved sanitation, and a real attempt to deal with the alarming indebtedness of the peasantry. Now what I would most earnestly and respectfully suggest is that we should select from each group such reforms as may be immediately urged with the greatest effect and press them forward in this country and in England with all the

energy we can command. In my humble opinion, our immediate demands should be :

(1) A reform of our legislative councils, i.e., raising the proportion of elected members to one half, requiring the budgets to be formally passed by the councils, and empowering the members to bring forward amendments, with safeguards for bringing debates to a close in a reasonable time. The presidents of the councils should have the power of veto. The Viceroy's Legislative Council consists, at present, of 25 members, of whom only five are elected, one by the Chamber of Commerce of Calcutta— a body of Europeans—and the other four by four provinces. We must ask for the proportion of elected members to be now raised to 12. Of this number one seat might be given to commerce and one to certain industries, and the remaining ten should be assigned to different provinces, two to each of the three older provinces, and one each to the remaining. And, to begin with, the right of members to move amendments may be confined to one amendment each. The two members for commerce and industries will generally be Europeans, and they will ordinarily vote with Government. Thus even if all the ten provincial members voted together, they would be only 10 out of 25. Ordinarily they will not be able to carry a motion against the Government, but on exceptional occasions they may obtain the support of two or three men from the other side, and then the moral effect of the situation will be considerable. In the provincial legislative councils, we must have an increase in the number of members, each district of a province being empowered to send a member. The objection that these bodies will, in that case, be somewhat unwieldy is not entitled to much weight.

(2) The appointment of at least three Indians to the Secretary of State's Council, to be returned, one each, by the three older provinces.

(3) The creation of advisory boards in all districts throughout India, whom the heads of districts should be bound to consult in important matters of administration concerning the public before taking action. For the present, their functions should be only advisory, the collectors or district magistrates being at liberty to set aside their advice at their discretion. Half the members of a Board should be elected representatives of the

different talukas or sub-divisions of the district, and the other half should consist of the principal district officers and such non-official gentlemen as the head of the district may appoint. These boards must not be confounded with what are known as district local boards. There is, at present, too much of what may be called secretariat rule with an excessive multiplication of central departments. District administration must be largely freed from this and reasonable opportunities afforded to the people concerned to influence its course, before final decisions are arrived at. If such boards are created, we may, in course of time, expect them to be entrusted with some real measure of control over the district administration. The late Mr. Ranade used to urge the importance of such boards very strongly. If ever we are to have real local government in matters of general administration, the creation of these boards will pave the way for it. One great evil of the present system of administration is its secrecy. This will be materially reduced, so far as district administration is concerned, by the step proposed.

(4) The recruitment of the judicial branch of the Indian Civil Service from the legel profession in india.

(5) The separation of judicial and executive functions.

(6) A reduction of military expenditure.

(7) A large extension of primary education.

(8) Facilities for industrial and technical education.

(9) An experimental measure to deal with the indebtedness of the peasantry over a selected area. I think, gentlemen, if we now concentrate all our energies on some such programme, we may within a r easonable time see results which will not be altogether disappointing. One thing is clear. The present is a specially favourable juncture for such an effect. In our country, there is sure to be a great rebound of public opinion after the repression to which it has been subjected during the last three years. And in England, for the first time since the Congress movement began, the Liberal and Radical party will come into real power. My recent visit to England...has satisfied me that a strong current has already set in there against that narrow and aggressive imperialism, which only the other day seemed to be carrying everything before it. The new Prime Minister is a tried and trusted friend of freedom. And as regards the new Secretary

of State for India, what shall I say ? Large numbers of educated
men in this country feel towards Mr. Morley as towards
a Master, and the heart hopes and yet it trembles, as it had
never hoped or trembled before. He, the reverent student of
Burke, the disciple of Mill, the friend and biographer of Gladstone—will he courageously apply their principles and his own to
the Government of the country, or will he too succumb to the
influences of the India Office around him, and thus cast a cruel
blight on hopes which his own writings have done so much to
foster ? We shall see ; but in any case his appointment, as
Secretary of State for India, indicates how strongly favourably
to our case the attitude of the new Ministry is. Mr. Ellis, the
new Under-Secretary of State for India, is openly known to be
a friend of our aspirations. A more gratifying combination of
circumstances could not be conceived, and it now rests with
us to turn it to the best advantage we can for our motherland.

Conclusion

Gentlemen, one word more and I have done. I have no wish
to underrate the difficulties that lie in our path, but I am convinced more than ever that they are not insuperable. Moreover,
the real moral interest of a struggle, such as we are engaged
in, lies not so much in the particular readjustment of present
institutions which we may succeed in securing, as in the strength
that the conflict brings us to be a permanent part of ourselves.
The whole life of a people, which is broader and deeper than
what is touched by purely political institutions, is enriched even
by failures, provided the effect has been all that it should be.
For such enrichment the present struggle is invaluable. "The
true end of our work", said Mr. Ranade nine years ago, "is to
renovate, to purify, and also to perfect the whole men by liberating his intellect, elevating his standard of duty, and developing
to the full all his powers. Till so renovated, purified, and
perfected, we can never hope to be what our ancestors once
were—a chosen people, to whom great tasks were allotted and by
whom great deeds were performed. Where this feeling animates
the worker, it is a matter of comparative indifference in what
particular direction it asserts itself and in what particular

method it proceeds to work. With a liberated manhood, with buoyant hope, with a faith that never shirks duty, with a sense of justice that deals fairly by all, with unclouded intellect and powers fully cultivated, and, lastly, with a love that overleaps all bounds, renovated India will take her proper rank among the nations of the world, and be the master of the situation and of her own destiny. This is the goal to be reached—this is the promised land. Happy are they, who see it in distant vision ; happeir those whom are permitted to work and clear the way on to it ; happiest they, who live to see it with their eyes and tread upon the holy soil once more. Famine and pestilence, oppression, and sorrow, will then be myths of the past, and the goods will once again descend to the earth and associate with men, as they did in times which we now call mythical." Gentle men, I can add nothing that may be worthy of being placed by the side of these beautiful words. I will only call to your mind the words of another great teacher of humanity who asks us to keep our faith in spite of trying circumstances and warns us against the presumption of despairing, because we do not see the whole future clearly before our eyes :

Our times are in His hand
Who saith, "A whole I planned,
Youth shows but half ; trust God ; see all, nor be afraid !"

2

Active and Passive Resistance*

Aurobindo Ghose

Organized resistance to an existing form of government may be undertaken either for the vindication of national liberty, or in order to substitute one form of government for another, or to remove particular objectionable features in the existing system without any entire or radical alteration of the whole, or simply for the redress of particular grievances.   Our political agitation in the nineteenth century was entirely confined to the smaller and narrower objects.   To replace an oppressive land revenue system by the security of a Permanent Settlement, to mitigate executive tyranny by the separation of judicial from executive functions, to diminish the drain on the   country naturally resulting from fareign rule   by more liberal employment of Indians in the services—to these half-way houses our wise men and political seers directed our steps—with this limited ideal they confined the rising hopes and imaginations of a mighty people reawakening after a great   downfall.   Their political inexperience   prevented   them from   realizing that these measures on which we have misspent half a century of unavailing effort, were not only paltry and partial in their scope but in their nature ineffective.   A Permanent Settlement can always be evaded by a   spendthrift Government bent on increasing its resources and unchecked   by any system of popular control; there is no limit to the possible number of cesses and local taxes

*Extracts from a series of articles written in April, 1907.

by which the Settlement could be practically violated without any direct infringement of its provisions. The mere deprivation of judicial functions will not disarm executive tyranny so long as both executive and judiciary are mainly white and subservient to a central authority irresponsible, alien and bureaucratic ; for the central authority can always tighten its grip on the judiciary of which it is the controller and paymaster and habituate it to a consistent support of executive action. Nor will Simultaneous Examinations and the liberal appointment of Indians mend the matter; for an Englishman services the Government as a member of the same ruling race and can afford to be occasionally independent ; but the Indian civilian is a serf masquerading as a heavenborn and can only deserve favour and promotion by his zeal in fastening the yoke heavier upon kis fellow-countrymen. As a rule the foreign Government can rely on the "native" civilian to be more zealously oppressive than even the average Anglo-Indian official. Neither would the panacea of Simultaneous Examinations really put an end to the burden of the drain. The Congress insistence on the Home Charges for a long time obscured the real accusation against British rule; for it substituted a particular grievance for a radical and congenital evil implied in the very existence of British control. The huge price India has to pay England for the inestimable privilege of being ruled by Englishmen is a small thing compared with the murderous drain by which we purchase the more exquisite privilege of being exploited by British capital. The diminution of Home charges will not prevent the gradual death by bleeding of which exploitation is the true and abiding cause. Thus, even for the partial objects they were intended to secure, the measures for which we petitioned and demanded in the last century were hopelessly ineffective. So was it with all the Congress nostrums ; they were palliatives which could not even be counted upon to palliate; the radical evil, uncured, would only be driven from one seat in the body politic to take refuge in others where it would soon declare its presence by equally troublesome symptoms. The only true cure for a bad and oppressive financial system is to give the control over taxation to the people whose money pays for the needs of Government. The only effective way of putting an end to executive tyranny is to make the people—and not an irresponsible Government—the controller and paymaster of both executive and judiciary. The only possible method of stopping the drain is to establish a popular government which may be relied on to foster and protect Indian commerce and Indian industry conducted by Indian capital and employing Indian labour. This is the object which the new politics, the politics of the twentieth century, places before the people of India in their resistance to the present system of Government—not tinkerings and palliatives but the substitution for the autocratic bureaucracy, which at present mis-governs us, of a free constitutional and democratic system of Government and the entire removal of foreign control in order to make way for perfect national liberty.

The redress of particular grievances and the reformation of particular objectionable features in a system of Government are sufficient objects for organized resistance only when the Government is indigenous and all classes have a recognized place in the political scheme of the State. They are not and cannot be a sufficient object in countries like Russia and India where the laws are made and administered by a handful of men, and a vast population, educated and uneducated alike, have no political right or duty except the duty of obedience and the right to assist in confirming their own servitude. They are still less a sufficient object when the despotic oligarchy is alien by race and has not even a permanent home in the country, for in that case the Government cannot be relied on to look after the general interest of the contrary. as in nations ruled by indigenous despotism; on the contrary, they are bound to place the interests of their own country and their own race first and foremost. Organized resistance in subject nations which mean to live and not to die, can have no less an object than an entire and radical change of the system of Government; only by becoming responsible to the people and drawn from the people can the Government be turned into a protector instead of an oppressor. But if the subject nation desires not a provincial existence and a maimed development but the full, vigorous and noble realization of its national existence, even a change in the system of Government will not be enough; it must aim not only at a national Government responsible to the people but a free national Government unhampered even in the least degree by foreign control.

It is not surprising that our politicians of the nineteenth century could not realize these elementary truths of modern politics. They had no national experience behind them of politics under modern conditions; they had no teachers except English books and English liberal "sympathisers" and "friends of India". Schooled by British patrons, trained to the fixed idea of English superiority and Indian inferiority, their imaginations could not embrace the idea of national liberty, and perhaps they did not even desire it at heart, preferring the comfortable case which at that time still seemed possible in a servitude under British protection, to the struggles and sacrifices of a hard and difficult independence. Taught to take their political lessons solely from the example of England and ignoring or not valuing the historical experience of the rest of the world, they could not even conceive of a truly popular and democratic Government in India except as the slow result of the development of centuries, progress broadening down from precedent to precedent. They could not then understand that the experience of an independent nation is not valid to guide a subject nation, unless and until the subject nation throws off the yoke and itself becomes independent. They could not realize that the slow, painful and ultra-cautious development, necessary in medieval and semi-medieval conditions when no experience of a stable popular Government had been gained, need not be repeated in the days of the steamship, railway and telegraph, when stable democratic systems are part of the world's secured and permanent heritage. The instructive spectacle of Asiatic nations demanding and receiving constitutional and parliamentary government as the price of a few years' struggle and civil turmoil, had not then been offered to the world. But even if the idea of such happening had occurred to the more sanguine spirits, they would have been prevented from putting it into words by their inability to discover any means towards its fulfilment. Their whole political outlook was bounded by the lessons of English history, and in English history they found only two methods of politics—the slow method of agitation and the swift decisive method of open struggle and revolt. Unaccustomed to independent political thinking, they did not notice the significant fact that the method of agitation only became effective in England when the people had already gained powerful voice in the Government. In order to secure that voice they had been compelled to resort no less than three times to the method of open struggle and revolt. Blind to the significance ot this fact, our nineteenth century politicians clung to the method of agitation, obstinately hoping against all experience and reason that it would somehow serve their purpose. From any idea of open struggle with the bureaucracy they shrank with terror and a sense of paralysis. Dominated by the idea of the overwhelming might of Britain and the abject weakness of India, their want of courage and faith in the nation, their rooted distrust of the national character, disbelief in Indian patriotism and blindness to the possibility of true political strength and virtue in the people, precluded them from discovering the rough and narrow way to salvation. Herein lies the superiority of the New School that they have an indomitable courage and faith in the nation and the people. By the strength of that courage and faith they have not only been able to enforce on the mind of the country a higher ideal but perceived an effective means to the realization of that ideal. By the strength of that courage and faith they have made such immense strides in the course of a few months. By the strength of that courage and faith they will dominate the future.

The new methods were first tried in the great Swadeshi outburst of the last two years—blindly, crudely, without leadership and organisation, but still with amazing results. The moving cause was a particular grievance, the partition of Bengal ; and to the removal of that grievance pettiest and narrowest of all political objects, our old leaders strove hard to confine the use of this new and mighty weapon. But the popular instinct was true to itself and would have done of it. At a bound we passed therefore from mere particular grievances, however serious and intolerable, to the use of passive resistance as a means of cure for the basest and evilest feature of the present system—the bleeding to death of a country by foreign exploitation. And from that stage we are steadily advancing, under the guidance of such able political thinking as modern India has not before seen and with the rising tide of popular opinion at our back, to the one true object of all resistance, passive or active, aggressive or defensive—the creation of a free popular Government and the vindication of Indian liberty.

3

Non-Cooperation with Evil*

M.K. Gandhi ·

The Poet of Asia, as Lord Hardinge called Dr. Tagore, is fast
becoming, if he has not already become, the Poet of the World.
Increasing prestige has brought to him increasing responsibility.
His greatest service to India must be his poetic interpretation of
India's message to the world. The Poet is therefore sincerely
anxious that India should deliver no false or feeble message in
her name. He is naturally jealous of his country's reputation.
He says he has striven hard to find himself in tune with the
present movement. He confesses that he is baffled. He can find
nothing for his lyre in the din and the bustle of non-cooperation.
In three forceful letters he has endeavoured to give expression to
his misgivings, and he has come to the conclusion that non-
cooperation is not dignified enough for the India of his vision,
that it is a doctrine of negation and despair. He fears that
it is a doctrine of separation, exclusiveness, narrowness and
negation;

No Indian can feel anything but pride in the Poet's exquisite
jealousy of India's honour. It is good that he should have
sent to us his misgivings in language at once beautiful and
clear.

In all humility, I shall endeavour to answer the Poet's doubts.

*M.K.Gandhi's reply to Tagore's criticism of his programme : from
Young India, 1919-1922, p. 347-352.

I may fail to convince him or the reader who may have been touched by his eloquence, but I would like to assure him and India that non-cooperation in conception is not any of the things he fears, and he need have no cause to be ashamed of his country for having adopted non-cooperation. If, in actual application, it appears in the end to have failed, it will be no more the fault of the doctrine, than it would be of Truth, if those who claim to apply it in practice do not appear to succeed. Non-cooperation may have come in advance of its time. India and the world must then wait, but there is no choice for India save between violence and non-cooperation.

Nor need the Poet fear that non-cooperation is intended to erect a Chinese Wall between India and the West. On the contrary, non-cooperation is intended to pave the way to real, honourable and voluntary cooperation based on mutual respect and trust. The present struggle is being waged against compulsory cooperation, against one-sided combination, against the armed imposition of modern methods of exploitation masquerading under the name of civiljzation.

Non-cooperation is a protest against an unwitting and unwilling participation in evil.

The Poet's concern is largely about the students. He is of opinion that they should not have been called upon to give up Government schools before they had other schools to go to. Here I must differ from him. I have never been able to make a fetish of literary training. My experience has proved to my satisfaction that literary training by itself adds not an inch to one's moral height and that character-building is independent of literary training. I am firmly of opinion that the Government schools have unmanned us, rendered us helpless and Godless. They have filled us with discontent, and providing no remedy for the discontent, have made us despondent. They have made us what we were intended to become—clerks and interpreters. A government builds its prestige upon the apparently voluntary association of the governed. And if it was wrong to cooperate with the Government in keeping us slaves, we were bound to begin with those institutions in which our association appeared to be most voluntary. The youth of a nation are its hope. I hold that, as soon as we discovered that the system of government was wholly, or mainly, evil, it became sinful for us to associate our children with it.

It is no argument against the soundness of the proposition laid down by me that the vast majority of the students went back after the first flush of enthusiasm. Their recantation is proof rather of the extent of our degradation than of the wrongness of the step. Experience has shown that the establishment of national schools has not resulted in drawing many more students. The strongest and the truest of them came out without any national schools to fall back upon, and I am convinced that these first withdrawals are rendering service of the highest order.

But the Poet's protest against the calling out of the boys is really a corollary to his objection to the very doctrine of non-cooperation. He has a horror of everything negative. His whole soul seems to rebel against the negative commandments of religion. I must give his objection in his down inimitable language. "R in support of the present movement has often said to me that passion for rejection is a stronger power in the beginning than the acceptance of an ideal. Though I know it to be a fact, I cannot take it as truth......Brahmavidya in India has for its object Mukti (emancipation), while Buddhism has Nirvana (extinction). Mukti draws our attention to the positive and Nirvana to the negative side of the truth. Therefore, he emphasized the fact of duhkha (misery) which had to be avoided and the Brahmavidya emphasized the fact of Ananda (joy) which had to be attained." In these and kindred passages, the reader will find the key to the Poet's mentality. In my humble opinion, rejection is as much an ideal as the acceptance of a thing. It is as necessary to reject untruth as it is to accept truth. All religions teach that two opposite forces act upon us and that the human endeavour consists in a series of eternal rejections and acceptances. Non-cooperation with evil is as much a duty as cooperatian with good. I venture to suggest that the Poet has done an unconscious injustice to Buddhism in describing Nirvana as merely a negative state. I make bold to say that Mukti (emancipation) is as much a negative state as Nirvana. Emancipation from or extinction of the bondage of the flesh leads to Ananda (eternal bliss). Let me close this part of my argument by drawing attention to the fact that the final word of the Upanishads (Brahmavidya) is Not. Neti (not this) was the best description the authors of the Upanishads were able to find for Brahman.

I therefore think that the Poet has been unnecessarily alarmed at the negative aspect of non-cooperation. We had lost the power of saying 'no'. It had become disloyal, almost sacriligious to say 'no' to the Government. This deliberate refusal to cooperate is like the necessary weeding process that a cultivator has to resort to before he sows. Weeding is as necessary to agriculture as sowing. Indeed, even whilst the crops are growing, the weeding fork, as every husbandman knows, is an instrument almost of daily use. The nation's non-cooperation is an invitation to the Government to cooperate with it on its own terms as is every nation's right and every good government's duty. Non-cooperation is the nation's notice that it is no longer satisfied to be in tutelage. The nation has taken to the harmless (for it), natural and religious doctrine of non-cooperation in the place of unnatural and irreligious doctrine of violence. And if India is ever to attain the Swaraj of the Poet's dream, she will do so only by non-violent non-cooperation. Let him deliver his message of peace to the world, and feel confident that India, through her non-cooperation, if she remains true to her pledge, will have exemplified his message. Non-cooperation is intended to give the very meaning to patriotism that the Poet is yearning after. An India prostrate at the feet of Europe can give no hope to humanity. An India awakened and free has a message of peace and goodwill to a groaning world. Non-cooperation is designed to supply her with a platform from which she will preach the message.

4

Freedom : The Basic Question*

M.K. Gandhi

I congratulate you on the resolution that you have just passed. I also congratulate the three comrades on the courage they have shown in pressing their amendments to a division, even though they knew that there was an overwhelming majority in favour of the resolution, and I congratulate the thirteen friends who voted against the resolution. In doing so, they had nothing to be ashamed of. For the last twenty years we have tried to learn not to lose courage even when we are in a hopeless minority and are laughed at. We have learned to hold on to our beliefs in the confidence that we are in the right. It behoves us to cultivate this courage of conviction, for it ennobles man and raises his moral stature. I was, therefore, glad to see that these friends had imbibed the principle which I have tried to follow for the last fifty years and more.

Having congratulated them on their courage, let me say that what they asked this committee to accept through their amendments was not the correct representation of the situation. These friends ought to have pondered over the appeal made to them by the Maulana to withdraw their amendments; they should have carefully followed the explanations given by Jawaharlal. Had they done so, it would have been clear to

---

*M.K. Gandhi's address to the All-India Congress Committee on 8 August, 1942.

them that the right which they now want the Congress to concede has already been conceded by the Congress.

Time was when every Musalman claimed the whole of India as his motherland. During the years that the Ali brothers were with me, the assumption underlying all their talks and discussions was that India belonged as much to the Musalmans as to the Hindus. I can testify to the fact that this was their innermost conviction and not a mask; I lived with them for years. I spent days and nights in their company. And I make bold to say that their utterances were the honest expression of their beliefs. I know there are some who say that I take things too readily at their face value, that I am gullible. I do not think I am such a simpleton, nor am I so gullible as these friends take me to be. But their criticism does not hurt me. I should prefer to be considered gullible rather than deceitful.

What these communist friends proposed through their amendments is nothing new. It has been repeated from thousands of platforms. Thousands of Musalmans have told me, that if Hindu-Muslim question was to be solved satisfactorily, it must be done in my lifetime. I should feel flattered at this; but how can I agree to a proposal which does not appeal to my reason ? Hindu-Muslim unity is not a new thing. Millions of Hindus and Musalmans have sought after it. I consciously strove for its achievement from my boyhood. While at school, I made it a point to cultivate the friendship of Muslim and Parsi co-students. I believed even at that tender age that the Hindus in India, if they wished to live in peace and amity with the other communities, should assiduously cultivate the virtue of neighbourliness. It did not matter, I felt, if I made no special effort to cultivate the friendship with Hindus, but I must make friends with at least a few Musalmans. It was as counsel for a Musalman merchant that I went to South Africa. I made friends with other Musalmans there, even with the opponents of my client, and gained a reputation for integrity and good faith. I had among my friends and co-workers Muslims as well as Parsis. I captured their hearts and when I left finally for India, I left them sad and shedding tears of grief at the separation.

In India too I continued my efforts and left no stone unturned to achieve that unity. It was my life-long aspiration

for it that made me offer my fullest cooperation to the Musalmans in the Khilafat movement. Muslims throghout the country
accepted me as their true friend.

How then is it that I have now come to be regarded as so
evil and detestable ? Had I any axe to grind in supporting the
Khilafat movement ? True, I did in my heart of hearts cherish a
hope that it might enable me to save the cow. I am a worshipper
of the cow. I believe the cow and myscelf to be the creation of
the same God, and I am prepared to sacrifice my life in order to
save the cow. But, whatever my philosophy of life and my
ultimate hopes, I joined the movement in no spirit of bargain. I
cooperated in the struggle for the Khilafat solely in order to discharge my obligation to my neighbour who, I saw, was in distress.
The Ali brothers, had they been alive today, would have testified
to the truth of this assertion. And so would many others bear me
out in that it was not a bargain on my part for saving the cow.
The cow, like the Khilafat, stood on her own merits. As an
honest man, a true neighbour and a faithful friend, it was
incumbent on me to stand by the Musalmans in the hour of
their trial.

In those days, I shocked the Hindus by dining with the
Musalmans, though with the passage of time they have now got
used to it. Maulana Bari told me, however, that though he
would insist on having me as his guest, he would not allow me
to dine with him, lest some day he should be accused of a
sinister motive. And so, whenever I had occasion to stay with
him, he called a Brahmana cook and made special arrangements
for separate cooking. Firangi Mahal, his residence, was an
old-styled structure with limited accommodation ; yet he cheer-
fully bore all hardships and carried out his resolve from which
I could not dislodge him. It was the spirit of courtesy, dignity
and nobility that inspired us in those days. The members of
each community vied with one another in accommodating members of sister communities. They respected one another's
religious feelings, and considered it a privilege to do so. Not a
trace of suspicion lurked in anybody's heart. Where has all
that dignity, that nobility of spirit, disappeared now ? I should
ask all Musalmans, including Quaid-i-Azam Jinnah, to recall
those glorious days and to find out what has brought us to the

present impasse. Quaid-i-Azam Jinnah himself was at one time a Congressman. If today the Congress has incurred his wrath, it is because the canker of suspicion has entered his heart. May God bless him with long life, but when I am gone, he will realize and admit that I had no designs on Musalmans and that I had never betrayed their interests. Where is the escape for me, if I injure their cause or betray their interests ? My life is entirely at their disposal. They are free to put an end to it, whenever they wish to do so. Assaults have been made on my life in the past, but God has spared me till now, and the assailants have repented for their action. But if someone were to shoot me in the belief that he was getting rid of a rascal, he would kill not the real Gandhi, but the one that appeared to him a rascal.

To those who have been indulging in a campaign of abuse and vilification I would say, "Islam enjoins you not to revile even an enemy. The Prophet treated even enemies with kindness and tried to win them over by his fairness and generosity. Are you followers of that Islam or of any other ? If you are followers of the true Islam, does it behove you to distrust the words of one who makes a public declaration of his faith ? You may take it from me that one day you will regret the fact that you distrusted and killed one who was a true and devoted friend of yours." It cuts me to the quick to see that the more I appeal and the more the Maulana importunes, the more intense does the campaign of vilification grow. To me, these abuses are like bullets. They can kill me, even as a bullet can put an end to my life. You may kill me. That will not hurt me. But what of those who indulge in abusing ? They bring discredit to Islam. For the fair name of Islam, I appeal to you to resist this unceasing campaign of abuse and vilification.

Maulana Saheb is being made a target for the filthiest abuse. Why ? Because he refuses to exert on me the pressure of his friendship. He realizes that it is a misuse of friendship to seek to compel a friend to accept as truth what he knows is an untruth.

To the Quaid-i-Azam I would say : "Whatever is true and valid in the claim for Pakistan is already in your hands. What is wrong and untenable is in nobody's gift, so that it can be made over to you.   Even if someone were to succeed in imposing an untruth on others, he would not be able to enjoy for long the fruits of such a coercion.   God dislikes pride and keeps away from it.   God would not tolerate a forcible imposition of an untruth."

The Quaid-i-Azam says that he is compelled to say bitter things but that he cannot help giving expression to his thoughts and his feelings.   Similarly I would say : I consider myself a friend of Musalmans. Why should I then not give expression to the things dearest to my heart, even at the cost of displeasing them ?   How can I conceal my innermost thoughts from them ? I should congratulate the Quaid-i-Azam on his frankness in giving expression to his thoughts and feelings, even if they sound bitter to his hearers.   But even so why should the Musalmans sitting here be reviled, if they do not see eye to eye with him ? If millions of Musalmans are with you can you not afford to ignore the handful of Musalmans who may appear to you to be misguided ?   Why should one with the following of several millions be afraid of a majority community, or of the minority being swamped by the majority ?   How did the Prophet work among the Arabs and the Musalmans ? How did he propagate Islam ?   Did he say he would propagate Islam only when he commanded a majority ?   I appeal to you for the sake of Islam to ponder over what I say.   There is neither fair play nor justice in saying that the Congress must accept a thing, even if it does not believe in it and even if it goes counter to principles it holds dear.

Rajaji said : "I do not believe in Pakistan. But Musalmans ask for it, Mr. Jinnah asks for it, and it has become an obsession with them.   Why not then say "yes" to them just now ?   The same Mr. Jinnah will later on realize the disadvantages of Pakistan and will forgo the demand." I said : "It is not fair to accept as true a thing which I hold to be untrue, and ask others to do so in the belief that the demand will not be pressed when the time comes for settling it finally.   If I hold the demand to be just, I should concede it this very day.   I should not agree to it merely in order to placate Jinnah Saheb.   Many friends have come and asked me to agree to it for the time being to placate Mr. Jinnah, disarm his suspicions and to see how he reacts to it.   But I cannot be party to a course of action with a false promise.   At any rate, it is not my method".

The Congress has no sanction but the moral one for enforcing its decisions.   It believes that true democracy can only be the outcome of non-violence.   The structure of a world federation can be raised only on a foundation of non-violence, and violence will have to be totally abjured from world affairs.   If this is true, the solution of Hindu-Muslim question, too, cannot be achieved by a resort to violence.   If the Hindus tyrannize over the Musalmans, with what face will they talk of a world federation ?   It is for the same reason that I do not believe in the possibility of establishing world peace through violence as the English and American statesmen propose to do.   The Congress has agreed to submitting all the differences to an impartial international tribunal and to abide by its decisions.   If even this fairest of proposals is unacceptable, the only course that remains open is that of the sword, of violence.   How can I persuade myself to agree to an impossibility ?   To demand the vivisection of a living organism is to ask for its very life.   It is a call to war. The Congress cannot be party to such a fratricidal war.   Those Hindus who, like Dr. Moonje and Shri Savarkar, believe in the doctrine of the sword may seek to keep the Musalmans under Hindu domination.   I do not represent that section.   I represent the Congress.   You want to kill the Congress which is the goose that lays golden eggs.   If you distrust the Congress, you may rest assured that there is to be perpetual war between the Hindus and the Musalmans, and the country will be doomed to continue warfare and bloodshed.   If such warfare is to be our lot, I shall not live to witness it.

It is for that reason that I say to Jinnah Saheb, "You may take it from me that whatever in your demand for Pakistan accords with considerations of justice and equity is lying in your pocket ; whatever in the demand is contrary to justice and equity you can take only by the sword and in no other manner."

There is much in my heart that I would like to pour out before this assembly.   One thing which was uppermost in my heart I have already dealt with.   You may take it from me that it is with me a matter of life and death.   If we Hindus and

Musalmans mean to achieve a heart unity, without the slightest mental reservation on the part of either, we must first unite in the effort to be free from the shackles of this empire. If Pakistan after all is to be a portion of India, what objection can there be for Musalmans against joining this struggle for India's freedom ? The Hindus and Musalmans must, therefore, unite in the first instance on the issue of fighting for freedom. Jinnah Saheb thinks the war will last long. I do not agree with him. If the war goes on for six months more, how shall we be able to save China ?

I, therefore, want freedom immediately, this very night, before dawn, if it can be had. Freedom cannot now wait for the realization of communal unity. If that unity is not achieved, sacrifices necessary for it will have to be much greater than would have otherwise sufficed. But the Congress must win freedom or be wiped out in the effort. And forget not that the freedom which the Congress is struggling to achieve will not be for the Congressmen alone but for all the forty crores of the Indian people. Congressmen must for ever remain humble servants of the people.

The Quaid-i-Azam has said that the Muslim League is prepared to take over the rule from the Britishers if they are prepared to hand it over to the Muslim League, for the British took over the empire from the hands of the Muslims. This, however, will be Muslim Raj. The offer made by Maulana Saheb and by me does not imply establishment of Muslim Raj or Muslim domination. The Congress does not believe in the domination of any group or any community. It believes in democracy which includes in its orbit Muslims, Hindus, Christians, Parsis, Jews—everyone of the communities inhabiting this vast country. If Muslim Raj is inevitable, then let it be; but how can we give it the stamp of our assent ? How can we agree to the domination of one community over the others ?

Millions of Musalmans in this country come from Hindu stock. How can their homeland be any other than India ? My eldest son embraced Islam some years back. What would his homeland be—Porbandar or the Punjab ? I ask the Musalmans : "If India is not your homeland, what other country do you belong to ? In what separate homeland would you put my son who embraced Islam ?" His mother wrote him a letter after his conversion, asking him if he had on embracing Islam given up drinking which Islam forbids to its followers. To those who gloated over the conversion, she wrote to say : "I do not mind his becoming a Musalman, so much as his drinking. Will you, as pious Musalmans, tolerate his drinking even after his conversion ? He has reduced himself to the state of a rake by drinking. If you are going to make a man of him again, his conversion will have been turned to good account. You will, therefore, please see that he as a Musalman abjures wine and woman. If that change does not come about, his conversion goes in vain and our non-co-operation with him will have to continue".

"India is without doubt the homeland of all the Musalmans inhabiting this country. Every Musalman should therefore co-operate in the fight for India's freedom. The Congress does not belong to any one class or community ; it belongs to the whole nation. It is open to Musalmans to take possession of the Congress. They can, if they like, swamp the Congress by their numbers, and can steer it along the course which appeals to them. The Congress is fighting not on behalf of the Hindus but on behalf of the whole nation, including the minorities. It would hurt me to hear of a single instance of a Musalman being killed by a Congressman. In the coming revolution, Congressmen, will sacrifice their lives in order to protect the Musalman against a Hindu's attack and *vice-versa*. It is a part of their creed, and is one of the essentials of non-violence. You will be expected on occasions like these not to lose your heads. Every Congressman, whether a Hindu or a Musalman, owes this duty to the organization to which he belongs. The Musalman who will act in this manner will render a service to Islam. Mutual trust is essential for success in the final nation-wide struggle that is to come.

I have said that much greater sacrifices will have to be made this time in the wake of our struggle because of the opposition from the Muslim Leage and from Englishmen. You have seen the secret circular issued by Sir Frederick Puckle. It is a suicidal course that he has taken. It contains an open incitement to organizations which crop up like mushrooms to combine to fight the Congress. We have thus to deal with an empire whose ways are crooked. Ours is a straight path which we can tread' even with our eyes closed. That is the beauty of Satyagraha.

In Satyagraha, there is no place for fraud or falsehood, or any kind of untruth. Fraud and untruth today are stalking the world. I cannot be a helpless witness to such a situation. I have travelled all over India as perhaps nobody in the present age has. The voiceless millions of the land saw in me their friend and representative, and I identified myself with them to an extent it was possible for a human being to do. I saw trust in their eyes, which I now want to turn to good account in fighting this empire upheld on untruth and violence. However gigantic the preparations that the empire has made, we must get out of its clutches. How can I remain silent at this supreme hour and hide my light under the bushel ? Shall I ask the Japanese to tarry awhile ? If today I sit quiet and inactive, God will take me to task for not using up the treasure He had given me, in the midst of the conflagration that is enveloping the whole world. Had the condition been different, I should have asked you to wait yet awhile. But the situation now has become intolerable, and the Congress has no other course left for it.

Nevertheless, the actual struggle does not commence this moment. You have only placed all your powers in my hands. I will now wait upon the Viceroy and plead with him for the acceptance of the Congress demand. That process is likely to take two or three weeks. What would you do in the meanwhile ? What is the programme for the interval, in which all can participate ? As you know, the spinning wheel is the first thing that occurs to me. I made the same answer to the Maulana. He would have none of it, though he understood its import later. The fourteenfold constructive programme is, of course, there for you to carry out. What more should you do ? I will tell you. Everyone of you should, from this moment onwards, consider yourself a free man or woman, and act as if you are free and are no longer under the heel of this imperialism.

It is not a make-believe that I am suggesting to you. It is the very essence of freedom. The bond of the slave is snapped the moment he considers himself to be a free being. He will plainly tell the master: "I was your bondslave till this moment, but I am a slave no longer. Yon may kill me if you like, but if you keep me alive, I wish to tell you that if you release me from the bondage, of your own accord, I will ask for nothing more from you. You used to feed and clothe me, though I could have provided food and clothing for myself by my labour. I hitherto depended on you instead of on God, for food and raiment. But God has now inspired me with an urge for freedom and I am today a free man, and will no longer depend on you."

You may take it from me that I am not going to strike a bargain with the Viceroy for ministries and the like. I am not going to be satisfied with anything short of complete freedom. May be, he will propose the abolition of salt tax, the drink evil, etc. But I will say : "Nothing less than freedom".

Here is a *mantra*, a short one, that I give you. You may imprint it on your hearts and let every breath of yours give expression to it. The *mantra* is : "Do or Die". We shall either free India or die in the attempt ; we shall not live to see the perpetuation of our salvery. Every true Congressman or woman will join the struggle with an inflexible determination not to remain alive to see the country in bondage and slavery. Let that be your pledge. Keep jails out of your consideration. If the Government keep me free, I will spare you the trouble of filling the jails. I will not put on the Goverment the strain of maintaining a large number of prisoners at a time, when it is in trouble. Let every man and woman live every moment of his or her life hereafter in the consciousness that he or she eats or lives for achieving freedom and will die, if need be, to attain that goal. Take a pledge, with God and your own conscience as witness, that you will no longer rest till freedom is achieved and will be prepared to lay down your lives in the attempt to achieve it. He who loses his life will gain it ; he who will seek to save it shall lose it. Freedom is not for the coward or the faint-hearted.

A word to the journalists. I congratulate you on the support you have hitherto given to the national demand. I know the restrictions and handicaps under which you have to labour. But I would now ask you to snap the chains that bind you. It should be the proud privilege of the newspapers to lead and set an example in laying down one's life for freedom. You have the pen which the Government can't suppress. I know you have large properties in the form of printing presses, etc., and you would be afraid lest the Government should attach them. I do not ask you to invite an attachment of the printing-press voluntarily. For myself, I would not suppress my pen even if the press was to be attached. As you know my press was attachh d in the past and returned later on. But I do not ask from you that final sacrifice. I suggest a middle way. You should now wind up your standing committee, and you may declare that you will give up writing under the present restrictions and take up the pen only when India has won her freedom. You may tell Sir Frederick Puckle that he can't expect from you a command performance, that his press notes are full of untruth, and that you will refuse to publish them. You will openly declare that you are whole-heartedly with the Congress. If you do this, you will have changed the atmosphere before the fight actually begins.

From the princes I ask with all respect due to them a very small thing. I am a well-wisher of the princes. I was born in a State. My grandfather refused to salute with his right hand any prince other than his own. But he did say to the prince, as I feel he ought to have said, that even his own master could not compel him, his minister, to act against his conscience. I have eaten the princes' salt and I would not be false to it. As a faithful servant, it is my duty to warn the princes that if they will act while I am still alive, the princes may come to occupy an honourable place in free India. In Jawaharlal's scheme of free India, no privileges or the privileged classes have a place. Jawaharlal considers all property to be State-owned. He wants planned economy. He wants to reconstruct India according to plan. He likes to fly; I do not. I have kept a place for the princes and the zamindars in India that I envisage. I would ask the princes in all humility to enjoy through renunciation. The princes may renounce ownership over their properties and become their trustees in the true sense of the term. I visualize God in the assemblage of people. The princes may say to their people : "You are the owners and masters of the State and we are your servants". I would ask the princes to become servants of the people and render to them an account of their own services. The empire too bestows power on the princes, but they should prefer to derive power from their own people ; and if they want to indulge in some innocent pleasures, they may seek to do so as servants of the people. I do not want the princes to live as paupers. But I would ask them : "Do you want to remain slaves for all time ? Why should you, instead of paying homage to a foreign power, not accept the sovereignty of your own people ?" You may write to the Political Department : "The people are now awake. How are we to withstand an avalanche before which even the large empires are crumbling ? We, therefore, shall belong to the people from today onwards. We shall sink or swim with them." Believe me, there is nothing unconstitutional in the course I am suggesting. There are, so far as I know, no treaties enabling the empire to coerce the princes. The people of the States will also declare that though they are the princes' subjects, they are part of the Indian nation and that they will accept the leadership of the princes, if the latter cast their lot with the people, but not otherwise. If this declaration enrages the princes and they choose to kill the people, the latter will meet death bravely and unflinchingly, but will not go back on their word.

Nothing, however, should be done secretly. This is an open rebellion. In this struggle secrecy is a sin. A free man would not engage in a secret movement. It is likely that when you gain freedom you will have a C.I.D. of your own, in spite of my advice to the contrary. But in the present struggle, we have to work openly and to receive bullets on our chest, without taking to heels.

I have a word to say to Government servants also. They may not, if they like, resign their posts yet. The late Justice Ranade did not resign his post, but he openly declared that he belonged to the Congress. He said to the Government that though he was a judge, he was a Congressman and would openly attend the sessions of the Congress, but that at the same time he would not let his political views warp his impartiality on the bench. He held Social Reform Conference in the very pandal of the Congress. I would ask all the Government servants to follow in the footsteps of Ranade and to declare their allegiance to the Congress as an answer to the secret circular issued by Sir Frederick Puckle.

This is all that I ask of you just now. I will now write to the Viceroy. You will be able to read the correspondence not just now but when I publish it with the Viceroy's consent. But you are free to aver that you support the demand to be put forth in my letter. A judge came to me and said : "We get secret circulars from high quarters. What are we to do ?" I replied, "If I were in your place, I would ignore the circulars. You may openly say to the Government : 'I have received your secret circular. I am, however, with the Congress. Though I serve the Government for my livelihood, I am not going to obey these secret circulars or to employ underhand methods.'"

Soldiers too are covered by the present programme. I do not ask them just now to resign their posts and to leave the army. The soldiers come to me, Jawaharlal and the Maulana and say : "We are wholly with you. We are tired of the Governmental tyranny." To these soldiers I would say : "You may say to the Government, 'Our hearts are with the Congress. We are not going to leave our posts. We will serve you so long as we receive your salaries. We will obey your just orders, but will refuse to fire on our own people.'"

To those who lack the courage to do this much I have nothing to say. They will go their own way. But if you can do this much, you may take it from me that the whole atmosphere will be electrified. Let the Government then shower bombs, if they like. But no power on earth will then be able to keep you in bondage any longer.

If the students want to join the struggle only to go back to their studies after a while, I would not invite them to it. For the present, however, till the time that I frame a programme for the struggle, I would ask the students to say to their professors : "We belong to the Congress. Do you belong to the Congress or to the Government ? If you belong to the Congress you need not vacate your posts. You will remain at your posts but teach us and land us unto freedom." In all fights for freedom, the world over, the students have made very large contributions·

If in the interval that is left to us before the actual fight begins, you do even the little I have suggested to you, you will have changed the atmosphere and will have prepared the ground for the next step.

There is much I should yet like to say. But my heart is heavy. I have already taken up much of your time. I have yet to say a few words in English also. I thank you for the patience and attention with which you have listened to me even at this late hour. It is just what true soldiers would do. For the last twenty-two years, I have controlled my speech and pen and have stored up my energy. He is a true Brahmachari who does not fritter away his energy. He will, therefore, always control his speech. That has been my conscious effort all these years. But today the occasion has come when I had to unburden my heart before you. I have done so, even though it meant putting a strain or your patience ; and I do not regret having done it. I have given you my message and through you I have delivered it to the whole of India.

5

Theory and Practice of Democracy[*]

B.R. Ambedkar

There is only one point of constitutional import to which I propose to make a reference. A serious complaint is made on the ground that there is too much of centralization and that the States have been reduced to Municipalities. It is clear that this view is not only an exaggeration, but is also founded on a misunderstanding of what exactly the Constitution contrives to do.

The second charge is that the Centre has been given the power to override the States. This charge must be admitted. But before condemning the Constitution for containing such overriding powers, certain considerations must be borne in mind. The first is that these overriding powers do not form the normal feature of the Constitution. Their use and operation are expressly confined to emergencies only. The second consideration is : Could we avoid giving overriding powers to the Centre when an emergency has arisen ? Those who do not admit the justification for such overriding powers to the Centre even in an emergency, do not seem to have a clear idea of the problem which lies at the root of the matter; The problem is so clearly set out by a writer in that well known magazine, *The Round Table* in its issue of December 1935, that I offer no apology for quoting the following extract from it. Says the

[*]Speech delivered at the Constituent Assembly on 25 November 1949.

writer :

"Political systems are a complex of rights and duties resting ultimately on the question, to whom or to what authority does the citizen owe allegiance. In normal affairs, the question is not present, for the law works smoothly and a man goes about his business obeying one authority in this set of matters and another authority in that. But in a moment of crisis, a conflict of claims may arise, and it is then apparent that ultimate allegiance cannot be divided. The issue of allegiance cannot be determined in the last resort by a juristic interpretation of statutes. The law must confirm to the facts or so much the worse for the law. When all formalism is stripped away, the bare question is, the authority commands the residual loyalty of the citizen. Is it the Centre or the Constituent State ?"

The solution of this problem depends upon one's answer to this question which is its crux. There can be no doubt that in the opinion of the vast majority of the people, the residual loyalty of the citizen in an emergency must be to the Centre and not to the constituent States. For, it is only the Centre which can work for a common end and for the general interest of a country as a whole. Herein lies the jurisdiction for giving to the Centre certain overriding powers to be used in an emergency. And, after all, what is the obligation imposed upon the constituent States by these emergency powers ? No more than this—that in an emergency, they should take into consideration alongside their own local interests, the opinions and interests of the nation as a whole. Only those who have not understood the problem can complain against this.

On 26 January 1950, India will be an independent country. What will happen to her independence ? Will she maintain her independence or will she lose it again ? This is the first thought that comes to my mind. It is not that India was never an independent country. The point is that she once lost the indipendence which she had. Will she lose it second time ? It is this thought that makes me most anxious for the future. What perturbs me greatly is the fact that not only India has once before lost her independence, but she lost it by the infidelity and treachery of some of her own people. In the invasion of Sind by Mohammed Bin Kasim, the Military Commanders of King

Dahar accepted bribes from the agents of Mohammed Bin Kasim and refused to fight on the side of their king. It was Jaichand who invited Mahommed Ghori to invade India and fight against Prithvi Raj and promised him the help of himself and the Solenki Kings. When Shivaji was fighting for the liberation of Hindus, the other Maratha noblemen and the Rajput Kings were fighting the battles on the side of Mogul emperors. When the Britsh were trying to destroy the Sikh rulers, Gulab Singh, their Principal command, sat silent and did not help to save the Sikh Kingdom. In 1875 when a large part of India had declared a war of Independence against the British the Sikhs stood and watched the event as silent spectators.

Will history repeat itself ? It is this thought which fills me with anxiety. This anxiety is deepened by the realization of the fact that in addition to our old enemies in the form of castes and creeds, we are going to have many political parties with diverse and opposite political creeds. Will Indians place the country above their creed or will they place the creed above the country ? I do not know. But this much is certain that if the parties place creed above country, our independence will be put in jeopardy a second time and probably be lost for ever. This eventuality we must all resolutely guard against. We must be determined to defend our independence with the last drop of our blood.

On 26 January 1950, India will be a democratic country in the sense that India from that date will have a government of the people, by the people and for the people. The same thought comes to my mind. What will happen to her democratic constitution? Will she be able to maintain it or will she loose it again? This is the second thought that comes to my mind and makes as anxious as the first.

It is not that India did not know what is Democracy. There was a time when India was studded with republics, and even where there were monarchies, they were either elected or limited, They were never absolute. It is not that India did not know parliaments or parliamentary procedure. A study of the Buddhist Bhikshi Sanghas discloses that not only there were parliaments—for the Sanghas were nothing but parliaments—but the Sanghas knew and observed all the rules of parliamentary procedure known to modern times. They had rules regarding seating arrangements, rules regarding Motions, Resolutions, Quorum, Whip, Counting of Votes, Voting by Ballot, Censure Motion, Regularization, Res Judicata, etc. Although these rules of parliamentary procedure were applied by Buddha to the meetings of the Sanghas, he must have borrowed them from the rules of the political Assemblies functioning in the country in his time.

This democratic system India lost. Will she lose it a second time ? I do not know. But it is quite possible in a country like India—where democracy from its long disuse must be regarded as something quite new—there is danger of democracy giving place to dictatorship. It is quite possible for this new-born democracy to retain its form but give place to dictatorship in fact. If there is a landslide, the danger of the second possibility becoming actuality is much greater.

If we wish to maintain democracy, not merely in form, but also in fact, what must we do ? The first thing in my judgement we must do is hold fast to constitutional methods of achieving our social and economic objectives. It means that we must abandon the bloody methods of civil disobedience, non-co-operation and satyagraha. Where there was no way left for constitutional methods for achieving economic and social objectives, there was a great deal of justification for constitutional methods. But where constitutional methods are open, there can be no justification for these unconstitutional methods. These methods are nothing but the Grammar of Anarchy and the sooner they are abandoned, the better for us.

The second thing we must do is to observe the caution which John Stuart Mill has given to all who are interested in the maintenance of democracy, namely, not "to lay their liberties at the feet of even a great man, or to turst him with powers which enable him to subvert their institutions." There is nothing wrong in being grateful to great men who have rendered life-long services to the country. But there are limits to gratefulness. As has been well said by the Irish patriot Daniel O' Connell, "no woman can be grateful at the cost of her chastity and no nation can be grateful at the cost of its liberty". The caution is far more necessary in the case of India than in the case of any other country. For in India, Bhakti or what may be called the path of devotion or hero-worship, plays a part in its politics unequalled in magnitude by the part it plays in the politics of any other country in the world. Bhakti in religion may be a road to the salvation of the soul. But in politics, Bhakti or hero-worship is a sure road to degradation and to eventual dictatorship.

The third thing we must do is not to be content with mere political democracy. We must make our political democracy a social democracy as well. Political democracy cannot last unless there lies at the base of it social democracy. What does social democracy mean? It means a way of life which recognizes liberty, equality and fraternity as the principles of life. These principles of liberty, equality and fraternity are not to be treated as separate items in a trinity. They form a union of trinity in the sense that to divorce one from the other is to defeat the very purpose of democracy. Liberty cannot be divorced from equality, equality cannot be divorced from liberty. Nor can liberty and equality be divorced from fraternity. Without equality liberty would produce the supremacy of the few over the many. Equality without liberty would kill individual initiative. Without fraternity, liberty and equality could not become a nature course of things. It would require a constable to endorse them. We must begin by acknowledging the fact that there is complete absence of two things in Indian society. One of these is equality. On the social plane we have in India a society based on the principle of graded inequality which means elevation for some and degradation for others. On the economic plane, we have a society in which there are some who have immense wealth as against many who live in abject poverty. On the 26th of Junuary 1950, we are going to enter into a life of contradictions. In politics we shall have equality and in social and economic life we shall have inequality. In politics we shall be recognizing the principle of one man one vote and one vote one value. In our social and economic life, we shall, by reason of our social and economic structure, continue to deny the principle of one man one value. How long shall we continue to live this life of contradictions? How long shall we continue to deny equality in our social and economic life? If we continue to deny it for long, we will do so only putting our political democracy in peril. We must remove this contradiction at the earliest possible moment or else those who suffer from inqulity will blow up the structure of political democracy which this Assembly has so laboriously built up.

The second thing we are wanting in is recognition of the principle of fraternity. What does fraternity mean ? Fraternity means a sense of common brotherhood of all Indians—of Indians being one people. It is the principle which gives unity and solidarity to social life. It is a difficult thing to achieve. How difficult it is can be realised from the story related by James Bryce in his volume on the American Commonwealth about the United States of America.

The story is—I propose to recount it in the words of Bryce himself—that : "Some years ago, the American Protestant Episcopal Church was occupied at its triennial Convention in revising its liturgy. It was thought desirable to introduce among the short sentence prayers a paryer for the whole people, and an eminent New England divine proposed the words, 'O Lord, bless our nation.' Accepted one afternoon, on the spur of the moment, the sentence was brought up next day for reconsideration, when so many objections were raised by the laity to the word "nation," as importing too definite a recognition of national unity, that it was dropped, and instead there were adopted the words, 'O Lord, bless the United States.'"

There was so little solidarity in the U.S.A. at the time when this incident occurred that the people of America did not think that they were a nation. If the people of the United States could not feel that they were a nation, how difficult it is for Indians to think that they are a nation ! I remember the days when politically-minded Indians resented the expression 'the people of India'. They preferred the expression 'the Indian nation'. I am of the opinion that in believing that we are a nation, we are cherishing a great delusion. How can people divided into several thousands of castes be a nation ? The sooner we realize that we are not yet a nation in the social and psychological sense of the word, the better for us. For then only we shall realize the ways and means of realizing the goal. The realization of this goal is going to be very difficult—far more difficult than it has been in the United States. The United States has no caste problem. In India there are castes. These castes are anti-national. In the first place because they bring about separation in life. They are anti-national also because they generate jealousy and antipathy between caste and caste. But we must overcome all these difficulties if we wish to become a nation in reality. For fraternity can be a fact only where there is a nation. Without fraternity, equality and liberty will be no deeper than coats of paint.

These are my reflections about the tasks that lie ahead of us. They may not be very pleasant to some. But there can be no gainsaying that political power in this country has too long been the monopoly of a few and the many are not only beasts of burden, but also beasts of prey. This monopoly has not merely deprived them of their chance of betterment, it has sapped them of what may be called the significance of life. These downtrodden classes are tired of being governed. They are impatient to govern themselves. This urge for self-realization devolves into a class struggle or class war. It would lead to a division of the House. That would indeed be a day of disaster. For as has been well said by Abraham Lincoln, a house divided against itself cannot stand very long. Therefore, the sooner room is made for the realization of that aspiration, the better for the few, the better for the country, the better for the maintenance of its independence and the better for the continuance of its democratic structure. This can only be done by the establishment of equality and fraternity in all spheres of life. That is why I have laid so much stress on them.

I do not wish to weary the House any further. Independence is no doubt a matter of joy. But let us not forget that this independence has thrown on us great responsibilities. By independence, we have lost the excuse of blaming the British for anything going wrong. If hereafter things go wrong, we will have nobody to blame except ourselves. There is great danger of things going wrong. Times are fast changing. People including our own are being moved by new ideologies. They are getting tired of Government by the people. They are prepared to have Government for the people and are indifferent whether it is Government of the people and by the people. If we wish to preserve the Constitution in which we have sought to enshrine the principle of Government of the people, for the people, and by the people, let us resolve not to be tardy in the recognition of the evils that lie across our path and which induce people to prefer Government for the people to Government by the people, not to be weak in our initiative to remove them. That is the only way to serve the country. I know of no better.

6

The Communist Challenge*

Polit Bureau, C.P.I.

The people's democratic front is the fighting front of all the anti-imperialist democratic forces, i.e., the workers, peasants, petty bourgeoisie and the middle bourgeoisie, with the parties, groups and individuals representing them. It is based on the firm alliance of the workers and the peasants led by the proletariat and its party, the Communist Party.

The working class and its party, the Communist Party, are the leader, guide and the architect of the people's democratic front. If the party has to fulfil such an historic task, it must have a thorough understanding of the scope and nature of the people's democratic front. It is, therefore, necessary to make a diligent study of the experiences of the international proletarian movement on this question : the party must make a study of its own past on this issue drawing proper lesson ; it must also master the strategy and tactics of the period and determinedly act to realise the people's democratic front.

In the earlier period, when our party was still young, the dominant tendency inside the party had been sectarian; it refused to work in the then existing trade-union organisations under the reformist leadership and insisted on setting up exclusively separate and independent trade unions, irrespective of the expedie-

*These are extracts from the draft resolution of the Polit Bureau of the Communist Party of India circulated among its members in November, 1950.

ncy of such a step and the result was a failure to forge a broad trade union unity—the lever for a national united front against imperialism.

The party refused to recognise the then still existing anti-imperialist role of the national reformist opposition of the Indian big business as represented by the Congress leadership, resulting in the failure to utilise the mass anti-imperialist organisations under Congress leadership, by joining them and working in them. It failed to participate in the anti-imperialist demonstrations and struggles, which were of course conducted under the bourgeois leadership in a typically reformist way, and failed to extend its mass influence.

The serious political, ideological and organisational differences that were prevailing inside the party had seriously impeded the unity of the proletariat and the party; the lack of such a unity had in turn seriously affected the struggle of that period to forge a revolutionary united front. These are in brief the lessons of the early period concerning the problem in discussion.

Following this, during the long period of 1935-48, when we were supposed to have corrected our former sectarian mistakes, we steadily landed ourselves in the reformist mistakes and the entire approach to the problem of united front had suffered serious right-opportunist deviations. Besides a number of other mistakes with regard to our approrch to the problem of allies, the main mistake of this period was in our conceding the national big bourgeoisie the character of a revolutionary opposition against imperialism. This basic mistake had led us to a number of errors, resulting in the failure to successfully build a revolutionary united front, a revolutionary working class movement and a strong party to assert the proletarian hegemony over the national-liberation movement.

The party leadership, while correctly stressing the necessity of working inside the mass anti-imperialist organisation under the Congress leadership, seriously underrated the significance of the building up of independent class and mass organisation and the party and actually building up of the Congress organisation was made the main plank in many places.

Secondly, while in the former sectarian period, the party refused to utilise the national reformist opposition of the big bourgeoisie to foreign rule, in the later period of right-reformism in the name of utilising that opposition of the big bourgeoisie, which of course was aggravated by the intensification of the crisis of world capitalism and the consequent rise of fascism, affording the proletariat a greater scope for the sweep of the revolution—we failed not only to expose the treacherous reformist ideology of Gandhism and its bourgeois exponents before .he people and isolate them ; but also by boosting of Nehru, Gandhi and national leadership to skies had helped to create further illusions in the people.

Thirdly, the party leadership failed to take note of the growing capitulatory tendencies on the part of the Congress leadership towards imperialism, which are particularly marked during the later period of the war itself in enunciating the policy of "Support Nehru government"—a government of compromise, collaboration and national betrayal. Thus when a complete break with and an irreconcilable opposition to the native big bourgeoisie was a historical task of the proletatriat, we pursued a policy of united front with it. And the result was the utter failure to fulfil the basic task of building up of a real fighting untied democratic front against both imperialism and native reaction and trailing behind the native big bourgeoisie.

Moreover, this right-reformist policy of the party, in the name of such 'national unity', had not only hindered the independent organisation and building up of workers', peasants' and other people's movement but also restricted the scope of the forms of struggle that were a dopted in the workers' and peasants' struggles. Not a few instances could be found during this period particularly in the later part of it—where militant and higher forms of struggle were discouraged under the pretext of 'inviting repression and danger of 'disruption', to forge a socalled united front ! This kind of trimming of the sails of the proletariat and its party to suite the vagaries and machinations of the native big bourgeoisie by restricting and confining the forms of struggle to the strictly 'peaceful and normal' methods did neither bring the realisation of a united front anywhere nearer, nor the people were rescued from the illusions of the bourgeois forms of struggle, helping them to take up and advance to higher and revolutionary forms of struggle.

And now, during the last two and a half years beginning with the second party congress during which a definite swing towards the discredited Titoist concept of monolithic front was observed (it persisted until the first resolution of the information bureau exposing the activities and policies of the Tito clique was publised and circulated) the struggle to correct this right-opportunist attitude towards united front has once again ended in a crude sectarian approach to the entire problem. While correctly breaking away from and taking up an irreconcilable opposition to the collaborationist bourgeoisie, we made a present to some of the democratic sections of the people and our allies such as the middle bourgeoisie and the rich peasantry to the class enemy, thus curtailing the scope and disrupting the formation of a wider united front against imperialist-big bourgeois-feudal combine which was absolutely necessary and quite possible at this stage.

The party leadership failed to fight the machinations of the big bourgeoisie and the socialists and others to disrupt the workingclass unity and to destroy the organised revolutionary workingclass movement. Not only the failure to fight out these disruptive moves of reaction and its lackeys but also the insistence on the sectarian organisational and mass front demands and launching of struggles by hurling in the vanguard sections, had only resulted in helping the enemy and failed to achive the desired workingclass unity.

The forms of struggle that were advocated during this period in the cities were 'putschist' in their nature, which failed to take note of the growing white terror, with the result that the party failed to unite its class in its struggle on the day-to-day demands not to speak of a broader unity with other sections of toiling and democratic masses

In the rural side, besides the disruption caused in the peasant front by the sectarian strategy, the forms of struggle the party leadership advocated were mass frontal clashes with the police and the military. This resulted in giving the upperhand to the enemy and facilitated a speedy smashup of our own forces. Instead of attacking the enemy from different angles and at different times, harassing, wearing out and delivering deadly blows, in short, instead of adopting guerilla partisan warfare as

the main form of struggle, the adventurist method of mass frontal clashes were resorted to, which has not only failed to unite the
toilers and other sections in the rural areas against the armed
offensive of the counterrevolution but only helped the vanguard
of the fighting people to get smashed quickly, resulting in the
disruption of the exiting fighting unity of the people.

To conclude, in brief, if right-reformism advocated and
pursued a policy of alliance with the class enemy in the name
of 'united front', left-sectarianism refused alliance with the
democratic classes and sections ; if right-opportunism, reeling
before the enemy's repression, retreated all along the line and
liquidated the struggles, left-adventurism refused to take note of
the growing white terror and attempted to push through the
classical insurrectionary fighting strategy; if right-reformism underrated the independent role of the proletariat and its mobilisation and tailed behind the bourgeoisie in the united front, left
sectarianism, in the name of independent strength, mobilisation
and the hegemony of the proletariat, undermined the formation
of a united workingclass movement as well as a fighting united
front of all democratic classes and groups. Thus the concept
of united democratic front in this period of left-sectarianism,
which started during the second congress with the Titoist idea of
a monolithic front, finally landed in absurd and vulgar liquidation of the very revolutionary understanding of a united democratic front in our country's war of liberation.

Drawing on these lessons, it is necessary to restate briefly the
correct viewpoint regarding the people's democratic front.

The people's democratic front the party visualises is a united
front of workers, peasants, petty bourgoisie and middle bourgeoisie, and the parties and groups representing them, based on
the minimum programme of our party and the fight for its realisation. Such minimum programme, in the opinion of the
revolutionary proletariat and the Communist Party, shall contain
all the basic demands that have been enumerated in the previous
section as the immediate programme of the people's democratic
revoltiuon. The Communist Party shall contain all the basic demands that have been enumerated in the pevious section as immediate programme of the people's revolution. The Communist
Party, while persistently fighting for the acceptance of this mini-

mum programme by all the allies in the front, does not demand of these allied classes or parties and groups representing them, the acceptance of the party's maximum programme, i.e., socialism. The party which has a single accepted ideology of Marxism-Leninism, has its own discipline based on democratic centralisation, and is agreed upon both maximum and minimum programmes, can alone be correctly characterised as monolithic. It would be utter nonsense to speak of a united front of several anti-imperialist and antifeudal classes as a monolithic organisation. And any insistence on the monolithic character of the united front would result either in liquidating the party by merging it in the front, and in sacrificing its independent existence as is evidenced in Yugoslavia or the front would get disrupted because of the insistence of such a monolithic nature.

The people's democratic front that the party visualises is a united front of armed struggle. Without such a front, the present ruling bloc of imperialists and their native satellites can never be defeated and overthrown from power and the realisation of a people's democratic order under which alone the successful implementation of the people's democratic front's programme is possible and fully realisable, can only be achieved through a united front of armed struggle.

But such a front on a countrywide scale cannot come into existence all at once. The development of such a front is a process of struggle for unity in action—beginning from joint demonstrations or action for the most easily understood demands of the different sections to the highest form of struggle for peace, land, bread and independence on a more permanent basis.

The most effective way to build such a front is to build it from below. It does not preclude agreements at the top between leaders and individuals of different organisations and parties. Such agreements often become essential to facilitate unity from below. But to achive this, the party has to systematically and persistently approach the different left parties, groups and individuals, patiently argue and thrash out the differing viewpoints and evolve the common basis of agreement for action. While doing so, the party has, at the same time, to expose the activities of the disruptive leaders before their ranks and masses and fight in a determined manner the influence of bourgeois nationalism that persists in them.

The people's democratic front can be materialised only if the proletariat and the Communist Party simultaneously fight for the just democratic demands of all the allied classes and groups on the one hand, and on the other, resist and fight back the vacillations, illusions and the narrow, sectional undemocratic demands against the proletariat and the people either by one or more of the allies in the front or the party or parties representing them. The building of such a united front and the struggle to realise it does not proceed over a straight and smoothly paved road on which all democratic forces can march in unison but over a difficult and strenuous path of unity and struggle within and sometimes without. Of course, it will neither be an irreconcilable struggle as between two hostile classes, trying to destroy each other nor a unity which excludes all struggle whatsoever.

The independence of the proletariat and the party for mobilisation and action is an indispensable condition for a seccessful building up of a people's democratic front. The independent strength and mobilisation of the proletariat and the party is the real lever on and the pivot around which the fighting unity of the democratic classes can be forged at all. The party bearing this truth in mind, has to undeviatingly act upto it. Consistent with this, the party neither demands the liquidation of other parties as a precondition to join the united front nor allows any such disruptive demands foisted on it by any class or classes and the party or parties in this democratic alliance.

The party would be prepared to work in cooperation with all the democratic and left parties, groups and their mass organisations and to invite them to join the people's democratic front. It reserves the right to criticise any individual, group or party which opposes, sabotages or disrupts a united action or the formation of such a united front. While it would reckon with the existing realities by recognising, co-operating and uniting with all the democratic left parties, it does not take upon itself the task of encouraging, forming and building up of such parties. The party on its own will simultaneously carry out the struggle to unite all the democratic classes under the direct leadership of the proletariat.

Our party in its struggle to build the people's democratic

front of armed struggle, reserves the right of propaganda and practice for the armed guerilla warfare as the principal form of struggle at the present stage of our national-liberation movement. But it neither chooses or attempts to foist this form of struggle on the classes or parties that are not yet convinced of it nor allows itself to be dictated to by the other parties on their own reformist form of struggle which they may believe as effective.

The party firmly believes that the efficacy of armed struggle can be best demonstrated as to make it acceptable by other parties, classes and groups in the democratic front if only it implements it basing on its own independent strength wherever and whenever it is capable of mobilising people for organising such struggles. In areas and territories where such armed resistance develops, the party visualises the alliance of different anti-imperialist parties and groups and the evolution of the people's democratic front of armed struggle comprising them on a local or territorial basis which in the process of development and expansion, will assume wider and wider character.

The party does neither make the acceptance of any particular form of struggle by other parties a precondition for either a united action or united front nor accepts the demand of giving up the armed struggle if demanded by others as a condition for the united front. As already explained in the foregoing pages, the party certainly takes up other forms of struggle also, wherever they are necessary and possible, as auxiliary to this main form. Accordingly the party would not only utilise all other conceivable legal and semilegal forms of struggle, but also co-operate in the forms of struggle the other parties would adopt in conducting mass struggles, even though the party believes that they are not really effective forms. While participating in them it expresses its criticism on these forms and patiently explains it to the fighting people and the parties concerned. Thus the forms of struggle it pursues and adopts from issue to issue are flexible so that a really revolutionary united front of armed struggle is created and developed.

Such, in brief, is our broad concept of a fighting people's democratic front.

7

Individual Freedom—The Touchstone*

Jawaharlal Nehru

The old civilisations with the many virtues that they possess, have obviously proved inadequate. The new western civilisation, with all its triumphs and achievements and also with its atomic bombs, also appears inadequate and, therefore, the feeling grows that there is something wrong with our civilisation. Indeed, essentially our problems are those of civilisation itself. Religion gave a certain moral and spiritual discipline; it also tried to perpetuate superstition and social usages. Indeed, those superstitions and social usages enmeshed and overwhelmed the real spirit or religion. Disillusionment followed. Communism comes in the wake of this disillusionment and offers some kind of faith and some kind of discipline. To some extent it fills a vacuum. It succeeds in some measure by giving a content to man's life. But in spite of its apparent success, it fails, partly but, because of its rigidity, even more so, because it ignores certain essential needs of human nature. There is much talk in communism of the contradictions of capitalist society, and there is truth in growing contradictions within the rigid frame-work of communism itself. Its suppression of individual freedom brings about powerful reactions. Its contempt for what might be called the moral and spiritual side of life not only ignores something that is basic in man, but also deprives human beha-

*From *The Basic Approach, A.I.C.C. Economic Review*, 15 August, 1958.

viour of standards and values. Its unfortunate association with violence encourages a certain evil tendency in human beings.

I have the greatest admiration for many of the achievements of the Soviet Union. Among these great achievements is the value attached to the child and the common man. Their system of education and health are probably the best in the world. But it is said, and rightly, that there is suppression of individual freedom there. And yet the spread of education in all its forms is itself a tremendous liberating force which ultimately will not tolerate that suppression of freedom. This again is another contradiction. Unfortunately, communism became too closely associated with the necessity for violence and unfortunately the idea which it placed before the world became a tainted one. Means distorted ends. We see here the powerful influence of wrong means and methods.

This is completely opposed to the peaceful approach which Gandhiji taught us. Communists as well as anti-communists both seem to imagine that a principle can only be stoutly defended by languages of violence, and by condemning those who do not accept it. For both of them there are no shades, there is only black and white. That is the old approach of the bigoted aspects of some religions. It is not the approach of tolerance, of feeling that perhaps others might have some share of the truth also. Speaking for myself, I find this approach wholly unscientific, unreasonable and uncivilised, whether it is applied in the realm of religion or economic theory or anything else. I prefer the old pagan approach to tolerance, apart from its religious aspects. But whatever we may think about it, we have arrived at a stage in the modern world when an attempt at forcible imposition of ideas on any large section of people is bound ultimately to fail. In present circumstances this will lead to war and tremendous destruction. There will be no victory, only defeat for everyone. Even this, we have seen, in the last year or two, that it is not easy for even great powers to reintroduce colonial control over territories which have recently become independent. This was exemplified by the Suez incident in 1956. Also what happened in Hungary demonstrated that the desire for national freedom is stronger even than any ideology and cannot ultimately be suppressed. What happened in Hungary was not essentially a conflict between communism and anti-communism. It represented nationalism striving for freedom from foreign control.

We talk of a welfare state and of democracy and socialism. They are good concepts but they hardly convey a clear and ambiguous meaning. This was the argument and then the question arose as to what our ultimate objective should be. Democracy and socialism are means to an end, not the end itself. We talk of the good of society. Is this something apart from and transcending the good of the individuals composing it ? If the individual is ignored and sacrificed for what is considered the good of the society is that the right objective to have ?

It was agreed that the individual should not so be sacrificed and indeed that real social progress will come only when opportunity is given to the individual to develop provided the individual is not a selected group, but comprises the whole community. The touchstone, therefore, should be how far any political or social theory enable the individual to rise above his petty self and thus think in terms of the good of all. The law of life should not be competition or acquisitiveness but co-operation, the good of each contributing to the good of all ; in such a society the emphasis will be on duties, not on right ; the rights will follow the performance of the duties. We have to give a new direction to education and evolve a new type of humanity.

But obviously it does not solve any of these problems and, in a sense, we remain where we were. In India we talk of the Welfare State and socialism. In a sense, every country whether it is capitalist, socialist or communist, accepts the ideal of the Welfare State. Capitalism, in a few countries at least, has achieved this common welfare to a very large extent, though it has far from solved its own problems and there is a basic lack of something vital.

Democracy allied to capitalism has undoubtedly toned down many of its evils and in fact is different now from what it was a generation or two go. In industrially advanced countries there has been a continuous and steady upward trend of economic development. Even the terrible losses of world wars have not prevented this trend in so far as these highly developed countries are concerned. Further, this economic development has spread, though in varying degrees, to all classes. This does not apply to countries which are industrially undeveloped. Indeed, in those countries the struggle for development is very difficult and some-time, in spite of efforts, not only do economic inequalities remain, but tend to become worse. Normally speaking, it may be said that the forces of a capitalist society, if left unchecked, tend to make the rich richer and the poor poorer and thus incr-ease the gap between them. This applies to countries as well as groups or regions or classes within the countries. Various democratic processes interfere with these normal trends. Capitalism itself has, therefore, developed some socialistic features even though its major aspects remain.

Socialism, of course, deliberately wants to interfere with the normal processes and thus not only adds to the productive forces but lessens inequalities. But, what is socialism ? It is difficult to give a precise answer and there are innumerable definitions of it. Some people probably think of socialism vaguely just as something which does good and which aims at equality. That does not take us very far. Socialism is basically a different approach from that of capitalism, though I think it is true that the wide gap between them tends to lessen because many of the ideas of socialism are gradually incorporated even in the capitalist structure. Socialism is after, all not only a way of life but a certain scientific approach to social and economic problems. If socialism is underdeveloped country, it does not suddenly make it any less backward. In fact we then have a backward and poverty-stricken socialism.

8

Emergency : The Congress Challenge*

1. Indira Gandhi on 26 June 1975

The president has proclaimed emergency. This is nothing to panic about.

I am sure you are all conscious of the deep and widespread conspiracy which has been brewing ever since I began to introduce certain progressive measures of benefit to the common man and woman of India. In the name of democracy it has been sought to negate the very functioning of democracy. Duly elected governments have not been allowed to function and in some cases force has been used to compel members to resign in order to dissolve lawfully elected assemblies. Agitations have surcharged the atmosphere, leading to violent incidents. The whole country was shocked at the brutal murder of my cabinet colleague, Shri L.N. Mishra. We also deeply deplore the dastradly attack on the Chief Justice of India.

Certain persons have gone to the length of inciting our armed forces to mutiny and our police to rebel. The fact that our defence forces and the police are diciplined and deeply patriotic and therefore will not be taken in, does not mitigate the seriousness of the provocation.

The forces of disintegration are in full play and communal

*Prime Minister Indira Gandhi's broadcasts to the nation on 26 June, 1975 and on 27 June 1975.

passions are being aroused, threatening our unity.

All manner of false allegations have been hurled at me. The Indian people have known me since my childhood. All my life has been in the service of our people. This is not a personal matter. It is not important whether I remain Prime Minister or not. However, the institution of the Prime Minister is important and the deliberate political attempts to denigrate it is not in the interest of democracy or of the nation.

We have watched these developments with utmost patience for long. Now we learn of new programmes challenging law and order throughout the country with a view to disrupting normal functioning. How can any Government worth the name stand by and allow the country's stability to be imperilled ? The action of a few are endangering the rights of the vast majority. Any situation which weakens the capacity of the national government to act decisively inside the country is bound to encourage dangers from outside. It is our paramount duty to safeguard unity and stability. The nation's integrity demands firm action.

The threat to internal stability also affects production and prospects of economic improvement. In the last few months the determined action we have taken has succeeded in largely checking the price rise. We have been actively considering further measures to strengthen the economy and to relieve the hardship of various sections, particularly the poor and vulnerable, those with fixed income. I shall announce them soon.

I should like to assure you that the new emergency proclamation will in no way affect the rights of law-abiding citizens. I am sure that internal conditions will speedily improve to enable us to dispense with this proclamation as soon as possible.

I have been overwhelmed by the messages of goodwill from all parts of India and all sections of the people.

May I appeal for your continued cooperation and trust in the days ahead ?

2. Indira Gandhi on 27 June 1975

I had told you yesterday morning that I would soon announce some economic measures. These will take a couple of days more. Today there are a few other matters to discuss with you.

What were the reasons for proclaiming emergency ?

A climate of violence and hatred had been created which resulted in the assassination of a cabinet minister and an attempt on the life of the Chief Justice. The opposition parties had chalked out a programme of countrywide bundhs, gheraos, agitations, disruption and incitement to industrial workers, police and defence forces in an attempt wholly to paralyse the central government. One of them went to the extent of saying that the armed forces should not carry out orders which they considered wrong.

This programme was to begin from the 19th of this month. We had no doubt that such a programme would have resulted in a grave threat to public order and damage to the economy beyond repair. This had to be prevented. The kind of programme envisaged by some of the opposition groups is not compatible with democracy, is anti-national by any test and could not be allowed.

Since the proclamation, there is normalcy all over the country, except for partial hartal and minor incidents in Gujarat. This sense of normalcy must be maintained. And there should be realisation that even in a democracy there are limits which cannot be crossed. Violent action and senseless Satyagrahas will pull down the whole edifice, which has been built over the years with such labour and hope. I trust it will be possible to lift the emergency soon.

You know that I have always believed in freedom of the press, and I still do, but like all freedoms it has to be exercised with responsibility and restraint. In situations of internal disturbance, whether language or communal riots, grave mischief has been done by irresponsible writing. We had to prevent such a situation. For some time several newspapers have deliberately distorted news and made malicious and provocative comments. The entire purpose is to bring about a situation of calmness and stability. The purpose of censorship is to restore a climate of trust. There has been delay in news from the AIR and newspapers. It took time to make all the necessary legal and administrative arrangements.

In the meantime, rumour-mongers and anti-social elements have had a field day and have spread stories of all kinds. I want to assure you that the leaders under arrest are being extended all courtesy and consideration.

Similarly, wild conjectures are circulating about impending nationalisation of industries, etc., and drastic new controls. We have no such plans.

Our purpose is to increase production, which will bring about greater employment and better distribution. One of the immediate needs is to supply power to agriculture and industry. We must alleviate the hardship of the poorer sections and middle classes. This morning I had a meeting with the secretaries to the Government of India and stressed the importance of making the administration more alert so that work is done more speedily and more efficiently.

This is a time for unity and discipline. I am fully confident with each day the situation will improve and that in this task our people in towns and villages will give us their full support, so that the country will be strengthened.

9

A Positive Response

Jayaprakash Narayan

Chandigarh
July 21, 1975.

Dear Prime Minister,

I am appalled at press reports of your speeches and inter-
views. (The very fact that you have to say something everyday
to justify your action implies a guilty conscience.) Having
muzzled the press and every kind of public dissent, you continue
with your distortions and untruths without fear of criticism or
contradiction. If you think that in this way you will be able to
justify yourself in the public eye and damn the opposition to
political perdition you are sorely mistaken. If you doubt this,
you may test it by revoking the emergency, restoring the people
their fundamental rights, restoring the freedom of press, releasing
all those whom you have imprisoned or dctained for no other
crime than performing a patriotic duty. Nine years, Madam, is
not a short perid of time for the people who are gifted with a
sixth sense, to have found you out.

The burden of your song, as I have been able to discover, is
that (a) there was a plan to paralyse the government and (b)
that one person had been trying to spread disaffection among
the ranks of civil and military forces. These seem to be your
major notes. But there have been also minor notes. Every now

and then, you have been doling out of your obiter dicta, such as the nation being more important than democracy and about the suitability of social democracy to India and more in the same vein.

As I am the villain of the piece, let me put the record straight. This may be of no interest to you—for all your distortions and untruths are wilful and deliberate but at least the truth would have been recorded.

About the plan to paralyse the government, there was no such plan and you know it. Let me state the facts.

Of all the states of India it was in Bihar alone there was a people's movement. But there too according to the Chief Minister's many statements, it has fizzled out long ago, if it had ever existed. But the truth is—and you should know if your ubiquitous intelligence have served you right—that it was spreading and percolating deep down in the countryside. Until the time of my arrest, Janta Sarkars were being formed from the village upwards to the block level. Later on, the process was to be taken up, hopefully, to the district and state level.

If you have cared to look into the programme of the Janta Sarkars, you would have found that for the most part it was constructive, such as : regarding the public distribution system, checking corruption at lower levels of administration, implementing the land reform laws, settling disputes through the age old custom of conciliation and arbitration, assuring a fair deal to Harijans, curbing such social evils as Tilak and Dahez, etc. There was nothing in all this that by any stretch of imagination could be called subversive. Only where the Janta Sarkars were solidly organised were such programmes as non-payment of taxes taken up. At the peak of the movenment, in urban areas an attempt was made for some days, through Dharna and picketting to stop the working of government offices. At Patna whenever the Assembly opened, attempts were made to persuade the members to resign and to prevent them peacefully from going in. All these were calculated programmes of civil disobedience and thousands of men and women were arrested all over the State.

If all this adds up to an attempt to paralyse the Bihar government, well, it was the same kind of attempt as was made during the freedom struggle through non-cooperation and satyagraha to paralyse the British government. But that was a government established by force, whereas the Bihar government and the legislature are both constitutionally established bodies. What right has anyone to ask an elected government and elected legislature to go? This is one of your favourite questions. But it has been answered umpteen times by competent persons, including well known constitutional lawyers. The answer is that in a democracy the people do have the right to ask for the resignation of an elected government if it has gone corrupt and has been misruling. And if there is a legislature that persists in supporting such a government it too must go, so that the people might choose better representatives.

But in that case how can it be determined what the people want in the usual democratic manner. In the case of Bihar the mammoth rallies and processions held in Patna, the thousands of constituency meetings held all over the state, the three day Bihar Bandh, the memorable happenings of the 4th November and the 'largest ever' meeting held at the Gandhi Maidan on November 18 were a convincing measure of the people's will. And what had the Bihar government and Congress to show on their side? The miserable counter-offensive of November 16 which had been master-minded by Mr Borooah and on which according to reliable reports, the fantastic sum of 60 lakhs of ruppes was spent. But if that was not conclusive enough proof, I had asked repeatedly for a plebiscite. But you were afraid to face the people.

While I am on the Bihar movement, let me mention another important point that would illumine the politics of such a type of movement. The students of Bihar did not start their movement just off the beat as it were. After formulating their demands at a conference they had met the Chief Minister and the Education Minister. They had several meetings. But unfortunately the inept and corrupt Bihar government did not take the students seriously. Then the latter gheraoed the Assembly. The sad event of that day precipitated the Bihar movement. Even then the students did not demand the resignation of the Ministry nor the dissolution of the Assembly. It was after several weeks during which firing, lathi charges and indiscriminate arrests took place that the Students' Action Committee felt compelled to put that demand. It was at that point that the Rubicon was crossed.

Thus in Bihar, the government was given a chance to settle the issues across the table. One of the demands of the students was unreasonable or non-negotiable. But the Bihar government preferred the method of struggle, i.e., unparalleled repression. It was the same in U.P. In either case the government rejected the path of negotiation, of trying to settle across the table and chose the path of strife. Had it been otherwise, there would have been no movement at all.

I have pondered over this riddle. Why did not those governments act wisely? The conclusion I have arrived at is that the main hurdle has been corruption. Somehow the government have been unable to deal with corruption in their ranks, particularly, at the top level: the ministerial level itself. And corruption has been the central point of the movement, particularly corruption in the government and the administration.

Be that as it may, except for Bihar there was no movement of its kind in any other state of India. In U.P. though Stayagraha had started in April, it was far from becoming a people's movement. In some other states though struggle committees had been formed, there seemed to be no possibility of a mass movement anywhere. And as the general election to the Lok Sabha was drawing near, the attention of the Opposition parties was turned more towards the coming electoral struggle involving civil disobedience.

Thus, the plan of which you speak, the plan to paralyse the government, is a figment of your imagination thought up to justify your totalitarian measures.

But suppose I grant you for a minute, for argument's sake, that there was such a plan, do you honestly believe that your erstwhile colleague, the former Deputy Prime Minister of India, and Chandra Shekhar, a member of the Congress Working Committee, were also a party to it? Then why have they also been arrested and many others like them?

No, dear Prime Minister, there was no plan to paralyse the government. If there was any plan, it was a simple, innocent and short-time plan to continue until the Supreme Court decided your appeal. It was this plan that was announced at the

Ramlila ground by Nanaji Deshmukh on 25 June and which was the subject of my speech that evening. The programme was for a selected number of persons to offer satyagraha before or near your residence in support of the demand that you should step down until the Supreme Court's jugment on your appeal. The programme was to continue for seven days in Delhi, after which it was to be taken up in the States. And, as I have said above, it was to last only until the judgement of the Supreme Court.

I do not see what is subversive or dangerous about it. In a democracy the citizen has an inalienable right to civil disobedience when he finds that other channels of redress or reform have dried up. It goes without saying that the satyagrahi willingly invites and accepts his lawful punishment. This is the new dimension added to democracy by Gandhi. What an irony that it should be obliterated in Gandhi's own India !

It should be noted—and it is a very important point—that even this programme of Satyagraha would not have occurred to the Opposition had you remained content quietly clinging on to your office. But you did not do it. Through your henchmen you had rallies and demonstrations organized in front of your residence begging you not to resign. You addressed these rallies and justifying your stand advanced spurious arguments and heaped calumny on the head of the opposition. An effigy of the High Court Judge was burnt before your residence and posters appeared in the city suggesting some kind of link between the judge and the CIA. When such despicable happenings were taking place every day, the Opposition had no alternative but to counteract the mischeif. And how did it decide to do it ? Not by rowdyism but by orderly Satyagraha, self-sacrifice.

It was this 'plan' and not any imaginary plan to paralyse the government that has aroused your ire and cost the people their liberties and dealt a death-blow to their democracy.

And why has the freedom of the press been suppressed ? Not because the Indian press was irresponsible, dishonest or anti-government. In fact, nowhere, under conditions of freedom is the press more responsible, reasonable and fair than it has been in India. The turth is that your anger against it was aroused because on the question of your resignation, after the

High Court's judgement, some of the papers took a line that was highly unpalatable to you. And when on the morrow of the Supreme Court judgement all the metropolitan papers, including the wavering Times of India, came out with well-reasoned and forceful editorials advising you to quit freedom of the press became too much for you to stomach. That cooked the goose of the Indian press, and you struck your deadly blow. It staggers one's imagination to think that so valuable a freedom of the press, the very life-breath of democracy, can be snuffed out because of the personal pique of a Prime Minister.

You have accused the Opposition of trying to lower the prestige and position of the country's Prime Minister. But in reality the boot is on the other leg. No one has done more to lower the position and prestige of that great office than yourself. Can one ever think of the Prime Minister of a democratic country who cannot even vote in his parliament because he has been found guilty of corrupt electoral practices ? (The Supreme Court may reverse the High Court's judgement—most probably it will, in this atmosphere of terror—but as long as that is not done your guilt and your deprivation of right to vote remain.

As for the 'one person' who is supposed to have tried to sow disaffection in the armed and police forces, he denies the charge. All that he has done is to make the men and officers of the Forces conscious of their duties and responsibilities. Whatever he has said in that connection is within the law : The Constitution, the Army Act and the Police Act.

So much for your major points : the plan to paralyse the government and the attempt to sow disaffection in the armed police and forces. Now a few of your minor points and obiter dicta.

You are reported to have said that democracy is not more important than the nation. Are you not presuming too much, Madam Prime Minister ? You are not the only one who cares for the nation. Among those whom you have detained or imprisoned there are many who have done much more for the nation than you. And everyone of them is as good a patriot as yourself. So, please do not apply salt to our wounds by lecturing to us about the nation.

Moreover, it is a false choice that you have formulated.

There is no choice between democracy and the nation. It was for the good of the nation that the people of India declared in their Constituent Assembly on 26th November 1949 that "we, the people of India, having solemnly resolved to constitute India into a Sovereign Democratic Republic...give to ourselves this Constitution". That democratic Constitution cannot be changed into a totalitarian one by a mere ordinance or law of Parliament. That can be done only by the people of India themselves in their new Constituent Assembly, especially elected for that specific purpose. If Justice, Liberty, Equality and Fraternity have not been rendered to 'all its citizens' even after a quarter of a century of signing of that Constitution, the fault is not that of the Constitution or of democracy but of the Congress party that has been in power in Delhi all these years. It is precisely because of that failure that there is so much unrest among the people and the youth. Repression is no remedy for that. One the other hand, it only compounds the failure.

I, no doubt, see that the papers are full these days of report of new policies, new drives, show of new enthusiasm. Apparently you are trying to make up for lost time, that is to say, you are making a show of doing here and now what you failed to do in nine years. But your twenty points will go the same way as your ten points did and the 'Stray Thoughts'*. But I assure you this time the people will not be fooled. And I assure you another thing too : a party of self-seekers and spineless opportunists and jee-huzurs ('yesmen') such as the Congress, alas, has become, can never do anything worthwhile. (Not all Congressmen are such. There are quite a few exceptions, such as those who have been deprived of their party membership and some of them their freedom so that according to the dharma of totalitarianism, there could be no criticism even within the party.) There will be a lot of propaganda and make-ado on paper but on the ground level the situation will not change the least. The condition of the poor—and they are the great majority over the greater part of the country—has been worsening over the past years. It would be enough if the downward trend were arrested. But, for that

---

*This refers to the note on economic policy that Mrs Gandhi sent to the AICC meeting held at Bangalore in July 1969.

your whole approach to politics and economics will have to change.

I have written the above in utter frankness without mincing words. I have done so not out of anger or so as to get even with you in words. No, that would be a show of impotence. Nor does it show any lack of appreciation for the care that is being taken on my health. I have done it only to place the naked truth before you, which you have been trying to cover up and distort.

Having performed this unpleasant duty, may I conclude with a few parting words of advice ? You know I am an old man. My life's work is done. And after Prabha's going I have nothing and no one to live for. My brother and nephew have their family and my younger sister—the elder one died years ago—has her sons and daughters. I have given all my life, after finishing education, to the country and asked for nothing in return.

Would you listen to the advice of such a man ? Please do not destory the foundations that the Father of the Nation, including your noble father, had laid down. There is nothing but strife and suffering along the path that you have taken. You inherited a great tradition, noble values and a working democracy. Do not leave behind a miserable wreck of all that. It would take a long time to put all that together again. For it would be put together again, I have no doubt. A people who fought British imperialism and humbled it cannot accept indefinitely the indignity and shame of totalitarianism. The spirit of man can never by vanquished, no matter how deeply suppressed. In establishing your personal dictatorship you have buried it deep. But it will rise from the grave. Even in Russia it is slowly coming up.

You have talked of social democracy. What a beautiful image those words call to the mind. But you have seen in eastern and central Europe how ugly the reality is : Naked dictatorship and, in the ultimate analysis, Russian overlordship. Please, please do not push India towards that terrible fate.

And may I ask to what purpose all these draconian measures? In order to be able to carry out your twenty points ? But who was preventing you from carrying out the ten points ? All the discontent, the protest, the Satyagraha were due precisely to

150   DEMOCRACY IN INDIA

the fact that you were not doing anything to implement your programme, inadequate as it was, to lighten the misery and burden under which the peeple and youth were groaning. This is what Chandra Shekhar, Mohan Dharia, Krishna Kant and their friends have been saying for which they have been punished.

You have talked of 'drift' in the country. But was that due to Opposition or to me ? The drift was because of your lack of decision and drive. You seem to act swiftly and dramatically only when your personal position is threatened. Once that is assured, the drift begins. Dear Indiraji, please do not identify yourself with the nation. You are not immortal, India is.

You have accused the Opposition and me of every kind of villainy. But let me assure you that if you do right things, for instance, your 20-points, tackling corruption at Ministerial levels, electoral reforms, etc., take the Opposition into confidence, heed its advice, you will receive the willing co-operation of every one of us. For that you need not destroy democracy. The ball is in your court. It is for you to decide.

With these parting words, let me bid you farewell. May God be with you.

Yours sincerely,
Jayaprakash

10

Constitution (44th Amendment) Bill

STATEMENT OF OBJECTS AND REASONS

A Constitution to be living must be growing. If the impediments to the growth of the Constitution are not removed, the Constitution will suffer a virtual atrophy. The question of amending the Constitution for removing the difficulties which have arisen in achieving the objective of socio-economic revolution, which would end poverty and ignorance and disease and inequality of opportunity, has been engaging the active attention of Government and the public for some years now.

2. The democratic institutions provided in the Constitution are basically sound and the path for progress does not lie in denigrating any of those institutions. However, there could be no denial that these institutions have been subjected to considerable stresses and strains and that vested interests have been trying to promote their selfish ends to the great detriment of public good.

3. It is, therefore, proposed to amend the Constitution to spell out expressly the high ideals of socialism, secularism and the integrity of the nation, to make the directive principles more comprehensive and give them precedence over those fundamental rights which have been allowed to be relied upon to frustrate socio-economic reforms for implementing the directive principles. It is also proposed to specify the fundamental duties of the citizens and make special provisions for dealing with anti-

national activities, whether by individuals or associations.

4.   Parliament and the State Legislatures embody the will of the people and the essence of democracy is that will of the people should prevail. Even though article 368 of the Constitution is clear and categoric with regard to the all inclusive nature of the amending power, it is considered necessary to put the matter beyond doubt. It is proposed to strengthen the presumption in favour of the constitutionality of legislation enacted by Parliament and State Legislatures by providing for a requirement as to the minimum number of Judges for determining questions as to the constitutionality of laws for a special majority of not less than two thirds for declaring any law to be constitutionally invalid. It is also proposed to take away the jurisdiction of High Courts with regard to determination of Constitutional validity of Central laws and confer exclusive jurisdiction in this behalf on the Supreme Court so as to avoid multiplicity of proceedings with regard to validity of the same Central law in different High Courts and the consequent possibility of the Central law being valid in one State and invalid in another State.

5.   To reduce the mounting arrears in High Courts and to secure the speedy disposal of service matters, revenue matters and certain other matters of special importance in the context of the socio-economic development and progress, it is considered expedient to provide for administrative and other tribunals for dealing with such matters while preserving the jurisdiction of the Supreme Court in regard to such matters under article 136 of the Constitution. It is also necessary to make certain modifications in the writ jurisdiction of the High Courts under article 226.

6.   It is proposed to avail of the present opportunity to make certain other amendments which have become necessary in the light of the working of the Constitution.

7.   The various amendments proposed in the Bill have been explained in the notes on clauses.

8.   The Bill seeks to achieve the above objects.

NEW DELHI;   **H.R.GOKHALE**
The 28th August, 1976.

TEXT OF BILL

Be it enacted by Parliament in the Twentyseventh Year of the Republic of India as follows:

1. (1) This Act may be called the Constitution (Fortyfourth Amendment) Act, 1976.

(2) It shall come into force on such date as the Central Government may, by notification in the Official Gazette, appoint and different dates may be appointed for different provisions of this Act.

Preamble

2. In the Preamble to the Constitution:

(a) for the words "SOVEREIGN DEMOCRATIC REPUBLIC", the words "SOVEREIGN SOCIALIST SECULAR DEMOCRATIC REPURLIC" shall be substituted; and

(b) for the words "unity of the Nation", the words "unity and integrity of the Nation" shall be substituted.

3. After article 31 of the Constitution, the following subheading shall be inserted, namely:

"Saving of Certain Laws".

4. In article 31C of the Constitution, for the words, brackets, letters and figures "the principles specified in clause (b) or clause (c) of article 39", the words and figures "all or any of the principles laid down in part IV" shall be substituted.

Anti-National Activities

5. After article 31C of the Constitution and before the subheading *"Right to Constitutional Remedies"*, the following article shall be inserted, namely:

'31D. (1) Notwithstanding anything contained in article 31, no law providing for—

(a) the prevention or prohibition of anti-national activities; or

(b) the prevention of formation of, or the prohibition of, anti-national associations,

shall be deemed to be void on the ground that it is inconsistent with, or takes away or abridges any of the rights conferred by article 14, article 19 or article 31.

(2) Notwithstanding anything in this Constitution, Parliament shall have, and the Legislature of a State shall not have, power to make laws with respect to any of the matters referred to in sub-clause (a) or sub-clause (b) of clause (1).

(3) Any law with respect to any matter referred to in sub-clause (a) or sub-clause (b) of clause (1) which is in force immediately before the commencement of section 5 of the Constitution (Forty-fourth Amendment) Act, 1976, shall continue in force until altered or repealed or amended by Parliament.

(4) In this article,—

(a) "association" means an association of persons ;

(b) "anti-national activity", in relation to an individual or association, means any action taken by such individual or association—

(i) which is intended, or which supports any claim, to bring about, on any ground whatsoever, the cession of a part of the territory of India or the secession of a part of the territory of India or which incites any individual or association to bring about such cession or secession:

(ii) which disclaims, questions, threatens, disrupts or is intended to threaten or disrupt the sovereignty and integrity of India or the security of the State or the unity of the nation ;

(iii) which is intended, or which is part of a scheme which is intended, to overthrow by force the Government as by law established ;

(iv) which is intended, or which is part of a scheme which is intended, to create internal disturbance or the disruption of public services ;

(v) which is intended, or which is part of a scheme which is intended, to threaten or disrupt harmony between different religious, racial, language or regional groups or castes or communities;

(c) "anti-national association" means an association—

(i) Which has for its object any anti-national activity ;

(ii) Which encourages or aids persons to undertake or engage in any anti-national activity ;

(iii) the members whereof undertake or engage in any anti-national activity.

Validity of State Laws

6. After article 32 of the constitution, the following article shall be inserted, namely:

"32A. Notwithstanding in article 32, the Supreme Court shall not consider the constitutional validity of any State law in any proceedings under that article unless the constitutional validity of any Central law is also in issue in such proceedings."

Opportunities to Children

7. In article 39 of the Constitution, for clause (ƒ), the following clause shall be substituted, namely:

"(ƒ) that children are giving opportunities and facilities to develop in a healthy manner and in conditions of freedom and dignity and that chilhood and youth are projected against exploitation and against moral and material abandonment."

Free Legal Aid

8. After article 39 of the Constitution, the following article shall be inserted, namely:

"39A. The State shall secure that the operation of the legal system promotes justice, on a basis of equal opportunity, and shall, in particular, provide free legal aid, by suitable legislation or schemes or any other way, to ensure that opportunities for securing justice are not denied to any citizen by reason of economic or other disabilities."

Workers' Participation in Management

9. After article 43 of the Constitution, the following article shall be inserted, namely:

"43A. The State shall take steps, by suitable legislation or in any other way, to secure the participation of workers in the management of undertakings, establishments or other organisations engaged in any industry."

Environment, Wild Life

10. After article 48 of the Constitution, the following

article shall be inserted, namely:

"48A   The State shall   endeavour to   protect   and   improve the environment and to safeguard the forests   and   wild   life   of the country.

11.   After Part IV of the Constitution, the following part shall be inserted, namely:

"PART IV A

FUNDAMENTAL DUTIES

51A.   It shall be the duty of every citizen of India—

(*a*)   to abide by the Constitution and respect its   ideals and institutions, the National Flag and the National Anthem ;

(*b*)   to cherish and follow the   noble   ideals   which   inspired our national struggle for   freedom ;

(*c*)   to uphold   and   protect   the   sovereignty,   unity   and integrity of India ;

(*d*)   to defend the country and render national service when called upon to do so ;

(*e*)   promote harmony and   the   spirit of   common   brother-hood   amongst   all   the   people of India transcending religious, linguistic and regional or   sectional diversities; to renounce prac-tices derogatory to the dignity of   women;

(*f*)   to value and preserve the rich heritage of our composite culture ;

(*g*)   to paotect and improve the natural   environment includ-ing forests, lakes, rivers and wild life, and to have compassion for living creatures ;

(*h*)   to   develop the   scientific   temper,   humanism and   the spirit of inquiry and reform;

(*i*)   to safeguard public property and to abjure violence;

(*j*)   to strive   towards   excellence   in all spheres of individual and collective   activity, so that the   nation constantly   rises to high r levels of endeavour and achievement."

Population and   Census

12.   In article 55 of the Constitution,   for the   *Explanation,* the following *Explanation* shall be substituted, namely:

'*Explanatian*—In this article, the expression "population" means the population as ascertained at the last preceding census of which the relevant figures have been published:

Provided that the reference in this *Explanation* to the last preceding census of which the relevant figures have been published shall until the relevant figures for the first census taken after the year 2000 have been published, be construed as a reference to the 1971 census."

Council of Ministers and President

13. In article 74 of the Constitution, for cluse (1), the following clause shall be substituted, namely:

"(1) There shall be a Council of Ministers with the Prime Minister at the head to aid and advise the President who shall in the exercise of his functions act in accordance with such advice."

14. In article 77 of the Constitution, after clause (3), the following clause shall be inserted, namely:

"(4) No court or other authority shall be entitled to require the production of any rules made under clause (3) for the more convenient transaction of the business of the Government of India."

15. In article 81 of the Constitution, to clause (3), the following proviso shall be added, namely:—

"Provided that the reference in this clause to the last preceding census of which the relevant figures have been published shall, until the relevant figures for the first census taken after the year 2000 have been published, be construed as a reference to 1971 census."

Allocation of Seats

16. In article 82 of the Constitution, after the proviso, the following provisos shall be inserted, namely:

"Provided further that such readjustment shall take effect from such date as the President may by order specify and until such readjustment takes effect, any election to the House may be

held on the basis of the territorial constituencies existing before
such readjustment:

Provided also that until the relevant figures for the first
census taken after the year 2000 have been published, it shall
not be necessary to readjust the allocation of seats in the House
of People to the States and the division of each State into territorial constituencies under this article."

Life of Parliament

17. (1) In article 83 of the Constitution, in clause (2), for
the words "five years" in the two places where they occur, the
words "six years" shall be substituted.

(2) The amendments made by sub-section (1) shall apply
to the House of People in existence on the date of coming into
force of this section.

Office of Profit

18. In article 100 of the Constitution, clauses (3) and (4)
shall be omitted.

19. In article 102 of the Constitution, for sub-clause (a) of
clause (1), the following sub-clause shall be substituted,
namely:

"(a) if he holds any such office of profit under the Government of any State as is declared by Parliament by law to
disqualify its holder."

President to Decide Disqualification

20. For article 103 of the Constitution, the following article
shall be substituted, namely:

"103. (1) If any question arises—

(a) as to whether a member of either House of Parliament
has become subject to any of the disqualifications mentioned in
clause (1) of article 102, or

(b) as to whether a person found guilty of a corrupt
practice at an election to a House of Parliament under any law
made by Parliament, shall be disqualified for being chosen as,

and for being, a member of either House of Parliament, or of a House of the Legislature of a State, or as to the period for which he shall be so disqualified, or as to the removal of, or the reduction of the period of, such disqualification,

the question shall be referred for the decision of the President and his decision shall be final.

(2) Before giving any decision on any such question, the president shall consult the Election Commission and the Election Commission may, for this purpose, make such inquiry as it thinks fit."

Powers of Parliament

21. In article 105 of the Constitution, for clause (3), the following clause shall be substituted, namely:

"(3) In other respects, the powers, privileges and immunities of each House of Parliament and of the members and the committees of each House shall be such as may, from time to time, be evolved by such House of Parliament."

House Quorum

22. In article 118 of the Constitution, in clause (1), after the words "its procedure", the brackets and words "(including the quorum to constitute meeting of the House)" shall be inserted.

Jurisdiction of Supreme Court and High Courts

23. After artice 131 of the Constitution, the following article shall be inserted, namely :

"131A. (1) Notwithstanding anything contained in any other provision of this Constitution, the Supreme Court shall, to the exclusion of any other court, have jurisdiction to detemine all questions relating to the constitutional validity of any Central law.

(2) Where a High Court is satisfied—

(a) that a case pending before it or before a court subordinate to it involves questions as to the constitutional validity of any Central law or, as the case maye be, of both Central and State laws; and (*b*) that the determination of such questions is necessary for the disposal of the case,

the High Court shall refer the questions for the decision of the Supreme Court.

(3) Without prejudice to the provisions of clause (2), where, on an application made by the Attorney-General of India, the Supreme Court is satisfied,—

(*a*) that a case pending before a High Court or before a court subordinate to a High Court involves questions as to the constitutional validity of any Central law or, as the case may be, of both Central and state laws; and

(*b*) that the determination of such questions is necessay for the disposal of the case,

the Supreme Court may require the High Court to refer the questions to it for its decision.

(4) When a reference is made under clause (2) or clause (3), the High Court shall stay all proceedings in respect of the case until the Supreme Court decides the questions so referred.

(5) The Supreme Court shall, after giving the parties an opportunity of being heard, decide the questions so referred, and may—

(*a*) either dispose of the case itself; or

(*b*) return the case to the High Court together with a copy of its judgment on such questions for disposal of the case in conformity with such judgment by the High Court or, as the case may be, the court subordinate to it."

24. After article 139 of the Constitution, the following article shall be inserted, namely :

"139A. (1) If, on an application made by the Attorney-General of India, the Supreme Court is satisfied that cases involving the same or substantially the same questions of law are pending before it and one or more High Courts or before two or more High Courts and that such questions are substantial questions of general importance, the Supreme Court may withdraw the case or cases pending before the High Court or the High Courts and dispose of all the cases itself.

(2) The Supreme Court may if it deems it expedient so to do for the ends of justice, transfer any case, appeal or other proceedings pending before any High Court to any other High

Court."

25. After article 144 of the Constitution, the following article shall be inserted, namely :

"144A (1) The minimum number of Judges of the Supreme Court who shall sit for the purpose of determining any question as to the constitutional validity of any Central law or State law shall be seven.

(2) A Central law or a State law shall not be declared to be constitutionally invalid by the Supreme Court unless a majority of not less than two-thirds of the Judges sitting for the purpose of determining the question as to the constitutional validity of such law hold it to be constitutionally invalid."

Central and State Accounts

26. In article 145 of the Constitution,—

(a) in clause (1), after sub-clause (c), the following sub-clause shall be inserted, namely :

"(cc) rules as to the proceedings in the court under articles 131A and 139A ;"

(b) in clause (2), for the words, brackets and figure "provisions of clause (3)", the words, figures, letter and brackets "provisions of article 144A, and of clause (3)" shall be substituted;

(c) in clause (3), for the words "The minimum number", the words, figures and letter "Subject to the provisions of article 144A, the minimum number" shall be substituted.

27. For article 150 of the Constitution, the following article shall be substituted, namely :

"150. The accounts of the Union and of the States shall be kept in such form as the President may, after consultation with the Comptroller and Auditor-General of India, prescribe,"

28. In article 166 of the Constitution, after clause (3), the following clause shall be inserted, namely :

"(4) No court or other authority shall be entitled to require the production of any rules made under clause (3) for the more convenient transaction of the business of the Government of the State."

29. In article 170 of the Constitution,

(a) for the *Explanation*, the following *Explanation* shall be substituted, namely :

'*Explanation*—In this clause, the expression "population" means the population as ascertained at the last preceding census of which the relevant figures have been published :

Provided that the reference in this *Explanation* to the last preceding census of which the relevant figures have been published shall, until the relevant figures for the first census taken after the year 2000 have been published, be construed as a reference to the 1971 census.",

(b) in clause (3), after the proviso, the following provisos shall be inserted, namely :

"Provided further that such reajdustment shall take effect from such date as the President may, by oader, specify and until such readjustment takes effect, any election to the Legislative Assembly may be held on the basis of the territorial constiuencies existing before such readjustment :

Provided also that until the relevant figures for the first census taken after the year 2000 have been published, it shall not be necessary to readjust the total number of seats in the Legislative Assembly of each State and the division of such State into territorial constituencies under this clause."

Life of State Assemblies

30. (1) In article 172 of the Constitution, in clause (1), for the words "five years" in the two places where they occur, the words "six years" shall be substituted,

(2) The amendments made by sub-section (1) shall apply to every Legislative Assembly in existence on the date of coming into force of this section.

31. In article 189 of the Constitution, clauses (3) and (4) shall be omitted.

32. In article 191 of the Constitution, for sub-clause (a) of clause (1), the following sub-clause shall be substituted, namely ;

"(a) if he holds any such office of profit under the Government of India or the Government of any State specified in the First Schedule as is declared by Parliament by law to disqualify its holder ;".

President to Decide Disqualification

33. For article 192 of the Constitution, the following article shall be substituted, namely :

"192. (1) If any question arises—

(a) as to whether a member of a House of the Legislature of a State has become subject to any of the disqualifications mentioned in clause (1) of article 191, or

(b) as to whether a person found guilty of a corrupt practice at an election to a House of the Legislature of a State under any law made by Parliament shall be disqualified for being chosen as, and for being, a member of either House of Parliament or of a House of the Legislature of a State, or as to the period for which he shall be so disqualified, or as to the removal of, or the reduction of the period of, such disqualification,

the question shall be referred for the decision of the President and his decision shall be final.

(2) Before giving any decision on any such question, the President shall consult the Election Commission and the Election Commission may, for this purpose, make such inquiry as it thinks fit."

34. In artice 194 of the Constitution, for clause (3) the following clause shall be substituted, namely :

"(3) In other respects, the powers, privileges and immunities of a House of the Legislature of a State, and of a State, and of the members and the committees of a House of such Legislature shall be as may from time to time be evolved by such House."

State Quorum

35. In article 208 of the Constitution, in clause (1), after the words "its procedure" the brackets and words "(including the quorum to constitute a meeting of the House)" shall be inserted.

36. In article 217 of the Constitution, in clause (2),—

(a) in sub-clause (b), the word "or" shall be inserted at

the end ;
    (*b*) after sub-clause (*b*) the following sub-clause shall be inserted, namely:
    (*c*) is, in the opinion of the President, a distinguished jurist.";
    (*c*) in the *Explanation*, in clause (*a*), for the words "has held judicial office", the words "has held judicial office or the office of a member of a tribunal or any post, under the Union or a State, requiring special knowledge of law" shall be substituted.
    37. In article 225 of the Constitution, the proviso shall be omitted.

Writ Powers of High Courts

    38. For article 226 of the Constitution, the following article shall be substituted, namely:
    "226. (1) Notwithstanding anything in article 32 but subject to the provisions of article 131A and article 226A, every High Court shall have power throughout the territories in relation to which it exercises jurisdiction to issue to any person or authority including in appropriate cases, any Government, within those territories directions, orders or writs, including writs in the nature of *habeas corpus*, *mandamus*, prohibition, *quo warranto* and *certiorari* or any of them,—
    (*a*) for the enforcement of any of the rights conferred by the provisions of Part III ; or
    (*b*) for the redress of any injury of a substantial nature by reason of the contravention of any other provision of this Constitution or any provision of any enactment or Ordinance or any order, rule, regulation, bye-law or other instrument made thereunder ; or
    (*c*) for the redress of any injury by reason of any illegality in any proceeding by or before any authority under any provision referred to in sub-clause (*b*) where such illegality has resulted in substantial failure of justice.
    (2) The power conferred by clause (1) to issue directions, orders or writs to any Government, authority or person may also be exercised by any High Court exercising jurisdiction in

relation to the territories within which the cause of action, wholly or in part, arises for the exercise of such power, notwithstanding that the seat of such Government or authority or the residence of such person is not within those territories.

(3) No petition for the redress of any injury referred to in sub-clause (b) or sub-clause (c) of clause (1) shall be entertained if any other remedy for redress is provided for by or under any other law for the time being in force.

(4) No interim order (whether by way of injunction or stay or in any other manner) shall be made on, or in any proceedings relating to, a petition under clause (1) unless—

(a) copies of such petition and of all documents in support of the plea for snch interim order are furnished to the party against whom such petition is filed or proposed to be filed ; and

(d) opportunity is given to such party to be heard in the matter.

(5) The High Court may dispense with the requirement of sub-clauses (a) and (b) of clause (4) and make an interim order as an exceptional measure if it is satisfied for reasons to be recorded in writing that it is neccessary so to do for preventing any loss being caused to the petitioner which cannot be adequately compensated in money but any such interim order shall, if it is not vacated earlier, cease to have effect on the expiry of a period of fourteen days from the date on which it is made unless the said requirements have been complied before the expiry of that period and the High Court has conti- nued the operation of the interim order.

(6) Notwithstanding anything in clause (4) or clause (5), no interim order (whether by way of injunction or stay or in any other manner) shall be made on, or in any proceeding relating to, a petition under clause (1) where such order will have the effect of delaying any inquiry into a matter of public impor- tance or any investigation or inquiry into an offence punishable with imprisonment or any action for the execution of any work or project of public utility, or the acquisition of any property for such execution, by the Government or any corporation owned or controlled by the Government.

(7) The power conferred on a High Court by this article

shall not be in derogation of the power conferred on he
Supreme Court by clause (2) of article 32."

39. After article 226 of the Constitution, the following
article shall be inserted, namely:

"226A. Notwithstanding anything in article 226, the High
Court shall not consider the constitutional validity of any
Central law in any proceedings under that article."

High Court Jurisdiction

40. In article 227 of the Constitution,—

(a) for clause (1), the following clause shall be substituted,
namely:

"(1) Every High Court shall have superintendence over all
courts subject to its appellate jurisdiction." ;

(b) after clause (4), the following clause shall be inserted,
namely ;

"(5) Nothing in the article shall be construed as giving to
a High Court any jurisdiction to question and judgment of any
inferior court which is not otherwise subject to appeal or
revision.

41. In article 228 of the Constitution, for the words "it
shall withdraw the case and may—", the words, figures and
letter "it shall withdraw the case and, subject to the provisions
of article 131A, may—" shall be substituted.

42. After article 228 of the Constitution, the following
article shall be inserted, namely :

"228A. (1) No High Court shall have jurisdiction to
declare any Central law to be constitutionally invalid.

(2) Subject to the provisions of article 131A, the High
Court may determine questions as to the constitutional validity
of State laws.

(3) The minimum number of Judges who shall sit for the
purpose of determining any question as to the constitutional
validity of any State law shall be five:

Provided that where the High Court consists of less than five
Judges all Judges of the High Court may sit and determine such
question.

(4) A State law shall not be declared to be constitutionally

invalid by the High Court unless—

(*a*) where the High Court consists of five Judges or more not less than two-thirds of the Judges sitting for the purpose of determining the validity of such law, hold it to be constitutionally invalid ; and

(*b*) where the High Court consists of less then five Judges, all the Judges of the High Court hold it to be constitutionally invalid.

(5) The provisions of this article shall have effect notwithstanding anything contained in this Part.

Explanation.—In computing the number of Judges of a High Court for the purposes of this article a Judge who is disqualified by reason of personal or pecuniary bias shall be excluded."

Deployment of Armed Force in States

43. After article 257 of the Constitution, the following article shall be inserted, namely :

257A. (1) The Government of India may deploy any armed force of the Union or any other force subject to the control of the Union for dealing with any grave situation of law and order in any State.

(2) Any armed force or other force or any contingent or unit thereof deployed under clause (1) in any State shall act in accordance with such directions as the Government of India may issue and shall not, save as otherwise provided in such directions, be subject to the superintendence or control of the State Government or any office or authority subordinate to the State Government.

(3) Parliament may, by law, specify the powers, function privileges and liabilities of the members of any force or any contingent or unit thereof deployed under clause (1) during the period of such deployment."

Public Servants' Enquiry Rules

44. In article 311 of the Constitution, in clause (2),—

(*a*) the words "and where it is proposed, after such inquiry, to impose on him any such penalty, until he has been given a reasonable opportunity of making representation on the penalty proposed, but only on the basis of the evidence adduced during such inquiry" shall be omitted ;

(*b*) for the words "provided that this clause shall not apply...", the following shall be substituted, namely :

"Provided that where it is proposed after such inquiry, to impose upon him any such penalty such penalty may be imposed on the basis of the evidence adduced during such inquiry and it shall not be necessary to give such person any opportunity of making representation on the penalty proposed :

Provided further that this clause shall not apply—".

45. In article 312 of the Constitution,—

(*a*) in clause (1),—

(*i*) for the word and figures "Part XI", the words and figuers "Chapter VI of Part VI or Part XI" shall be substituted ;

(*ii*) after the words "all-India judicial services" the brackets and word "(including an All-India Judicial Service)" shall be inserted ;

(*b*) after clause (2), the following clauses shall be inserted, namely:—

"(3) The all-India judicial service referred to in clause (1) shall not include any post inferior to that of a district judge as defined in article 236,

(4) The law providing for the creation of all-India judicial service aforesaid may contain such provisions for giving effect to the provision of that law and no such law shall be deemed to be an amendment of this Constitution for the purposes of article 368."

Administrative Tribunals

46. After Part XIV of the Constitution, the following Part shall be inserted, namely :

PART XIVA

TRIBUNALS

323A. (1) Parliament may, by law, provide for the adjudication or trial by administrative tribunals of disputes and complaints with respect to recruitment and conditions of service of perons appointed to public services and posts in connection with the affairs of the Union or of any State or of any local or other authority within he territory of India or under the control of the Government of India or of any corporation owned or controlled by the Government.

(2) A law made under clause (1) may—

(a) Provide for the establishment of an administrative tribunal for the Union and a separate administrative tribunal for each State or for two or more States ;

(b) specify the jurisdiction, powers (including the power to punish for contempt) and authority which may be exercised by each of the said tribunals ;

(c) provide for the procedure (including provisions as to limitation and rules of evidence) to be followed by the said tribunals ;

(d) exclude the jurisdiction of all courts, except the jurisdiction of the Supreme Court under article 136, with respect to the disputes or complaints referred to in clause (1) ;

(e) provide for the transfer to each such administrative tribunal of any cases pending before any court or other authority immediately before the establishment of such tribunal as would have been within the jurisdiction of such tribunal if the causes of action on which such suits or proceedings are based had arisen after such establishment ;

(f) repeal or amend any order made by the President under clause (3) of article 371D ;

(g) contain such supplemental, incidental and consequential provision (including provisions as to fees) as Parliament may deem necessary for the effective functioning of, and for the speedy disposal of cases by, and the enforcement of the orders of, such tribunals.

(3) The provisions of this article shall have effect notwithstanding anything in any other provision of this Constitution or in any other law for the time being in force.

Tribunals for Other Matters

323B. (1) The appropriate Legislature may, by law, provide

for the adjudication, or trial by tribunals of any disputes complaints, or offences with respect to all or any of the matters
specified in clause (2) with respect to which such Legislature has
power to make laws.

(2) The matters referred to in clause (1) are the following,
namely :

(*a*) levy, assessment, collection and enforcement of any tax ;

(*b*) foreign exchange, import and export across custom
frontiers ;

(*c*) industrial and labour disputes ;

(*d*) land reforms by way of acquisition by the State of any
estate as defined in article 31A or of any rights therein or the
extinguishment or modification of any such rights or by way of
ceiling on agricultural land or in any other way ;

(*e*) ceiling on urban property ;

(*f*) elections to either House of Parliament or the House or
either House of the Legislature of a State, but excluding the
matters referred to in article 329 and article 329A :

(*g*) production, procurement, supply and distribution of foodstuffs (including edible oilseeds and oils) and such other goods
as the President may, by public notification, declare to be
essential goods for the purpose of this article and control of
prices of such goods ;

(*h*) offences against laws with respect to any of the matters
specified in sub-clauses (*a*) to (*g*) and fees in respect of any of
those matters ;

(*i*) any matters incidental to any of the matters specified in
sub-clauses (*a*) to (*h*).

(3) A law made under clause (1) may—

(*a*) provide for the establishment of a hierarchy of tribunals ;

(*b*) specify the jurisdiction, powers (including the power to
punish for contempt) and authority which may be exercised by
each of the said tribunals ;

(*c*) provide for the procedure (including provisions as to
limitation and rules of evidence) to be followed by the said
tribunals;

(*d*) exclude the jurisdiction of all courts except the jurisdiction of the Supreme Court under article 136 with respect to all
or any of the matters falling within the jurisdiction of the said

tribunals ;

(*e*) provide for the transfer to each such tribunal of any court or any other authority immediately before the establishment of such tribunal as would have been within the jurisdiction of such tribunal if the causes of action on which suits or proceedings are based had arisen after such establishment ;

(*f*) contain such supplemental, incidental and consequential provisions (including provision as to fees) as the appropriate Legislature may deem necessary for the effective functioning of, and for the speedy disposal of cases by, and the enforcement of the orders of such tribunals.

(4) The provisions of this article shall have effect notwithstanding anything in any other provision of this Constitution or in any other law for the time being in force.

Explanation—In this article, "appropriate Legislature", in relation to any matters means, or as the case may be, a State Legislature competent to make laws with respect to such matters in accordance with the provisions of Part XI.'

47. . In article 330 of the Constitution, the following *Explanation* shall be inserted at the end, namely :

Explanation—In this article and in article 332, the expression "population as ascertained at the last preceding census of which the relevant figures have been published.

Provided that the reference in this *Explanation* to the last preceding census of which the relevant figures have been published shall, until the relevant figures for the first census taken after the year 2000 have been published be construed as a reference to the 1971 census.'

Proclamation of Emergency

48. In article 352 of the Constitution,

(*a*) in clause (1), after the words "make a declaration to that effect,', the following shall be inserted, namely :

"in respect of the whole of India or of such part of the territory thereof as may be specified in the Proclamation",

(*b*) in clause (2) in sub-clause (*a*), after the words "revoked", the words "or varied" shall be inserted ;

(*c*) after clause (2), the following clause shall be inserted, namely :

"(2A) Where a Proclamation issued under clause (1) is varied by a subsequent Proclamation, the provisions of clause (2) shall, so far as may be, apply in relation to such subsequent Proclamation as they apply in relation to a Proclamation issued under clause (1)."

49. To article 353 of the Constitution, the following proviso shall be added. namely :

"Provided that where a Proclamation of Emergency is in operation only in any part of the territory of India,—

(*i*) the executive power of the Union to give directions under clause (*a*), and

(*ii*) the power of Parliament to make laws under clause (*b*), shall also extend to any State other than a State in which or in any part of which the Proclamation of Emergency is in operation if and in so far as the security of India or any part of the territory thereof is threatened by activities in or in relation to the part of the territory of India in which the Proclamation of Emergency is in operation."

50. In article 338 of the Constitution, in clause (4) for the word "six months" wherever they occur, the words "one year" shall be substitued.

51. (1) In article 357 of the Constitution, for clause (2) the following clause shall be substituted, namely :

"(2) Any law made in exercise of the power of the Legislature of the State by Parliament or the President or other authority referred to in sub-clause (*a*) of clause (1) which Parliament or such other authority would not, but for the issue of a Proclamation under article 356, have been competent to make shall, after the proclamation has ceased to operate, continue in force until altered or repealed or amended by a competent Legislature or other authority".

(2) The amendment made by sub-section (1) shall apply to any law referred to in clause (2) of article 357 of the Constitution which is in force immediately before the coming into force of this section.

52. To article 358 of the Constitution, the following proviso shall be added, namely :

"Provided that where a Proclamation of Emergency is in operation only in any part of the territory of India, any such law may be made, or any such executive action may be taken, under this article in relation to or in any State or Union terr. itory specified in the First Schedule in which or in any part of which the Proclamation of Emergency is not in operation if and in so far as the security of India or any part of the territory thereof is threatened by activities in or in relation to the part of the territory of India in which the Proclamation of Emergency is in operation."

53. In article 359 of the Constitution,—

(a) to clause (1A), the following proviso shall be added, namely :

"Provided that where a Proclamation of Emergeacy is in operation only in any part of the territory of India, any such law may be made, or any such executive action may be taken, under this article in relation to or in any State or Union territory speci- fied in the First Schedule in which or in any part of which the Proclamation of Emergency is not in operation, if and in so far as the security of India or any part of the territory thereof is threatened by activities in or in relation to the part of the terr- itory of India in which the proclamation of Emergeney is in operation.";

(b) to clause (2), the following proviso shall be added, namely :

"Provided that where a Proclamation of Emergency is in operation only in a part of the territory of India, any such order shall not extend to any other part of the territory of India unless the President, being satisfied that the security of India or any part of the territory thereof is threatened by activities in or in relation to the part of the territory of India in which the Proclamation of Emergency is in operation, considers such extension to be necessary."

54. In article 366 of the Constitution,—

(a) after clause (4), the following clause shall be inserted, namely :

'(4A) "Central law" means any law other than a State law,'

(b) after clause (26), the following clause shall be inserted.

namely :

'(26A) "State law" means—

(a) a State Act or an Act of the Legislature of a Union territory ;

(b) an Ordinance promulgated by the Governor of a State under article 213 or by the Administrator of a Union territory under article 239B ;

(c) any provision with respect to a matter in the State List in a Central Act made before the commencement of this Constitution ;

(d) any provision with respect to a matter in this State List or the Concurrent List in a Province Act ;

(e) any notification, order, scheme, rule, regulation or bye-law or any other instrument having the force of law made under any Act, Ordinance or provisions referred to in sub-clause (a), sub-clause (b), sub-clause (c) or sub clause (d); and

(f) any other law (including any usage or custom having the force of law) with respect to a matter in the State List.

Courts Barred on Constitution Amendments

55. In article 368 of the Constitution, after clause (3), the following clause shall be inserted, namely :

"(4) No amendment of this Constitution (including the provisions of Part III) made or purporting to have been made under this article [whether before or after the commencement of section 55 of the Constitution (Forty-fourth Amendment) Act, 1976] shall be called in question in any court except upon the ground that it has not been made in accordance with the procedure laid down by this article."

56. In article 371 F of the Constitution, in clause (c), for the words "five years", the words "six years" shall be substituted and for the words "four years" in the two places where they occur, the words "five years" shall be substituted.

Seventh Schedule Amended

57. In the Seventh Schedule to the Constitution—

(a) in List I—Union List, after entry 2, the following entry shall be inserted, namely :

"2A. Deployment of any armed force of the Union or any other force subject to the control of the Union or any contingent or unit thereof in any State in aid of the civil powers, jurisdiction, privileges and liabilities of the members of such forces while on such deployment.";

(b) in List II—State List,—

(i) in entry 1, for the words "the use of naval, military or air force or any other armed force of the Union", the words "the use of any naval, military or air force or any other armed forces of the Union or of any other force subject to the control of the Union or of any contingent or unit thereof" shall be substituted ;

(ii) for entry 2, the following entry shall be substituted, namely :

"2. Police (including railways and village police) subject to the provisions of entry 2A of List I.",

(iii) in entry 3, the words "Administration of justice; constitution and organisation of all courts, except the Supreme Court and the High Court ;" shall be omitted ;

(iv) entries 11, 19, 20 and 29 shall be omitted ;

(v) in entry 55, the words "and advertisements broadcast by radio or television" shall be inserted at the end ;

(c) in List III—Concurrent List,—

(i) after entry II, the following entry shall be inserted, namely :

"11A. Administration of justice ; constitution and organisation of all courts, except the Supreme Court and the High Courts.";

(ii) after entry 17, the following entries shall be inserted, namely :

"17A. Forests.

17B. Protection of wild animals and birds.";

(iii) after entry 22, the following entry shall be inserted, namely :

"20A. Population control and family planning."

(iv) for entry 25, the following entry shall be substituted, namely :

"25. Education, including technical education, medical

education and universities, subject to the provisions of entries 63, 64, 65 and 66 of List I; vocational and technical training of labour.";

(v) after entry 33, the following entry shall be inserted, namely :

"33A. Weights and measures except establishment of standards".

Pending Petitions

58. (1) Notwithstanding anything contained in the Constitution every petition made under article 226 of the Constitution, before the appointed day and pending before any High Court immediately before that day (such petition being referred to in this section as a pending petition) and any interim order (whether by way of injunction or stay or in any other manner) made on or in any proceedings relating to, such petition before that day shall be dealt with in accordance with the provisions of article 226 as substituted by section 38.

(2) In particular, and without prejudice to the generality of the provisions of sub-section (1), every pending petition before a High Court which would not have been admitted by the High Court under the provisions of article 226 as substituted by section 38 if such petition had been made after the appointed day, shall abate and any interim order (whether by way of injunction or stay or in any other manner) made on or in any proceedings relating to, such petition shall stand vacated.

Provided that nothing contained in this sub-section shall affect the right of the petitioner to seek relief under any other law for the time being in force in respect of the matter to which such petition relates and in computing the period of limitation, if any, for seeking such relief, the period during which the proceedings relating to such petition were pending in the High Court shall be excluded.

(3) Every interim order (whether by way of injunction or stay or in any other manner) which was made before the appointed day, on or in any proceedings relating to, a pending petition [not being a pending petition which has abated under sub-section (2)], and which is in force on that day, shall, unless

before the appointed day copies of such pending petition and of documents in support of the plea for such interim order had been furnished to the party against whom such interim order was made and an opportunity had been given to such party to be heard in the matter, cease to have effect (if not vacated earlier),—

(a) on the expiry of a period of one month from the appointed day, if the copies of such pending petition and the documents in support of the plea for the interim order are not furnished to such party before the expiry of the said period of one month ; or

(b) on the expiry of a period of four months from the appointed day, if the copies referred to in clause (a) have been furnished to such party within the period of one month referred to in that clause but such party has not been given an opportunity to be heard in the matter before the expiry of the said period of four months.

(4) Notwithstanding anything contained in sub-section (3) every interim order (whether by way of injunction or stay or in any other manner) which was made before the appointed day or in any proceedings relating to a pending petition [not being a pending petition which has abated under sub-section (2), and which is in force on that day, shall, if such order has the effect of delaying any inquiry into a matter of public importance or any investigation or inquiry into an offence punishable with imprisonment or any action for the execution of any work or project or public utility, or the acquisition of any property for such execution, by the Government or any corporation owned or controlled by the Govenment, stand vacated.

Explanation— In this section, "appointed day" means the date on which section 38 comes into force.

Removal of Difficulties

59. (1) If any difficulty arises in giving effect to the provisions of the Constitution as amended by this Act (including any difficulty in relation to the transition from the provisions of the Constitution as they stood immediately before the date of the President's assent to this Act to the provisions of the Constitn-

tion as amended by this Act), the President may, by order, make
such provisions, including any adaptation or modification of
any provision of the Constitution, as appear to him to be necessary or expedient for the purpose of removing the difficulty:

Provided that no such order shall be made after the expiry
of two years from the date of such assent.

(2) Every order made undar sub-section (1) shall, as soon
as may be after it is made, be laid before each House of
Parliament.

NOTES ON CLAUSES

Clause 2.—The concepts of secularism, socialism and integrity
of the Nation are implicit in the Constitution. These have been
clearly spelt out in the amendments to the Preamble.

Clause 4.—Article 31C, as presently worded, saves only laws
giving effect to the directive principles specified in clause (*b*) and
clause (*c*) of article 39 from attack on the ground of infringement
of fundamental rights contained in articles 14, 19 and 31. The
amendment seeks to widen the scope of the artiele so as to cover
all the directive principles enumerated in Part IV ;

Clause 5.—The amendment provides for the making of a
Parliamentary law to prevent or prohibit anti-national activities
and to prevent or prohibit the formation of anti-national associations. The expressions 'anti-national activities' and 'anti-national associations' have been defined in detail. The law made by
virtue of this amendment shall not be deemed to be void on the
ground that it takes away or abridges any of the fundamental
rights conferred by articles 14, 19 and 31.

Clause 6.—This clause seeks to insert a new article 32A to
provide that the Supreme Court shall have no jurisdiction to
decide the constitutional validity of a State law in any proceeding
under article 32 unless the validity of a Central law is also in
issue in such proceedings. The High Court will have no jurisdiction in such cases.

Clauses 7 to 10.—Article 30 is being amended to emphasize
the constructive role of the State with regard to children.

New directives are being added in Part IV to provide for—
(1) free legal aid to economically backward classes ;

(2) participation of workers in the management of organisations engaged in any industry ;

(3) protection and improvement of environment and safeguarding of forests and wild life.

Clause 11.—The Constitution does not contain any provisions specifying the fnndamental duties of the citizens. New Part IVA proposed in this clause enumerates these fundamental duties.

Clause 13—The President acts on the advice of the Council of Ministers. It is being made explicit by this amendment that he shall be bound by such advice.

Clauses 14 *and* 28—Article 77 (3) provides for the framing of rules for the convenient transaction of Government business which rules are treated by the Government as confidential. However, as courts have been found to summon these rules for production, it is considered that this should be prevented. A new clause is, therefore, being added to provide that no court or authority shall compel their production.

A similar provision is being made in article 166.

Clauses 12, 15. 16, 29 *and* 47.—In the context of the intensification of the family planning programmes of the Government, it is considered that not only the allocation of seats in the House of the people to the States and the total number of seats in Legislative Assemblies of the States but also the extent of parliamentary and assembly constituencies and the reservation of seats for Scheduled Castes and Scheduled Tribes as determined on the basis of the 1971 census, should be frozen till the year 2001. It s accordingly, proposed to amend the relevant articles, namely, articles 81 and 82 relating to the Lok Sabha, article 170 relating to the Legislative Assemblies of States, article 55 relating to the manner of election of the President and articles 330 and 332 relating to reservation of seats for Scheduled Castes and Scheduled Tribes in the Lok Sabha and the Legislative Assemblies of States. Provision is also being made to the effect that whenever after a census, delimitation is undertaken, such delimitation is to take effect from the date to be specified by the President.

Clauses 17, 30 *and* 56—It is proposed to change the duration of the Lok Sabha and the State Legislative Assemblies from five to six years. A consequential amendment is made in article

371F (*c*) relating to Sikkim Legislative Assembly.

Clauses 18, 22, 31 *and* 35—Presently under article 100 the quorum for constituting a meeting of either House of Parliament is one-tenth of the total numer of members. This provision can only be altered by a Parliamentary law. The relevant provisions are proposed to be omitted from article 100 and power is being taken to do it by means of rules under asticle 118. Similar provisions are being made in relation to the State Legislatures by amending articles 189 and 208.

Clauses 19 *and* 32—sub-clause (a) of clause (1) of article 102 provides that a person shall be disqualified for being chosen as, and for being, a member of either House of Parliament if he holds an office of profit under the Government of India or the Government of any State, other than an office declared by Parliament by law not to disqualify its holder. The existing position has led to a great deal of uncertainty. The sub-clause is sought to be amended to provide that a person shall be so disqualified if he holds any such office of profit under the Government of India or the Government of any State as is declared by Parliament by law to disqualify its holder.

Similar provision is being made in article 119 (1) (a) relating to State Legislatures but the power to specify the office will vest in Parliament instead of in the State Legislature.

Clauses 20 *and* 33—The amendment proposed in clause 20 enlarges the scope of article 103. The question as to whether a member has become subject of any disqualification mentioned in clause (1) of article 102 as also the question whether a person is disqualified for being chosen as a member of either House of Parliament, etc., on the ground of being found guilty of a corrupt practice, including the question as to the period of disqualification or as to the removal or the reduction of the period of such disqualification, shall be decided by the President after consulting the Election Commission which is empowered to hold an inquiry in this behalf. It is proposed to amend article 192 on smilar lines.

Clauses 21 *and* 34—This clause seeks to amend clause (3) of article 105 which provides that the powers, privileges and immunities of each House of Commons or of its members and committees until they are defined by a Parliamentary law. The amendment proposed is that the powers, privileges and immunities aforesaid of either House of Parliament and of the members and the committees thereof shall he evolved by such House from time to time. A similar modification is being made in clause (3) of article 194 which relates to State Legislatures.

Clauses 23,24 *and* 25.—Presently, the Constitutional validity of a Central law can be questioned either before the Supreme Court or the High Court. This scheme is being altered as it is felt that if a number of High Courts give differing judgements as regards the validity of a Central law, the implementation of the Central law will become difficult. It is, therefore, proposed to invest the Supreme Court with exclusive jurisdiction as re- gards determination of the constitutional validity of Central laws. Where a case involves constitutional validity of both a Central and a State law, the Supreme Court alone will have jurisdiction to determine the constitutional validity of such laws. Where cases involving the same or substantially the same ques- tions of law of general importance are pending before the Supreme Court and one or more High Courts before two or more High Courts, the Attorney-General can move the Supreme Court to withdraw the cases pending before the High Court of High Courts to itself and dispose of the same. Further, the Supreme Court is being empowered to transfer cases from the High Court to another High Court if it is expedient for the ends of justice so to do.

It is also being provided that the minimum number of Judges of the Supreme Court who shall sit for determining any question as to the constiutional validity of a Central law or of a Central and a State law shall be not less than seven and that a Central or a State law shall not be declared to be constitutionally invalid unless not less than two-thirds of the judges hearing the cases hold the same to be constitutionally invalid.

Clause 26—This amendment makes some consequential chan- ges in article 145 following the insertion of new article 131A, 139A and 144A,

Clause 27.—At present the Comptroller and Auditor-Gene- ral has the power to prescribe the form in which the account of Union and of the States shall be maintained. Consequent on the decision of Government to separate the accounts from audit, this power is being given to the President, to be exercised after consultation with the Comptroller by amending article 150.

Clause 36.—This amendment relates to the qualification to be fulfilled by a person for appointment as a High Court Judge. Sub-clause (b) of clause (2) of article 217 is being amended to provide that a distinguished jurist is also qualified for appointment as a High Court Judge. This amendment also provides that hereafter the period spent by a person, after he became an advocate, as a member of a Tribunal or as the incumbent of any post, under the Union or a State, requiring special knowledge in law shall be taken into account for the purpose of computing the period during which such person has been an advocate.

Clause 37.—This is a consequential amendment of article 225 following insertion of new article 323B which provides for the exclusion of the jurisdiction of the High Courts and the Supreme Court (except the jurisdiction under article 136) and for the setting up of tribunals, in respect of certain specified matters including matters concerning the revenue.

Clauses 38 *and* 58.—Clause 38 seeks to amend article 226 to a significant extent. While the High Courts continue to enjoy their power to enforce fundamental rights, they cannot hereafter exercise jurisdiction in every case where there is an invasion of a legal right which, so far, they have been doing by virtue of the jurisdiction conferred by the expression 'for any other purpose' which is being deleted now. Instead, the High Courts are being vested with a restricted jurisdiction. They can exercise jurisdiction in (a) cases where there is a contravention of a statutory provision causing substantial injury to the petitioner, and (b) cases where there is an illegality resulting in substantial failure of justice. In either case, the petitioner has to satisfy the court that he has no other remedy.

Provision is being made under clause 31 that the High Court shall not issue an interim order ordinarily except upon notice to the other side and after giving the other side an opportunity to be heard. An exception is made in cases where the loss or damage to the petitoner cannot be compensated in money. Notwithstanding this exception, the High Conrts shall have no power to grant an interim order in any case where the effect of such order is to delay any inquiry into a matter of public work/ project of public utility, etc.

Provision is also being made in clause 58 to cover petitions pending in the High Courts.

Clause 39 and 42.—These amendments seek to exclude from the jurisdiction of High Courts questions as to constitutional validity of Central laws and provide for the minimum number of Judges of a High Court who shall sit for determining any questions as to the constitutional validity of a State law. The minimum number is fixed at five but where a High Court consists of less than five Judges, all the Judge of the High Court sitting together can here such questions. Any Judge disqualified by reason of pecuniary or personal bias has to be excluded in computing the number of Judges of the High Court. Where the number of Judges hearing a questions as to the constitutional invalidity shall be by a majority of not less than two-thirds and where the number of Judges is less than five, the law in issue cannot be declared to be constitutionally invalid unless all the Judges hold it to be constitutionally invalid.

Clause 40.—This clause seeks to amend article 227 to omit the reference to tribunals occurring in clause (1) of the article and make it clear that nothing in that article shall be construed as giving to a High Court any jurisdiction to question any judgment of any inferior court which is not otherwise subject to appeal or revision.

Clause 41.—This amendment is consequential to the insertion of new article 131A.

Clause 43.—By this amendment a new article 257A is inserted to empower the Union to send any armed force of the Union for dealing with any grave situation of law and order in any State. Such force shall act in accordance with the directions of the Central Government and shall not be subject to the control of the State Government. Provision is also being made to empower Parliament to define the powers, functions and the liabilities of the members of such forces.

Clause 44.—This clause seeks to amend article 311 (2) denying the Government servant the opportunity to make a representation at the second stage of the inquiry against the penalty proposed to be imposed on him.

Clause 45.—This clause seeks to amend article 312 of the

Constitution relating to all-India Services to provide for the creation of all-India JudicialService by a Parliamentary law. Such Service shall not include any post inferior to that of a district judge.

Clause 46.—This clause seeks to insert a new Part XIVA, which consists of article 323A and 323B. The former providesfor the setting up of Administrative Tribunals by a Parliamentary aw for determining disputes relating to the recruitment and conditions of service of Union Government servants and servants of the State including the employees of any local or other authority within the territory of India or under the control of the Government of India or of a corporation owned or controlled by the Government. Such law will provide for the constitution of a tribunal for the Union and for a separate tribunal for each State or for two or more States and define the jurisdiction and powers of such tribunals.

New article 323B provides for the creation of tribunals for the determination of disputes, complaints and offences respecting the various matters specified therin.

Clauses 48, 49, 52 *and* 53.—At present a Proclamation of Emergency cannot be made in respect of a part of the country. The amendments proposed in these clauses are for enabling the President to make a Proclamation of Emergency in respect of a part of the country or, as the case may be, to restrict a Proclamation of Emergency made in respect of the country as a whole to a part of the country.

Clauses 50 *and* 51.—Under the existing article 356, a proclamation approved by Parliament ceases to be in operation after a period of six months unless revoked earlier and can be renewed for a period of six months at a time but in no case beyond a total period of three years. The period of six months is now being enlarged to one year. Clause (2) of article 357 is being substitued by a new clause to the effect that any law made by Parliament or the President or any other authority in exercise of the powers of the State Legislature under article 356 shall continue in force until altered, repealed or amended by the competent Legislature or other authority.

Clause 54.—By this amendment, the expressions 'Central law' and 'State law' are being defined. This has become necessary because of the divison of jurisdiction between the Supreme

Court and the High Conrts as regards the determination of the Constitutional validity of Central and State laws.

Clause 55.—This clause seeks to amend article 368 to clarify the true scope of that article.

Clause 57.—The amendments made by this clause seek either to amend the existing entries in the lists of the Seventh Schedule or to transpose certain entries of subjects in certain entries from one List to another. The entries or subjects which have been transposed from List II to List III are : (1) administration of justice, constitution and organisation of all courts except the Supreme Court and High Courts, (2) education, (3) weights and measures, (4) forests, and (5) protection of wild animals and birds. It is also proposed that taxes on advertisements broadcast by radio or television should be excluded from the purview of entry 55 of the State List.

Clause 59.—This clause provides for the removal of difficulties.

11

Criticisms of the Amendments

A. A National Seminar Consensus

An all-India seminar discussed the Constitution (44th Amendment) Bill and related matters on October 16 and 17 in New Delhi.

Participants in the seminar were prominent political leaders, jurists, parliamentarians and academicians. Speakers were C. K. Daphtary, V. M. Tarkunde, H. V. Kamath, A. K. Gopalan, E.M.S. Namboodiripad, P. Ramamurti, Somnath Chatterjee, Tridib Chaudhary, Asoka Mehta, Charan Singh, Era Sezhiyan, Amar Chakravarty, S. M. Joshi, Satish Chandra, Soli Sorabjee, G. Swaminathan, Sher Singh, Lily Thomas, John Manjooran, Rama Reddy, O. P. Thyagi, H. M. Patel, S. L. Saxena and Krishna Kant.

The following is the text of the consensus adopted at the seminar :

This nationl seminar is of the considered opinion that enactment of the Constitution (44th Amendment) Bill by the present Parliament should not be proceeded with on grounds both of procedure and substance. There is in the country, on account of the emergency, a climate of oppression and fear in wich no free and open debate is possible. Leaders of political parties and of public opinion are in jail, meetings have until recently been almost totally banned and are even now only allowed in restricted hall meetings and the press has been effectively gagged. The denial of the fundamental freedom of expression and of association and the erosion of judicial processes have created a situation in which it is impossible for the people to know, discuss and understand the sweeping and drastic constitutional amendments being proposed in their name, but certainly not to their benefit although this is so alleged.

The ruling party sought no mandate in 1971 for the kind of changes now proposed and statements to the contrary bear no relation to fact. Furthermore, the fifth Lok Sabha concluded its normal five-year tenure last March and is now serving an extended term under emergency decree. For it to consider the making of what would virtually be a new Constitution on the basis of 43 per cent votes cast under very different circumstances, six years ago, would be a fraudulent exercise of power. The honest and democratic alternative would be for the Government to face the people, whom it claims to serve, in fair and free elections which are in any case long overdue. Not to do so, and to rush the 44th amendment through what is a rump Parliament, in an atmosphere in which no free debate has been permitted or is indeed possible, would be to institutionalise the emergency with added powers and present the people with a fait accompli.

According to the statement of objects and reasons appended to the Bill, the 44th amendment is intended to remove the difficulties which have arisen in achieving the objective of socio-economic revolution "which would end poverty, ignorance and disease and inequality of opportunity". The assertion will not bear scrutiny.

After the amendment to Article 31, the present Constitution has placed no impediment on genuine socio-economic reform and the Government has failed to point out a single measure that it has brought forward during the past five years or would like to introduce in the future which could not or cannot be enacted and implemented given the political will. Nor is it true to say that the doctrine of the sanctity of the 'basic structure' of the Constitution propounded by the Supreme Court in the Keshavananda Bharati judgement has obstructed social and economic change. Indeed, the Supreme Court ruled in that case that the right to property is not a part of the basic structure of the Constitution. None of the provisions of the 44th amendment, however, seeks to restrict the constitutional right to property as such. It is quite clear that the objectives of the Government are very different and the adoption of the 44th amendment would in effect establish a constitutional dictatorship. It is pertinent to point out that the policies of the Government pursued so fas have not helped the poor but the rich and led to concentration of wealth.

It would be relevant in this connection to refer to certain of the other constitutional amendments made after the proclamation of the internal emergency on June 26, 1972. The 38th amendment places even a mala fide declaration of emergency beyond scrutiny of the courts. The 39th amendment, which was struck down by the Supreme Court, sought to place the Prime Minister's election beyond challenge even if it was obtained by resort to 'corrupt practice'. The 40th Amendment Bill, which has so far only been adopted by the Rajya Sabha, seeks to confer absolute and permanent immunity on the President, Vice-President, Prime Minister, Speaker and Governors against any proceeding even for criminal offences committed by them, either during their tenure of offce or even prior to their assuming that office. Furthermore, several draconian measures having a bearing on free and fair elections, individual liberty and democratic freedoms, and freedom of the press have been given absolute consۑitutional immunity by their inclusion in the 9th Schedule of the Constitution.

The 44th amendment would now practically abrogate the citizens' fundamental rights altogether by expanding the scope of Article 31c to place any legislation purporting to further any of the directive principles beyond judicial challenge on the ground of violating the right to equality and the other fundamental freedams. The scope of the directive principles is all-inclusive, ranging from the welfare of the citizen to international peace.

The proposed new Article 31d, relating to so-called anti-national activities and anti-national associations, is again so wide as to pave the way for virtual one-party rule, any anti-governmental activity being treated as anti-national. Any laws enacted with the object of banning so-called anti-national activities or associations are proposed to be placed beyond judicial review even if they violate fundamental rights. The liberties of the citizen are sought to be furthei curtailed by prescribing a set of so-called fundamental duties.

The effect of these proposals, in sum, would be to deprive the ultimate sovereign, namely, the people, of rights and leave them only with duties. Conversely, the servants of the people, namely, the executive, would be placed in a position of owning all manner of rights and owing no duties.

The effect of the 44th amendment will be to eliminate the whole system of checks and balances provided in the Constitution and leave the way clear for the arbitrary exercise of executive authority to the detriment of the citizen. In a number of important matters such as taxation, labour disputes, elections, service matters, procurement and distribution of foodstuffs and other essential goods, land reforms, trade, foreign exchange, and urban property ceilings, the jurisdiction of the High Courts is sought to be substituted by that of tribunals which would be clearly amenable to executive pressures.

This would deny the citizen impartial justice in these matters of deep concern to him while the right to appeal to the Supreme Court would be illusory for the common man in view of the prohibitive costs involved. The residual powers of the High Courts are further curtailed by the proposed amendment to Article 226 relating to writ jurisdiction.

Moreover, the High Courts are precluded from determining the validity of even a rule or a notification issued under Central Acts.

Article 368 is sought to be amended so as to enable Parliament to alter even the basic structure of the Constitution including such features as democracy, republicanism, division of power and the federal character of the Indian polity. While the courts are totally precluded from considering the validity of any constitutional amendment, howsoever draconian or anti-people, the ordinary laws may only be struck down by a two-thirds majority in a bench of seven judges in the Supreme Court and five judges in High Courts. This would virually mean that a judge deciding in favour of the Government would have twice the judicial power enjoyed by a judge deciding otherwise.

Even the limited powers given to the President to caution and advise the central executive against hasty or ill-conceived measures are to be taken away.

The central executive is also seeking to usurp Parliament's powers to modify any provision in the Constitution for the professed purpose of removing difficulties. This very wide power bears no comparison with the far more limited removal-of-difficulties power given to the President under the existing Article 392 of the Constitution.

The federal character of the Constitution is also weakened, by the 44th amendment, by enhancing the powers of the centre at the expense of the states and more particularly by enabling the Government of India to deploy the armed or police forces of the union in the states without the consent of the state Governments, "for dealing with any grave situation of law and order in any state."

Other examples of the erosion of the independent authority of constitutional officers or agencies such as the Election Commission, the Union Public Service Commission and the Comptroller and Auditor-General are to be found in the transference of certain of their powers and initiatives to the central executive or bodies subordinate to it under various proposed amendments. In particular, the manner in which the accounts of the union and of the states shall be kept will, under a proposed amendment, henceforward be prescribed by the central executive. This could open the door for financial manipulation to serve partisan interest. Even the amendment to preclude the production in any court of law of rules made for the transaction of official business at the centre or in the states must be viewed with suspicion as being opposed to the salutary principles of open government.

The net effect of the 44th amendment is to take away the rights and powers of the President, the legislatures, the judiciary, the states, the UPSC, the Election Commission and the Comptroller and Auditor-General. In each case, power is transferred not just to the central executive but to the chief executive, namely, the Prime Minister, who emerges all-powerful and above the law. Such an enormous accretion of power in the hands of a single person is dangerous and liable to misuse. However, in view of recent experience of the arbitrary exercise of authority, such a total concentration of power cannot be regarded as innocent or accidental and would spell the end to individual liberty and democratic institutions which millions of Indians have unitedly struggled to win and uphold.

The Government has ironically included in the 44th amendment a fundamental duty that enjoins the citizen "to cherish and follow the noble ideals which inspired our national struggle for freedom." This national seminar would like to remind the Government and the people of those ideals and, in particular, of Gandhiji's injunction that the right means are as important as right ends. In the present instance, however, the attempted forced passage of the 44th amendment constituted an exercise in wrong means to attain wrong ends.

Let the Government go to the people. Let there be fair and free elections in an environment free of fear and intimidation. At such an election it would be possible to place before the people for their consideration a number of constitutional changes and safeguards that will enlarge the democratic rights of the people and ensure that the country never again face the danger of the overthrow of democracy and liberty through apparently constitutional processes. Some of these matters are :

1. restating the conditions in which an emergency may be declared;
2. safeguards for preventing an abuse of the emergency provisions;
3. safeguards against the arbitrary suspension of State Governments;
4. the limits within which fundamental rights and other liberties may be suspended;
5. better ensuring of the independence of the judiciary;
6. organisation and constitution of the Election Commission;
7. provisions relating to preventive detention;
8. the ordinance-making powers of the President and the Governors;
9. an impartial mode of appointment of Governors;
10. provision in Article 368 to preclude any amendment in the basic structure of the Constitution.

B. E.M.S. Namboodiripad : C.P.I.(M)'s Position

If the Government has 'an open mind" on the amendments

to the Constitution as Law Minister Gokhale asserted in Bombay on October 8, it should drop the idea of rushing the Constitution (44th Amendment) Bill through the session of Parliament that is opening on October 25.

Firstly, as has been pointed out by all the opposition parties and a large number of eminent non-party individuals, it is totally undemocratic and beyond its legitimate powers for a Parliament, which has outlived its original term of five years and is continuing only thanks to the emergency, to make any amendments to the Constitution.

Secondly, and still more important, the amendments proposed now are so sweeping that they overturn the basic structure itself of the Constitution enacted in the name of "We, the pepole of India". It alters— and alters in an anti-democratic direction—the relationship between the citizens of India and the state, between the Centre and the States as well as among the executive, judical and legislative arms of state power.

It is not necessary in this article to go into the various provisions of the amending bill in order to show how it subverts the entire democratic framework of the Constitution, since we have dealt in detail with them in the Polit Bureau's comprehensive critique of the recommendations of the Swaran Singh Committee and elsewhere. We may, however, sum up our arguments in brief :

1. An important aspect of democracy, in so far as it pertains to the relations between the citizens and the state, is the fundamental rights spelt out in Part III of the Constitution. This is being thrown overboard now. Once the amending bill is enacted, there is nothing that stands in the way of the ruling party, with a majority in Parliament. in abrogating every one of the fundamental rights, including even the right to live.

(2) An equally important aspect of democracy is the paocess of democratic election, making even the highest dignitaries in the state answerable to and removable by the elected representatives of the people who themselves are answerable to and removable by the adult citizens of the country at least once in five years. This, too, is being done away with (a) by the provisions that have already been made putting certain dignitaries on a pedestal higher than the other citizens of India and

(b)   by enabling the executive, through its majority in Parliament, to make still further alterations, not excluding the total abolition of the electoral process itself.

(3) A vital provision in the existing Constitution safeguarding the interests of every citizen of India is that, if she or he is harassed or unjustly dealt with by the executive authorities, relief can be sought through the appropriate procedure of writs in the High Courts or the Supreme Court.   This, too, is being done away with.   A host of subjects like service matters, labour disputes, revenue, procurement and supply, etc., are being taken away from the jurisdiction of courts.   This, in fact, is an attack on the rights of the citizens, rather than a restriction on the powers of courts.

(4)   It is from here that we go into the controversial question of the role of the judiciary.   While our Party and other left and democratic parties have never subscribed to the "theory" of "supremacy of the judiciary" nor ever forgotten the class character of the judiciary and the many reactionary judgements that have been given, we recognise that in a number of cases, the judiciary has acted as a check on the arbitrary actions of the executive authorities as well as in scrutinising legislation adopted with a view to checking whether the rights of the citizens are being curtailed.   What the amending bill does is to strengthen the executive not only in relation to the judiciary but in relation to the people at large.

(5) One of the vital principles laid down during the days of the freedom struggle, and written into the Canstitution, is the federal character of the Indian Republic, the federating states exercising wide power in the fields allotted to them.   In the very process of drafting the Constitution, however, this principle was watered down, so that the states were made dependent on the Centre. This process got aggravated in the 25-year working of the Constitution.   Now comes the Constitution (44th Amending) Bill which makes the Indian Union still more Centralised, still less federal, by (a) removing important subjects like education and forests from the state list, (b) enabling the Centre to take over the key aspect of police administration whenever and wherever it wants, and (c) providing for an all-India judicial service over which the states will have no control.

The proposed amendments also threaten the harmonious development of the various nationalities of the country since even any efforts by linguistic nationalities to oppose the compulsory imposition of Hindi and champion the cause of equality of all Indian languages can be termed "separatist" and hence "anti-national" and suppressed under the "law."

(6) Finally, and above all, the amending bill enables the executive aothorities (through the control they exercise on Parliament) to make any amendment that they may like to make in the future. No further encroachment into the rights of citizens as against the state or into those of states as against the Centre will be liable to be questioned anywhere. This, too, in a situation where even elected Members of Parliament have no fundamental rights and can be kept in indefinite detention without trial. There is no authority to question the action of the executive authorities if they take it into their heads to detain without trial the entire opposition in Parliament and as many within the ruling party itself as are found inconvenient to the leaders of the ruling party.

It is such a Parliament that is being empowered to amend any part of the Constitution, including the preamble which declares India to be a sovereign democratic republic. The very body which is now asked to add "socialist and secular" can tomorrow be asked to replace "republic" by "monarchy".

It is amazing that a piece of legislation that has the potentiality of being used to transform the democratic republic into its very opposite is claimed as a weapon in the hands of the progressives to be used against the reactionaries The reality is that this is the culmination of a long process through which the executive authorities have been arrogating to themselves power that had been denied to them when the Constitution was drawn up.

There is no need for speculation on where this will lead. There is the living experience of the people that the extensive powers, with which the executive authorities are vested even in the present Constitution, have been used not to restrict and eliminate but to strengthen and enrich the monopolists and landlords. They have been used not to protect the interest of, but to attack, the workers, the peasants, the middle class employees, etc. Not even the most ardent defenders of the ruling party would deny that during the 26 years of the working of the Constitution, the rich have become richer and the poor are being further impoverished. It is the very same executive authorities that are now being clothed with still more extensive powers enabling them to deal with the common people in the way in which any despotic regime anywhere in the world has dealt with the common people. Though the present amendments to the Constitution are being proposed in the name of making "radical social changes", meeting "the ends of social justice", etc., they are so anti-democratic that they will only result in more social injustice with the process of the rich getting richer further accelerated, with a simultaneous acceleration of the poverty of the mass of the people and the loss of their democratic rights. It is not for nothing that those who talk so much about "radical social change" and "social justice" refuse to exclude the rights to property from the fundamental rights or amend it so that only the poor and middle property owners will have that right and the landlords and monopolists will not be able to exercise it.

It should be clear from all this that the CPI (M) cannot have anything to do with the process through which the Government wants to push through this obnoxious piece of legislation. But it certainly wants to, and will enlighten the people— despite the limitations of all the restrictions that have been imposed by the Government on such a process of enlightening the people—on the gravity of the situation that will arise if the Constitution (44th Amendment) Bill is passed into law.

The chairman of the Congress Constitution Reforms Committee, Sardar Swaran Singh, makes it a grievance that the CPI (M) and other parties of the opposition are carrying on a campaign among the people against the amending bill, rather than discuss with his committee the lines along which the Constitution is to be amended. Does he mean to say that the "national debate" on constitutional changes about which the leaders of his party and the Government are continuously talking, is to be confined to discussions with his committee ?

We, on the other hand, hold that it is the right of every patriotic and democratic party, and individual in the country to express freely on what the Government proposes to do with the Constitution. It is this right of every section of the people to participate in the national debate that is denied when the entire opposition is prevented from the holding public meetings and sometimes even hall meetings to discuss constitutional changes. This, too, under conditions in which, even if meetings are allowed, several leaders of opposition parties cannot address them.

Let Sardar Sawarn Singh first create conditions in which leaders and activists of all opposition parties can freely participate in the national debate through meetings, seminars, news-columns, etc., before demanding that the opposition should go for discussions with his committee.

Let him recall that the Constitution being sought to be amended now was "adopted, enacted and given ourselves to" by "We, the people of India." Any far-reaching changes in it should be made by the entire people and definitely not by a Parliament which has outlived its term and with all the restrictions on free debate that are still continuing.

This, the CPI (M) has proposed, requires a referendum which can be prepared for only by a new Parliament elected under such conditions of political activity as existed before the declaration of the Emergency.

October 11, 1976

12

The Janata Party Manifesto*

The forthcoming Lok Sabha poll constitutes the most crucial election that the country has had since Independence. The choice before the electorate is clear. It is a choice between freedom and slavery ; between democracy and dictatorship ; between abdicating the power of the people or asserting it ; between the Gandhian path and the way that has led many nations down the precipice of dictatorship, instability, military adventure and national ruin.

Our people are being asked to make this choice in most abnormal circumstances. The Emergency that was declared on June 25, 1975 has not been withdrawn. The sweeping and draconian powers with which the Government armed itself, remain intact. Fundamental rights have not been restored. The citizen has no protection against arbitrary arrest and in definite incarceration. The courts have been deprived of vital powers. MISA, with all its obnoxious provisions, continues in force. The Prevention of Publication of Objectionable Matters Act has been entrenched in the Constitution. The Press is not free. Thousands of political workers are still under detention in different parts of the country. The Constitution has been amended and laws fashioned to sanctify the ruling party's definition of a "committed" judiciary, a "committed" press and a "committed" bureaucracy. The monopolistic control of All India Radio, Doordarshan and Samachar, that involuntarily "nationalised" news agency, is be-

*This manifesto was for the election of March 1977.

ing used to convert these mass media into instruments of party propaganda and deny the Opposition fair opportunity to present its point of view to the people.

The Government has made this crucial election a grossly unequal contest in relation to time, resources and the continuing application of Emergency provisions. History is replete with instances where those who conspire against the rights of the people attempt to undermine freedom by portraying it as a luxury, dear only to those who wish to defend property and privilege. They cleverly conceal the fact that fundamental freedoms are weapons that the oppressed and the poor need to fight tyranny, exploitation and injustice, vested interests and opportunist governments. Bread cannot be juxtaposed against liberty. The two are inseparable.

Nightmare of Fear

The months through which the country has passed since the declaration of the so-called internal Emergency have been a nightmare of fear and humiliation, reminiscent of the days of foreign domination. A fresh Emergency was invoked after the judgement of the Allahabad High Court and verdict of the people in Gujarat. Behind the cover of censorship, a reign of terror was unleashed with the massive deployment of police and para-military forces. Indiscriminate arrest became the order of the day. A pall of fear was thrown over the country. The rule of law ceased to exit. The right of habeas corpus was taken away. The judicial process was gravely undermined and the citizen was placed at the mercy of the State. The courts were solemnly told that while the Emergency lasted, they were powerless to protect the citizen even if he should be starved to death or shot. The concept of equality before law, precious to any democratic society, was jettisoned, and a constitutional amendment was sought to be enacted to confer immunity on the individual holding the office of Prime Minister. The Representation of the People Act was amended to redefine corrupt practices and to legalise what was considered and found corrupt before the Emergency. The Press was gagged. Hundreds of printing presses were sealed. Papers and journals were compelled to close down. The acade-

mic world was not left untouched. Innumerable teachers and
students were arrested. All democratic rights were whittled away.

Extra-Constitutional Power Centres

Extra-constitutional centres of power were built up in the
Government and permitted to wield enormous official power
without the trammels of legality or accountability. Consummate efforts were made to destroy the distinction between party
and State that characterises a democratic polity.

Onslaught on Working Class

The worker found his cherished and hard-won rights eroded.
Even the tardy increase in his dearness allowance was impound-
ed. He was robbed of his bonus. The instruments of power
were abused to suppress or subvert independent trade unions.
Trade union workers were thrown into jail and attempts were
made to manipulate union elections and bring these organisations under the control of the ruling party. While workers were
denied the right of strike, employers were left free to declare
lock-outs and to lay off workers with impunity, and aided to
fatten on new concessions and new agreements with multinationals.

42nd Amendment

The Constitution was amended to sanctify and institutionalise a total concentration of power in the hands of one individual
—the Prime Minister. The authoritarian trends that had unfo
ded themselves over the past few years were embodied in th
42nd Amendment which was bulldozed through Parliament. To
call it an amendment is a misnomer. It is a betrayal of the
testament of faith that the founding fathers bequeathed
to the people and it subverts the basic structure of the
1950 Constitution. It vitiates the federal principle and upsets
the nice balance between the people and Parliament, Parliament
and the judiciary, the judiciary and the executive, the State and
the Centre, the citizen and the Government. It is the culmina-

tion of a conspiracy to devalue democracy that started with the erosion of the cabinet system, the deliberate and consummate scuttling of democratic processes in the ruling party, and the concentration of all power in the hands of a leader who has been sought to be identified with the nation or even to be placed above it.

The Emergency has succeeded only in generating an atmosphere of fear and insecurity. The question before the electorate is whether whatever might have been achieved during the past 19 months was achieved because of the Emergency or whether the price in freedom, human rights and long-term economic and social destabilisation that the country has had to pay was necessary for, or commensurate with, whatever has supposedly been achived.

"Gains" of the Emergency ?

The ruling party claims gains in production on account of the Emergency. Some increases in production have indeed been registered after earlier lags on account of the Government's own failures. At the same time, innumerable large and medium units and thousands of small units have been shut down during this same period. The cotton textile, jute and engineering industries are passing through one of the gravest recessions they have ever experienced. The steel industry today produces less than the target that it was set to achieve in 1965-66, and even this connot be absorbed by the domestic economy because of a crisis investment. The Government has itself admitted that over half million workers were laid-off in the first six months of the Emergency. This large and cruel figure does not include the thousands who have been retrenched. The number of those who have been put out of employment since the Emergency exceeds 1.5 million. Real wages have fallen.

Prices

The ruling party claims that the Emergency has brought price down. Its own indices belie this claim. The final Fifth Plan document notes that prices started declining from September 1974—nine months before the Emergency was proclaimed. It says that wholesale prices declined by 7% between September 1974 and March 1975, thanks largely to an excellent harvest. However, in the past eleven months prices have risen by 12% and are now higher than they were before the Emergency. The retail price index has not been released since August 1976. The recent increase in the prices of commodities like sugar, cotton and oilseeds, all of which affect the common man directly, has been the result of speculation. Why has the Government failed to deal with those speculators and hoarders in spite of the unlimited powers in its armoury ?

Export-Led Growth

The ruling party claims that the Emergency has led to an increase in export and foreign exchange reserves. Today, higher export in many fields like steel, cement and aluminium are a symptom of the deep recession in our own country, or the result of a deliberate attempt to promote exports at the cost of domestic consumption. This is all the more distressing when we observe that some of the commodities exported have been sold at a loss while others, like sugar, are daily necessities whose export has led to shortage in the demoestic market and a consequential rise in prices. In the name of adopting a strategy of export-led growth, we are in danger of scuttling the perspective of development that flows from the Gandhian ideals that we cherish. If we do not encourage the production of wage goods that our people need and, instead, allow Indian and international industrial interests to get together and give priority to the production of capital-intensive export goods that the advanced countries fancy, the masses must suffer and unemployment will mount.

Hungry Millions

A buffer stock of foodgrains is essential. However, the fact is that 17 million tonnes of grain are currently being held in reserve while millions of Indians go hungry for lack of employment and purchasing power. Some of this grain should obviously have been utilised for providing mass employment under imaginatively conceived food-for-work schemes.

Smuggling and Tax Evasion

The ruling party claims that the Emergency has enabled it to check smuggling and other economic offences. The claim is fallacious. Anti-smuggling and other measures were belatedly adopted by the Government six months before the Emergency was proclaimed in the wake of a public outcry for stern action. In fact, smugglers, back-marketeers, tax dodgers and foreign exchange racketeers were long permitted to buy immunity through contributions to the coffers of the ruling party.

Compulsory Family Planning

The Government again claims that the Emergency has been a boost to the drive for family planning. In fact, a distinct disservice has been done to this national cause by abandoning methods of persuasion and education and by invoking coercive force and compulsion. Panic and anger have culminated in resort to firing and terror. Thousands of Government employees and teachers have been denied their emoluments or other benefits for months for failure to deliver prescribed 'sterilization quotas'. In many states, ration cards and permits of various kinds are issued only to those who have undergone sterilization. Unsuspecting and ineligible persons have been herded and forcibly taken to sterilization camps. Human dignity has been set at naught by these indefensible actions. The Janta Party will institute an inquiry into allegations of excesses.

Jhuggis Demolished

The callous manner in which jhuggi colonies and pucca buildings in other areas have been razed to the ground in Delhi and elsewhere follow the same arrogant and coercive pattern. New ghettoes of the poor have been built to relocate these unfortunate people on the periphery of metropolitan centres. These are scarcely better than planned slums and have divorced large pop-

ulations from the economic activities in which they were engaged.

Rising Corruption

It is claimed by the ruling party that the Emergency has enabled it to root out corruption. The experience of the common
citizen is otherwise. The assumption of arbitrary power by the
Government and its delegation even to petty officials in the different fields of administration has led to a vast increase in corruption. Today any minion of the Government can threaten the
use of the absolute powers that he enjoys or imagines he enjoys
under the Emergency to blackmail or extort ransoms or bribes
from the poor citizen who has no means of redress. The Emergency has, in fact, exposed the common man to the extortions
of policemen, petty officers and ruling party militants. The
revenue intelligence and enforcement agencies have been grossly
misused in many instances for political and partisan ends.

Stagnant Economy

The economy has stagnated. On an average, per capita income
has grown by less than one per cent per annum. The per capita
availability of essential goods like pulses, cloth and foodgrain has
been stationary and in certain cases, has actually fallen. The
rate of net investment has not risen above the level obtaining in
the early 1960s. Current steel production is less than the target
set in the Third Plan. The current output of coal is no more
than the target for 1965-66. Foodgrain production has touched
118 million tonnes less than the Fourth Plan target. Over 68%
of the people are today below the poverty line, 28% more than a
quarter century ago.

Indices of Failure

Illiteracy, unemployment and rural pauperisation have increased. There are 11 million unemployed on the live-register
today most of whom belong to the category of the educated unemployed. Only a fraction of the unemployed register, and total

unemployment is known to be several times higher. An increasing number of industries has gone 'sick' and official policy has created a vested interest in sickness. Banking has been politicised and threatens to place the entire credit structure in jeopardy. Investment, whether public or private, has not revived. The 'final version' of the Fifth Five-Year Plan, despite increased financial outlays, constitutes a smaller plan in real terms and targets than the earlier draft Plan. With one or two exceptions, such as oil, all critical targets, whether in respect of agriculture, industry or the social services, have scaled down. The minimum needs programme, once said to be the hallmark of the Fifth Plan, has been decimated.

The record of the last decade has thus been a record of failure and stagnation, growing inequalities, continuing injustice and a widening gap between promise and fulfilment. There has been alienation, disenchantment and cynicism.

Against this background, it is easy to see that the real reasons that prompted the ruling party to invoke the emergency were the need to cover up the hollowness of its programme of "garibi hatao", mask its retreat from planning and a genuinely socialist ideology, and move towards the assumption of absolute power.

Emergence of Janata Party

It is in response to this situation—in order to defend the people's democratic rights and livelihood—that the Janata Party has come into being. It is not a mere alliance of parties but a new national party to which the Congress (O), the Bharatiya Lok Dal, the Jana Sangh, the Socialist Party, Independent Congressmen and many others stand firmly committed. This manifesto is a solemn reaffirmation of that common resolve.

The Party acknowledges with pride and humility the heroism of tens of thousands of unknown Indians, men, women and children, in every part of the country and in all walks of life, who have kept aloft the banner of freedom during the Emergency. It salutes the martyrs who have fallen or suffered in the struggle and pledges that these sacrifices shall not go in vain.

Gandhian Values

The traumatic experience of the Emergency has been a great eye-opener. We have had a taste of what happens when democracy is eclipsed. The time has come to examine whether we have not strayed from the path that we walked when we fought for Independence ; whether we have adhered to the ends and means that Gandhiji placed before us, and the values which led us to Independence and brought the masses into their own.

The Janata Party is dedicated to the values and ideals of Gandhiji. It is dedicated to the task of building up a democratic and socialist state in India, drawing inspiration from our rich heritage and the noble traditions of our struggle for independence and freedom.

Decentralisation

A high degree of centralisation or the concentration of power is inconsistent with democracy. The Party, therefore, believes in a polity that ensures decentralisation of economic and political power. This is essential for the maximisation of individual initiative and popular participation in development and administration. The fundamental freedoms of speech, association and expression, judicial independence and equality before law are absolutely essential if people are to retain democratic control over the exercise of power.

Executive, Judiciary and Satyagraha

Public workers and public servants should maintain the highest standards of probity and integrity, and set an example of simplicity and selfless service. They should conduct themselves as true servants of the people, and not as masters or rulers. Self-restraint and the rule of law are the source of social discipline. An independent judiciary is the shield of the citizen against attacks from fellow citizens, employers or the State itself. If all else fails, the ultimate guarantee of democracy and the final safeguard against exploitation and abuse of power is Satyagraha, or peaceful, non-violent resistance.

Austerity

The Party affirms the right of peaceful and democratic dissent. It believes that fundamental freedoms are not only compatible with but necessary for real economic freedom and progress, and for the elimination of exploitation. The test of progress towards socialism and democracy lies in the life of the poorest and the lowest strata of society, and the extent to which equality of opportunity becomes real, and discrimination and exploitation cease. The party, therefore, will orient its planning to three objectives and give priority to the task of raising the living standards and status of the poorest and weakest sections. It will level down as much as level up and redistribute incomes and wealth to build a just society in which austerity and sharing will replace pomp, ostentatious consumption and waste.

Devolution and Participation

Government of and by the people can have no meaning without the widest possible popular participation at all levels. The Janata Party will work for such devolution and decentralisation of power as is necessary for the attainment of these objectives. It will attempt to evolve a national consensus on the desirability of smaller districts and smaller development blocks so as to encourage democratic participation and sound ecnomic management, and micro-planning from below. Panchayat institutions and Municipalities will be revitalised and vested with larger powers and responsibility so that they may play their true role as basic organs of popular government, initiative and planning. Regular ond periodic elections to these bodies will be statutorily guaranteed.

Political Charter

As a party wedded to the ideals of freedom and democracy, it believes that fearlessness is of the essence. It will, therefore, take immediate steps to free the people from the bondage of fear. It will restore to the citizen his fundamental freedoms and to the judiciary its rightful role.

To generate fearlessness and to revive democracy, the Janata Party will :

(1) Lift the Emergency ;

(2) Restore the fundamental freedoms that have been suspended by Presidential Order ;

(3) Repeal MISA, release all political detenus, and review all other unjust laws ;

(4) Enact laws to ensure that no political or social organisation is banned without independent judicial enquiry ;

(5) Seek to rescind the 42nd Amendment ;

(6) Amend Article 352 of the Constitution to prevent its abuse in the interest of an individual or group ;

(7) Move to amend Article 356 to ensure that the power to impose President's Rule in the States is not misused to benefit the ruling party or any favoured faction within it ;

(8) Introduce electoral reforms after a careful consideration of suggestions made by various committees including the Tarkunde Committee and, in particular, consider proposals for recall of errant legislators and for reducing election costs, as well as for reducing voting age from 21 to 18 ;

(9) Repeal the amendment to the Representation of the People Act which redefines corrupt practice and places electoral offences by certain individuals beyond the scrutiny of the courts ;

(10) Re-establish the rule of law ;

(11) Restore the authority of the judiciary and safeguard the independence and integrity of the Bar ;

(12) Ensure that all individuals, including those who hold high office, are equal before law ;

(13) Assure the right to peaceful and non-violent protest ;

(14) Abolish censorship and end all harassment to newspapers, journals, publishers and printing presses ;

(15) Safeguard the freedom of the press by repealing the Prevention of Publication of Objectionable Matters Act, and restore the immunity that the Press previously enjoyed in reporting legislative proceedings ;

(16) Ensure that All-India Radio, Doordarshan and the

Films Division are converted into genuinely autonomous bodies that are politically objective and free from governmental interference ;

(17) Ensure that news agencies are completely independent of the Government and are not given the right to mono-poly ;

(18) Delete property from the list of Fundamental Rights and, instead, affirm the right to work ;

(19) Ensure that Government employees are not victimised, are freed of political pressure, and are not compelled to execute illegal orders and unlawful actions. Their right to access to Courts will be restored.

A New Economic Policy

Social justice is not an abstract concept indicating good intentions, but is a basic philosophy which must be translated into action and lead to the welfare of the masses on the princi-ple of equality and prosperity for all. There cannot be two societies, rich and poor, in which the latter category is made to subserve the goals of elitism, consumerism and urbanism. The Gandhian values of "antyodaya" and austerity must be accepted and implemented if the vicious circle of the poor becoming poorer and the rich richer is to be broken. Hence the Janata Party affirms the right to work. This can become a realisable ideal only if we move towords the establishment of an eoonomy in which agriculture and cottage and small industries have pri-macy, and are not sacrificed to the big machine and the big city. Modernisation of industry must be based on improved tech-nology. But the only way to steer clear of the evils of capitalism and state capitalism and to ensure full employment and the decentralisation of economic power is to follow the Gandhian precept that whatever can be produced efficiently by decentra-lised industry should be so produced. There is room for heavy and large-scale industry, but only where it is not possible to organise such production satisfactorily in the cottage and small scale sector. This spirit must inform the nation's economic policy.

Delete Property as Fundamental Right

The Government has time and again resorted to the plea

that fundamental rights and judicial processes have had to be curtailed in order to protect and further progressive social and economic measures and to prevent vested interests from thwarting them by resort to the courts. This is totally fallacious. Indeed, an official task force set up by the Planning Commission reported in 1974 that land reform measures had not been implemented because of a clear lack of political will.

In order to remove this specious alibi once and for all, the Janata Party will move to delete property from the fundamental rights chapter of the Constitution, leaving it as an ordinary statutory right like any other which may be enforced in a court of law. As a corollary to this, it will also delete the Ninth Schedule to the Constitution which was originally intended to protect vulnerable land legislation but which has increasingly come to be employed to entrench such repressive and unjust laws as MISA, the Prevention of Publication of Objectionable Matters Act and the recent amendment to the Representation of the People Act.

End Destitution in 10 Years

The Janata Party believes that it is possible to eliminate destitution within a decade by raising every family above the poverty line. To this end, it will base its planning and policies on the Directive Principles of the Constitution and particularly Article 41 which lays down that "The State shall within the limits of its economic capacity and development, make effective provision for securing the right to work, to education, and to public assistance in cases of unemployment, old age, sickness and disablement, and in other cases of undeserved want."

Full Employment Strategy

It will attempt to achieve this objective through appropriate economic policies that promote self-employment and provide employment, education and social services to every citizen. It regards employment as a basic instrument rather than as a distant objective of development and social justice.

The country's growing population is both the consequence

and cause of its poverty. Yet we cannot forget that our people
are our wealth. It is estimated that the country will have a
population of over 900 million by the year 2000 A.D. 125 million people will be added to the labour force in the next 25
years. These new entrants cannot be absorbed in the cities
which have already become vast camping sites for migrants from
rural areas who are being squeezed off the land and from other
traditional occupations. Cities have their place. But if rural
India cannot provide economic opportunity and creative out-
lets for the growing masses in the countryside, we will be forced
along the capital-intensive, urban-oriented and centralized path
of development followed in the West. Gandhiji warned us
against the danger and futility of attempting to borrow or trans-
plant the Western system of industrialisation without adapting
it to the conditions and requirements of our country.

New Planning Priorities

The experience of the past three decades has only underlined
the relevance and validity of the values that Gandhiji placed
before us. A quarter-century of planning under the leadership
of the ruling party has failed to provide adequately the mass of
the people with any one of the six basic necessities of life, food,
safe drinking water, clothing, housing, education, and health
care. The Janata Party will, therefore, re-orient planning goals
and priorities to adopt a pattern of development based on an
appropriate technology that answers our need to find full
employment and a better life for our people and to steer clear of
the evils of capitalist or totalitarian industrialisation. There
must be safeguards against pollution and environmental degradation and an accent on conservation and the exploitation of
renewable resources and recycling principles.

Primacy of Agriculture

In the economic sphere the Janata Party will accord primacy
to agriculture and rural reconstruction which must constitute
the base of our development and planning. The relative neglect
of the rural sector has created a dangerous imbalance in the

economy. The farmer has been consistently denied reasonable and fair prices for what he produces. Allocations for agriculture and related development have been grossly inadequate and the need for improving conditions in the villages has received scarce attention. Typically, as many as 116,000 villages do not have even the most elementary facilities for drinking water.

Rural-Urban Disparities

The paucity of farm incomes and rural employment has led to tardy capital formation in the village sector. The Janata Party will not only check growing disparities between town and country but pledges itself to initiate a comprehensive new village movement and promote rural growth centres. The farmer must get remunerative prices based on a principle of parity that balances the prices at which he sells his produce and the price he pays for the goods he buys. If the rural sector is to grow and flourish, it must be accorded favourable terms of trade as a matter of overall national policy. The farmer must be assured of inputs at reasonable prices. The agricultural sector must be provided with infrastructure facilities for extension, irrigation, land and water development, credit processing and marketing and also related technical and maintenance services.

Agrarian Reform

The party is committed to agrarian reforms covering tenurial relationships, ownership and consolidation of holdings. The party notes that owing to the tardy and insincere implementation of land ceiling legislation, the available surplus land declared, much less distributed, has been pitifully small. The party will honestly implement land legislation, provide machinery for scrutinising fraudulent transfers and dispossession and plug such loopholes as have come to light. Landlordism will be abolished. Surplus lands and other reclaimed lands will be distributed among the landless, particularly Harijans and Adivasis. They will also be provided the wherewithal effectively to cultivate their holdings. Once these reforms have been effectively implemented, the party will make sure that uncertainty about frequent changes does not affect production or create instability in the agricultural sector.

Dynamic Approach to Rural Development

Integrated rural development demands a dynamic approach. Agriculture itself must be made more productive through proper land and water conservation and utilisation, agrarian reforms, mixed farming, animal husbandry, aqua-culture, and the organization of agro and rural-based industries. Facilities should be available in the countryside for the processing of agricultural produce. Dairying has a great future based on the wealth of Indian cattle which can be upgraded. The Janata Party believes that these objectives can not be realised without an adequate increase in the allocation of funds to the agricultural sector. Rural resources, whether mobilised through banks or otherwise should be reinvested in rural development.

The Janata Party will exempt holding below 2.5 hectares from payment of land revenue. Care will be taken to see that this does not in any way impair their titles to the land by universalising the issue of passbooks to farmers. Recent increases in land revenue in some states have raised the incidence of this levy by as much as five times. These increases will be reviewed.

Traditional rural artisans like blacksmiths, carpenters, weavers, leather workers and potters constitute a vast repository of skills and potential for increased prodution and additonal employment. Recourse to modern technology and managment are necessary to improve their tools, skills and market potential and provide a wider functional range for their products.

Stress on Wage Goods

The Janata Party believes that the time has come for a fresh lcok at the pattern and perspective of industrialisation. Our twin objectives must be to produce the wage goods necessary for mass consumption and to choose a pattern of industrialisation that will provide full employment to our people. Without adequate emphasis on the production of mass consumption goods, we will not be able to hold back inflation, ensure the minimum needs of the population, and secure a base from which further development can be launched. It is mistaken to succumb to the lure of Western models.

Appropriate Technology for Swadeshi

The Janata Party wants the benefits of science and technology to reach all our people. It is not opposed to advanced technology but it firmly believes this can be harnessed to our needs only if we employ appropriate technology—simple or sophisticated—that is compatible with the environment and, while maximising employment, will yield optimum socio-economic benefits in the circumstances that prevail in our country. The Party will, therefore, review industrial and locational policies to derive the fullest advantage from the choice of appropritate technology in different sectors. Appropriate technology is a means of promoting individual and community self-reliance through a swadeshi movement.

Demarcated Areas of Production

Such an approach will prevent growth of monopolies and the concentration of economic power, increase production, reduce the problems of urban conglomerations, take industry and employment to smaller towns and rural areas, and create modern mini-industries in textile, sugar, paper, dairy, cement, pottery and other sectors. There must be a shift from capital-intensive to employment-oriented technologies which are conducive to decentralised operation on low energy systems. Such a policy will also have its implications in the field of credit and marketing. Appropriate measures will have to be taken to demarcate areas cf differential technology and to provide for statutory reservations of spheres of production for small scale and cottage industries.

The Party will see that financial and credit institutions earmark 20-25 per cent of their credit for projects and purposes designed to benefit that large segment of our population presently living below the poverty line. This must be over and above the allocation for agriculture.

End Monopoly

While economic and industrial self-reliance must remain our

goal, we must guard against the growth of monopoly and concentration of economic power. The Monopolies Commission has
been allowed to become moribund in order to benefit monopoly
capital and attract multinationals. The Janata Party will correct
this trend.

Wage and Price Policy

The Janata Party believes that economic policies should subserve the interests of workers in the agricultural and industrial
sectors. It will accordingly affirm the rights of workers and trade
unions. The Party will introduce legislation to assure minimum
wages for all categories of workers. Such minimum wages should
be sufficient for the maintenance of the worker and his family.

While it believes that the erosion in real wages caused by fluc-
tuations in price and the value of money should be neutralised
by dearness allowance the Party realises that one answer to the
difficulties experienced in this field lies in the formulation and
implementation of an equitable national wage and price policy
in which the ruling party has singularly failed. The Janata Party
will lose no time in formulating and implementing a national
wage and price policy based on the following principles :

(*i*) A fair wage must be the minimum wage ;

(*ii*) Workers must derive proportional benefits from increases in productivity ;

(*iii*) The party accepts the principle of bonus as a deferred
wage. It will safeguard the legitimate interests of the working
class with due regard to the need for increased productivity :

(*iv*) A wage and price policy must ensure that income disparities are reduced. Steps will be taken to see that minimum
incomes rise rapidly so that the difference between the minima
and maxima income, after tax, is reduced to 1:20. It will
strive progressively futher to reduce the differential to 1:10 within a decade by a policy of income redistribution that raises
floor levels and discourages bloated incomes.

(*v*) The prices of essential commodities will not be allowed
to rise beyond the capacity of the common man to pay. Therefore, as long as shortago, persist, a well-organised public distribution system is absolutely necessary, coupled with a consu-

mer movement to maintain vigilance over prices and quality.

(vi) Consistent with the Gandhian attitude to labour and industry, the Janata Party believes that workers must be trained as partners in industry. They must not only receive adequate wages and bonus, but also be enabled to participate in management and equity. To attain these objectives, representatives of the workers will be provided with opportunites for training in managerial skills and provision will be made to ensure that specific quotas of new equity will be set apart for workers.

Taxation

The burden of taxation today falls heavily on the common man because of the levy of a number of excise duties and sales tax on articles of mass consumption. The incidence of indirect taxtion on the poorer sections has increased many time since Independence. The operation of sales tax has also led to malpractices and harassment. The Janata Party considers it desirable to replace sales tax with appropriate excise duties coupled with a formula which would ensure that the states derive steadily increasing shares from the total collections, thus maintaining the element of elasticity that is today being provided by sales tax. The Party will work towards a redistributive tax policy and will strongly encourage savings. As far as direct taxation is concerned, it will raise the minimum exemption limit for income tax to Rs. 10,000.

Energy and Transport

The Janata Party attached the highest importance to the development of cheap, alternative sources of energy and mass transport facilities. It will give high priority in working out schemes for the utilisation of solar energy, wind and tidal power, biogas, and other non-conventional sources of energy, and synthesize these in a national energy policy. This is necessary to promote a decentralised and labour-intensive economy and the goal of Swadeshi.

National Water Policy

A national water policy and priorities for the use of water

with water-budgeting and water-audit are essential. The Party will establish river basin commissions for the integrated development of watersheds, to provide protection from recurrent cataclysmic floods and erosion, and to utilize fully the potential for groundwater, surface irrigation, hydro-electricity, navigation and pisciculture.

Drinking water is a basic need. The Party will formulate and execute a programme to provide every hamlet and village with an assured water supply within five to seven years.

ECONOMIC CHARTER

The Janata Party's Economic programme envisages :

1. Deletion of property as a fundamental right ;
2. Affirmation of the right to work and a full employment strategy;
3. Strees on Gandhian values of austerity, 'Antyodaya' and a decentralised economy ;
4. An end to destitution within ten years ;
5. Appropriate technology for self-reliance ;
6. New planning priorities, notably the primacy of agriculture, agrarian reforms and more favourable terms of trade and higher allocations for the rural sector ;
7. Narrowing down of rural-urban disparities and a new rural-urban nexus ;
8. Emphasis on wage goods production for mass consumption ;
9. Statutory reservation of spheres of production for small-scale and cottage industries ;
10. A wage and price policy ; raising the minimum tax exemption limit to Rs. 10,000 and exemption of land revenue on all holdings below 2.5 hectares ;
11. Redistributive taxation and excise in lieu of sales tax ;
12. Formulation of a national water policy and a national energy policy.
13. Environmental care.

Social Policy

The Party is conscious of the crucial role that social policy and social service have to play in raising living standards. It will formulate and implement a comprehensive and integrated programme of social services, particularly in the fields of education, health, housing and social insurance.

Population Planning

The Janata Party fully accepts the vital need for family planning as a means of individual and national development and well being. But it does not believe that a programme of this kind should be tarnished and brutalised by the use of force or compulsion of any kind. The coercive methods employed in the recent past constitute a gross violation of human rights and dignity and are in fact counter-productive. The Party will set up a committee to look into complaints of excesses in this regard. The Party sees family planning as an integral part of a larger population policy package, comprehending education, health, maternity and child care, family welfare and women's rights, nutrition, employment and rising living standards. To isolate family planning is foolish and futile.

New Directions in Education

The Janata Party attaches the highest importance to the development and enrichment of our vast human potential. Investment in man is a critical factor that determines the direction and degree of development. The Party will take steps to see that education up to the middle level is provided to all within the next 12 years or less. The present system of education must be reformed to allow for non-formal, multi-point entry, continuing and formal education with part-time and locally available non-professional teachers wherever necessary. The content of education must be functional and related to the lives of the people and the environment in which it is imparted. It must be related to the perspective of social needs. The concept of the dignity of labour must be inculcated through work-experience. Education must imbue the country's youth with the moral and social values and skills that we wish to develop. Opportunities must be provided for earning-while-learning at all levels. The range of scholarships must be extended for deserving students and educational grants given to families belonging to the scheduled castes and tribes.

Ending Illiteracy

The Janata Party will seek to improve the village school and make it a focal centre for development. Adults without schooling will be provided with non-formal, part-time and functional education. Illiteracy will be eradicated within five to ten years. Teacher training will be strengthened and measures taken to revise the catastrophic fall in educational standards.

Higher and technical education will be similarly restructured. The tendency hitherto has been to follow western world models involving extremely capital-intensive systems. This has resulted in unhealthy trends and in the multiplication of unemployed educated youth in urban areas on the one hand and extreme shortage of trained professional personnel in the rural areas on the other. To remove this anomaly, the Janata Party advocates short courses without sacrificing standards, improvments in the curriclum, and other corrective measures.

Languages

The Party will develop the people's languages and utilise them progressively in higher education, administration and the court. It will faithfully implement the three-language formula. The rights of linguistic minorities will be protected. Urdu and Sindhi, which are spoken by large sections, will be accorded due importance and encouragement.

Health to the Millions

The Party will devote special attention to providing health facilities to the rural areas and all vulnerable sections of the population including the urban poor. It will attempt to bring simple medical aid within the reach of every citizen by organising a cadre of medical, para-medical and community health workers, among whom trained practitioners of indigenous systems of medicine will be a part. These cadres will form a pyramid with appropriate referal, dispensary, hospital and specialised services at the higher rungs. Adequate emphasis will be placed on preventive health, provision of safe drinking water, programmes to ensure sanitation and immunisation in the rural areas and the production of inexpensive durgs and medicines. The party will attempt progressively to improve the quality of the contributory health insurance scheme and extend its coverage to all those who are in employment. The possibility of supplementing this with group health insurance schemes for rural communities will be explored.

Housing for the Poor

The present scheme of providing housing sites to the rural poor remains inadequate and has sometimes even been illusory. The Janata Party will undertake programmes of public housing and will formulate proposals to make credit easily available to genuine housing cooperatives in the rural and urban areas. It will encourage low-cost building and develop means and organisations to translate these concepts into practice. Urban policy will be designed to locate working class housing near places of work and to develop composite neighbourhoods rather than segregated areas for rich and poor.

Policy Regarding Urbanisation

The Janata Party sees urbanisation and rural development as two facets of the same coin. It will frame a national population and employment policy geared to developing a harmonious hierarchy of settlements, rising from the village and rural growth centres upwards. A new rural-urban nexus must be forged that is egalitarian and productive and not discriminatory and exploitative. The growth of megacities will be discouraged through fiscal and other measures and medium and small settlements assisted to grow as employment and service centres.

The Janata Party is for the prevention of the growth of slumcities and for the improvement of slums where they exist. Urban government will be reorganised and made efficient and more representative.

New Village Movement

The new village movement we envisage will bring new life, hope and dignity to rural India seen as viable communities of functional rural clusters with improved dwellings, clean water and modern sanitation, a congenial environment, dependable and convenient energy supplies, adequate transport and communication facilities that link it to the larger world, suitable health and educational services, access to credit and markets, culturally invigorated and no longer compartmentalised by barriers of caste and fedual distinctions based on land-ownership or occupation.

The new village will be the focus of modern farms and thriving workshops, providing gainful and varied employment for all. Privation, dirt, durdgery and dead habit will be no more. Women will emerge into their own. The money-lender and bonded labour will be things of the past. The new village will be open to science and technology. It will have live democratic institutions in its panchayats, youth clubs and mahila mandals and facilities for recreation and entertainment.

Social Security

The old, infirm, orphaned, handicapped, retired and other disabled or retarded persons have a legitimate claim on society. The Janata Party will seek to build up a comprehensive social insurance scheme covering old age and disability.

Women's Rights

Women constitute half the population of our country. No progress is possible if their problems and interests do not receive due attention. The Janata Party believes in the equality of all citizens. It will, therefore, ensure to women equal remuneration and equal opporunities in all walks of life. The education and training of women and their status in every sector of employment, including the household sector, must receive special attention. The drudgery of democratic work must be relieved and simple conveniences provided. Dowry is a social evil that must be rooted out completely. The party will give due consideration to the many valuable suggestions contained in the recently-published report on the Status of Women in India.

Children and Youth

The childern of India are its future. They have a right to health, education, recreation, employment and opportunities for cultural pursuits. The Party will formulate and implement programmes of student and youth service and will encourage physical fitness and sports. It will attempt to provide youth with increasing opportunities to assume responsibility in every sphere and sector of life. Student Unions and other democratic rights will be restored.

Minorities

The Janata Party is pledged to preserving the secular and richly diverse character of our State. It will accord the highest respect to the rights and legitimate needs of the minorities. It believes that all citizens are equal and should be treated as equals and that they should have full protection against discrimination of any kind. There are numerous complaints about discrimination against minorities in industry, trade, commerce and in the matter of employment. The Janata Party pledges itself to prevent any discrimination against the minorities religious, culture or linguistic, or against any citizens or group of citizens in the country.

Civil Rights Commission

The Party will establish a Civil Rights Commission, an independent and autonomous body, competent to ensure that the minorities, scheduled castes and tribes and other backward classes do not suffer from discrimination or inequality

New Deal for Weaker Sections

It is a matter of deep shame that even three decades after the advent of independence, the social and economic condition of the weaker sections of our society, particularly the scheduled castes and tribes, continue to be abject. They are still subject to many forms of discrimination and have been victims of foul atrocities. The average income of most of these groups is below the subsistance level. Their social and economic backwardness have made it difficult for them to take full advantage of even the limited opportunities and facilities available. This in turn affects and inhibits the avenues of employment and promotion open to them, and the acquisition of the skill necessary to take up projects for self-employment or cooperative efforts in the fields of agriculture, industry and trade.

The Janata Party believes that the disparities that separate these members of our society from the more educationally and economically advanced sections cannot be radically reduced without a policy of special treatment in their favour. It will accordingly provide preferential opportunities for education and self-employment to these sections In this connection it will reserve between 25 and 33 per cent of all appointments to government service for the backward classes, as recommended by the Kalelkar Commission. Harijans will be provided house-sites.

Ending Untouchability

The stigma of untouchability must be effaced through legal and educational measures and by social action. The carrying of head-loads for scavenging will be banned and alternative facilities provided. The Party will formulate a special programme within the framework of the five year plans for the substantial advancement of the scheduled castes and tribes and other backward classes and will provide adequate funds for the purpose. Special machinery will be set up to implement the programme and assure fulfilment of the relevant constitution guarantees.

Caste distinction must be ended.

Tribal Interests

The land and forest rights of the scheduled tribes will be safe-guarded. Forest policies should not be formulated or imple-mented at the cost of the Adivasis. Nor should forest contrac-tors be permitted to exploit these simple people. Forest village should be converted into revenue villages.

Trible cultures are part of India's varied heritage and shall be given due protection and encouragement.

Backward Areas

Special plans will be drawn up for backward and neglected regions such as the Northeast, J and K, the Himalayan belt, the desert areas and Kutch, the Sunderbans, the Malnad Tract and the Outer Islands.

Cancer of Corruption

The Janata Party will take immediate and firm steps to rid public life of the corruption that has crept into it at all levels especially after the Emergency. Unless those who hold office at the highest levels, including ministers, legislators and bureau-crats, set an example in probity and honesty, it will be impossi-ble to restore integrity in public life. The Party will, therefore, take drastic measures in this field. It will ensure that every one of its officers and cadres adheres to the highest norms of integrity. It will give effect to the recommendations of the Santhanam Committee on corruption in the administration and public life. It will also enact the long-pending Lokpal and Lokayukt Bill and will bring the Prime Minister and Chief Ministers within its purview.

The object must be to devise and establish special procedures and agencies for the automatic cognisance of complaints of corruption and misuse of authority so that allegations against persons in high places, not excluding the Prime Minister and Chief Ministers, are investigated and disposed of independently of the pleasure of the Government. The Party will enact a law requiring holders of public office to declare their assets immediately on assuming and demitting office.

People's Initiative

The Party will respect and foster the creative urges of the people and promote popular initiative. It will, accordingly, give every support to constructive voluntary action in all fields. Likewise, it will promote the arts and our tremendously rich folk culture in all regions.

Legal Reform

The Party will introduce reforms to make justice speedy and inexpensive and bring it within the reach of the poor through legal aid. It deplores the punitive transfer and supersession of judges and will take steps to review all such processes as have tended to undermine the independence and integrity of the Bench and Bar.

SOCIAL CHARTER

The Janata Party's Social Charter will comprise :
1. Education reform with middle schooling for all within 12 years ;
2. Eradication of illiteracy ;
3. Safe drinking water for all ;
4. Stress on community and preventive health, and measures towards group health insurance ;
5. A New Village movement ;
6. Low-cost building and mass public housing ;
7. A policy regarding urbanisation ;
8. A comprehensive scheme of social insurance ;
9. Family Planning as part of a large population policy package, without coercion ;
10. A new deal for the scheduled castes and tribes with special machinery to guarantee their rights and interests ;
11. A Civil Rights Commission ;
12. Automatic machinery for combating corruption ;
13. Women's rights and youth welfare ;

14. Legal aid and inexpensive justice ;
15. Fostering people's initiative and voluntary action.

Foreign Policy

The Janata Party's foreign policy will reflect the nation's enlightened interest and its aspirations and priorities at home. It will oppose all forms of colonialism, neo-colonialism and racialism. It stands for friendship for all. It is committed to genuine non-alignment free from attachment to any power bloc. It will strive for the peaceful settlement of all international disputes and will work with other Third World nations to establish a new and just international economic order.

The Party will strive to resolve such outstanding issues as remain with some of its neighbours and will consciously promote a good-neighbour policy. It stands for regional cooperation for the common good, and for global detente free of new blocs or spheres of influence and based on universal and general armament.

It will uphold Human Rights and denounce their violation wherever and whenever this might occur.

Defence

A constructive and imaginative foreign policy is a country's best defence. The Party will, however, fully maintain defence preparedness and ensure that the superior training and strategy of the armed forces is matched with the best possible weaponry and equipment, indigenously produced or procured from varied and dependable sources that will not be cut off in a crisis, with due regard to cost-effectiveness.

It will review the force levels and role of such para-military establishments as the B.S.F.

The Indian armed forces constitute a splendid pool of trained and disciplined manpower which should be not lost to the nation on early retirement. Special schemes will be sought to utilise ex-servicemen for various constructive purposes including land and water conservation programmes which call for a variety of organisational and technical skills.

Open Government in New Society

The Janata Party promises as open government in a free society and will not misuse the intelligence services and governmental authority for personal or partisan ends. It will open and sustain a dialogue with the people at all levels and on all issues. The New Society it promises is not empty rhetoric like the ruling party's socialism of and for the new political zamindars and vested interests it has created. It will build from the bottom upwards, before all else to raise the marginal man above the poverty line in consonance with the Gandhian philosophy of "Antoydaya". This calls for a new type of planning, a new approach to administration, new values, and an altogether new ethos.

Faith in the Future

The Janata Party has faith in the future of India because it has unstinted faith in the Indian people—their traditions, their values, their courage, their humanism and their dedication. The people know just how near the precipice the country has been brought by our present rulers, and for what ends.

Steeled by this experience and determined to live as free people, the Janata Party calls on every citizen to rally and fight the tyranny so that we may all, with goodwill and civility, join together in building the future : a free and just society.

Onward To Victory, Freedom, Progress

Hindu Sectarian Challenge*

K. P. Karunakaran

In the vast literature on the political developments on modern India, one finds only infrequent and inadequate references to the Hindu Mahasabha. From 1915, the year of its establishment as an all-India organisation, to 1948 when Gandhi's martyrdom at the hands of a fanatical Hindu gave it a shock from which it never recovered, the Mahasabha functioned as a political organisation with its own clearcut objectives. The fact that unlike the Muslim League—the communal organisation of the Muslims—the Hindu Mahasabha could not fulfil its objectives, does not make, a study of its political philosophy and practice, insignificant. On the other hand, such a study will throw much light on the political attitude of the people of India by drawing attention to those ideologies and theories which they rejected. Moreover, one cannot deny that the Hindu Mahasabha has given a legacy of its own to free India. The most dominant political forces in the country have, no doubt, rejected this philosophy of the Hindu Mahasabha. But some other parties have not done so. And in times of crises such as those created by the India-Pakistan war, these organizations, the appeal of which is restricted to some regions of India, are in a position to exercise a decisive influence in the political life of the country and in regard to the formulation of policies by the Government.

Before 1947, the Hindu Mahasabha was the most important

*A note on the legacy of the Hindu Mahasabha.

organisation which championed Hindu communalism. The word communalism has acquired a special meaning in India. In the sense it is understood now in India, it was first used in the nineteenth century. According to the shorter Oxford Dictionary, it meant "of or pertaining to any of the racial or religious communities, especially in India". The Dictionary of Sociology defines communalism as "a theory of government based on maximum autonomy for all local minority groups" and adds : "As commonly used in India the term refers (a) to the practice of assigning a certain number of seats in the legislatures of eleven British Provinces to each religious groups, and (b) to the struggle for power (in the form of additional seats)". Broadly speaking, one can say that communalism in India meant that philosophy which stood for the promotion of the interests of a particular religious community or the members of a particular caste.

It is interesting to recall that although the Muslim League and the Hindu Mahasabha were referred to as communal bodies by those who were opposed to them, their own votaries never accepted this description of those organizations. Both the Hindu Mahasabhites and the Muslim Leaguers claimed that they were Nationalists and they were also in agreement in holding the view that the Hindus and Muslims were two separate nations.

M. S. Aney, who was associated with the Hindu Mahasabha once observed :

> Without any fear of contradiction, the Hindus are a Nation or nationality by themselves. They have a common literature which regulate and govern their life even in minute details. They have developed a common outlook on life which is decidedly different from that of any other people...The Hindus in the North and in the South, in spite of superficial differences have common basis for their magnificent architecture, painting, music, dancing and several other fine arts. No sane man can question the proposition that the Hindus are a Nation.

A Hindu Mahasabha leader who explained the differences between the Mahasabha and the Congress in a book regretted that a leader of Babu Rajendra Prasad's standing made the assertion that there was one nation in India without citing any historical evidence. Countering Maulana Azad's claim that the language, poetry, literature, culture, art, dress, manners and customs were the common achievement of the Hindus and the Muslims, he explains the Hindu Mahasabha's stand :

> What a vicious circle of deception and hypocrisy which Congress leaders have immersed themselves in. Is it possible to deceive all peoples for all times ? Certainly not. The truth is that eleven hundred years of history of mutual conflicts have left behind a legacy of bitter memories, communal hatred and religious intolerance. Can the great Maulana afford to ignore the wide gulf between the Hindu and the Muslim cultures, the differences in physical features of the two communities, their arts, literature, and the very preliminary difference in their dress, not to speak of their customs and manners.

M.A. Jinnah, who is referred to as the architect of Pakistan, agreed with this view ; but he drew different conclusion from this process of reasoning. He often maintained that the problem in India was not of an intercommunal character, but of an international one. On 17 September 1944, he wrote to Gandhi :

> We (the Muslims) maintain the Muslims and Hindus are two major nations by any definition or test as a nation. We are a nation of a hundred million, and what is more, we are a nation with our own distinctive culture, civilization, language and literature, art and architecture, names and nomenclature, sense of values and proportion, legal laws and moral codes, customs and calendar, history and traditions, aptitudes and ambitions ; in short, we have our own distinctive outlook on life. By all the canons of international law, we are a nation.

Dr. B.R. Ambedkar, who expressed similar views, was neither a member of the Hindu Mahasabha nor a Muslim Leaguer. He was the leader of the Scheduled Caste Federation which represented some sections of Hindus who belonged to low castes. He said :

> In the religious field Hindus draw their inspirations from the Ramayana, Mahabharatha and the Geeta. The

Musalmans, on the other hand, derive their inspiration from the Quran and the Hadis. Thus, the things that divide are far more vital than the things that unite. In depending on certain common features of Hindu or Muhammedan special life, in relying upon common language, common race and common country the Hindu is mistaking what is accidental and superficial for what is essential and fundamental. The politicial and religious antagonisms divide the Hindus and Musalmans far more deeply than the so-called common things are able to blend together.

A small grogp of Muslim leaders, often referred to as the Nationalist Muslims, and leaders like Gandhi and Nehru challenged those assertions and highlighted those aspects of social and political life which bound all the people of India. Elaborating upon the unity of India, Nehru wrote :

The idea of a united and a free India gripped the people... To combat this, the British Government tried to lay stress on the religious differences and adopted a policy which encouraged them and brought them into conflict with each other. It has had a measure of success but nationalism, in India as in other countries and the East, is the dominant urge of the times and must triumph. This nationalism is being tempered today by the economic urge, but this is still further removed from the medieval outlook which thinks in terms of religious groupings in political affairs... Religious differences affect politics less and less, though sometimes they distract attention. There is no religious or cultural conflict in India. What is called the religious or communal problem is really a dispute among upper class people for the division of the spoils of office or of representation in legislature.

Gandhi, who approached the problem from an angle which is entirely different from that of Nehru, very often came to an identical conclusion. His difference in approach is evident from the fact that he did not discount the importance of religion. He declared : "India was prominently the land of religion. It was the first and last duty of an Indian to maintain it as such. They should draw their strength from the soul, from God. If they

adhered to that path, Swarajya which they were aspiring to and
working for, would become their handmaid." But by religion
Gandhi did not mean Hinduism but religion as such.   His
prayer meetings very often started with hymns from various
religions.   He attached equal sanctity to Gita, Bible and Quran.
He once observed :

> I am proud to belong to that Hinduism, which is all-
> inclusive, and which stands for tolerance... Hindustan of
> my conception is all-sufficing to me.   It certainly
> includes the Vedas, but it includes also much more. I can
> detect no inconsistency in declaring that I can. without in
> any way whatsoever impairing the dignity of Hinduism,
> pay equal homage to the best of Islam, Christianity,
> Zoroastrianism and Judaism.

On the matter of inter-relation between religion and politics,
Gandhi held the view that "Religion is a personal matter which
should have no place in politics. It is in the unnatural condition of foreign domination that we have unnatural divisions
according to religion. Foreign domination going, we should
laugh at our folly in having clung to false ideals and
slogans."

It is significant that the Nationalist Muslims as a group did
not go to the extent of Gandhi and Nehru in declaring that the
Hindu-Muslim conflicts were purely the creation of the British
Government. Addressing the Indian National Congress from
the presidential chair, M.A. Ansari put forward the view which
was shared by many others :

> The political and religious differences which are straining
> the relations between the two communities are but outward
> manifestations of a deeper conflict, not peculiar to India
> or unknown to history. It is essentially a problem of two
> different cultures, each with its own outlook on life,
> coming in close contact with one another.

A study of the political philosophy and of the Hindu
Mahasabha can be undertaken only in the background of these
various views of important individuals which very often came
into conflict and clashed with one another.   There were also
many conflicts between the various organizations they represented and led. The Indian National Congress and the Muslim

League were only the most important among them. There were many caste organizations and religious-cum-political bodies of such group of people as the Sikhs. The anti-Brahmin movement in the South and in Maharashtra acted and interacted on many political movements of India in this period. The various statements made by the spokesmen of British Government in this period on the political situation in India and the constitutional changes introduced by the Government made their impact on Indian politics. The aim of this paper is confined to examination of the political philosophy and practice of the Hindu Mahasabha. As this is done in isolation, the reader is requested to view them in the background of other important political events and constitutional developments. For reasons of brevity, they are not related here. Moreover, very competent studies on these aspects of Indian politics are available.

The Formative Phase of the Hindu Mahasabha

The Hindu Mahasabha was established in the Punjab as a provincial organization in 1907. Later it was this provincial Hindu Mahasabha of the Punjab which took the necessary steps to organize the All-India Mahasabha. The all-India organization came into being in 1915, when a conference was held at Hardwar under the presidentship of the Maharaja of Kasimbazaar. By the time some attempts were thus made to organize the Hindu Mahasabha on a national scale, the Indian National Congress had completed thirty years of its existence and the Muslim League nine years. The Congress had also many achievements to its credit. The Muslim League had also won some of its communal political demands. Thus the Hindu Mahasabha made a late start.

But the spirit of communalism was present in the thinking of a large number of Hindus much earlier. The political thought and activities of the "Extremist" leaders of the Indian National Congress like B.G. Tilak, B.C. Pal and Lajpat Rai bear the mark of Hindu revivalism. To them and to many of their followers during 1905-1912, Hindu religious scriptures were a source of inspiration and courage. According to Aurobindo Ghose, another prominent Extremist leader of this period, "Natio-

nalism is a religion that has come from God... If you are going to be a Nationalist, if you are going to assent to this religion
of Nationalism, you must do it in religious spirit". Of course,
Ghose did not say "Hindu" religion ; but many of his other
speeches and activities made it clear that he was primarily interested in making an appeal to the Hindus. On another occasion
he explicitly said : "I say no longer that nationalism is a creed
a religion, a faith ; I say that it is the Sanathana Dharma
which for us is nationalism. This Hindu nation was born with
Sanathana Dharma; with it it moves and with it it grows." Speaking on the same lines, Bipin Chandra Pal, another leader, said :
"Behind the new nationalism in India stands the old Vedan-
tism of the Hindus... The spiritual note of present nationalist
movement in India is entirely derived from this revived Vedantic
thought." Some of the political agitations in this period also
referred to India as mother goddess and extensively used other
idioms and symbols which made an appeal primarily to the
Hindus. The organization of Durga Pujas and Shivaji and Gan-
esh festivals were connected against foreign political domination
of India, but they did antagonize some Muslims and made
them feel that they were not a part and parcel of those
agitations.

Even the concept that the Hindus were a separate political
entity was not absent from the minds of the Congress leaders
in this period. For instance, Lala Lajpat Rai wrote : "As at
present situated the absence of such an organization (Hindu political or semi-political organization) places the Hindus at distinct
disadvantage, and takes away from them, the chances of a
united action or of a united expression of opinion upon matters,
which affect the unity, prosperity, the well being and generally
the interests of Hindus all over India." Lajpat Rai was a
Congressman, when he made this observation. Later, he
worked simultaneously in the Congress and the Hindu Mahasabha, Tilak was also interested in promoting Hindu solidarity.

The Indian National Congress, as an organisation, did not
accept the political philosophy of these extremist leaders. When
Gandhi became its supreme leader, he did everything possible
to promote Hindu-Muslim unity and made the Muslims feel
that they were partners in the struggle against the foreign

domination. After 1921, the Hindu communalists were out of their elements in the Congress and some of them left the organization and a few others became inactive. The Congress however, was never completely free from their influence.

In the Hindu Mahasabha they had a separate organization which was completely devoted to the promotion of Hindu interests. Since its formation in 1915 up to 1923 it did not make much impact on the political scene. The Lucknow Pact concluded between the Congress leaders and the Muslim League leaders was a heavy blow to the Hindu communalism. Much more damaging to the forces of communalism were the powerful non-cooperation and Khilafat movements launched under the guidance of Gandhi during 1919-1921. Referring to the work of Hindu Mahasabha up to 1923 one of its founder members said : "The Sabha went on holding annual general and special meetings at intervals, for the purpose of passing resolutions on subjects of general Hindu interests. But as to ameliorating and improving the conditions of all classes of Hindu community it did practically nothing."

In this period there was no clarity of thinking and no determination of purpose among the Hindu Mahasabha leaders even on such social questions as untouchability which was connected with religion. Referring to the state of affairs in this period Swami Shraddhanand wrote : "There has been a general feeling that in its early phases the Hindu Mahasabha was essentially a social and religious organization for the upliftment of the Hindu community. Contrary to this, one finds that it did practically nothing to the end." In many respects, the Hindu Mahasabha took an orthodox view. Some of its prominent members maintained that initiating the untouchables with sacred teaching of the Vedas and allowing them to dine with high caste people were against the 'shastras' and customs of Sanathana Dharma. They were also opposed to the legislation which wanted to validate inter-caste marriages. Owing to the propaganda of its leaders there was a general feeling that in its early phase the Hindu Mahasabha was essentially a social and religious organization with the objectives of uplifting the lower classes and of promoting Hindu solidarity. But neither the character of the leadership nor its social base allowed it to fulfil these functions. The

DOCUMENTS   235

leaders and the members of the Sabha belonged to the high
caste and they had vested interests in maintaining the hierachi-
cal order of the Hindu society and in preserving hereditary
priesthood and faith in the miracles.

While the Sabha, in its early phase, did not fulfil its professed social and religious objectives, it expressed its strong views on
many political questions of the day. In the first general session
of the Hindu Mahasabha a resolution was adopted protesting
against the decision to give separate representation to the Muslims in imperial councils and other legislative bodies. All kinds
of communal representation was condemned at the All-India
Conference of Hindu Mahasabha held in 1918 The resolutions
and speeches at the conference of the Hindu Mahasabha clearly
indicated that it was from the beginning a political organization.

The Search for Identity

From 1923 onwards, the Hindu Mahasabha began to emerge
as a separate entity. In 1933, when Bhai Parmanand became
the President, the Mahasabha's separation from the Congress
was complete. One can say that the period from 1923 to 1933
was the second phase of the Hindu Mahasabha—a phase in
which it was gradually trying to evolve its separate entity.

Throughout this period, however, as the most important
leaders of the Mahasabha were Congressmen like Pandit Madan
Mohan Malaviya and Lajpat Rai who were great admirers of
Mahatma Gandhi, the Hindu Mahasabha was not in a position
to develop its image as a political party with its own distinctive
programme. As the loyalty of these Hindu Mahasabha leaders
was divided, there were many contradictions and inconsistencies
in the activities of the organization.

Some of the leaders who were members of both the
Congress and the Hindu Mahasabha spoke with one accent on
the Congress platforms and with another in the Hindu
Mahasabha meetings. Addressing the annual conference of
the Hindu Mahasabha Lajpat Rai said in 1925 :

> every Muslim, man or woman, is a proselytising agent of
> Islam. The success so far gained by them is a memorable
> monument to their faith and tenacity of purpose as it is to
> our irreligion, indifference and the present sociology and
> orthodoxy of the Hindus together with the power trial,

mildness and docility of temper, and their indulgence, sentimentalism of various kinds of their own creations such as the excesses of Bhakti, Sampradaya and Ahimsa and non-violence... the chief causes to the monumental success of Islam in India, their daily work of proselyti- sation and of building their community brick by brick, was so organized and without any noise, that the hope was that if they can choose once reach the Hindus at par by assimilation of the untouchables in themselves, their aggressiveness in which they feel supreme confidence will stand them a push to the mild Hindu as to send him down headlong along the inclined plane of estimation. Thus they were dreaming of absorbing the whole of Hindu India into themselves so that the whole of Hindustan may ultimately belong to them.

With this understanding of the social and political situation in India, it is not surprising that Lajpat Rai laid down the following as the objectives of the All India Hindu Mahasabha throughout the length and breadth of the country.

To provide relief to such Hindus, men and women, who need help in times of communal riots and disturbances. Re-conversion of Hindus who have been forcibly converted to Islam. To organize gymnasiums for the use of Hindu young men and women. To organize Seva samithis... To represent communal interests of the Hindus in all political controversies.

These programmes were placed before the Hindu Mahasabha in a period when the Indian National Congress, under Gandhi's leadership, was engaged in promoting Hindu-Muslim unity and concentrated on the political struggle of the Indian people as a whole from the British domination.

In 1925 the Mahasabha appointed a committee under Lajpat Rai to "ascertain and formulate Hindu opinion on the subject of Hindu-Muslim problem in relation to the question of further constitutional reforms. The aim was to give a distinct political orientation to the activities of the Mahasabha. Bhai Parmanand, who was gradually emerging as an important leader of the organization, began to express the view that Congressmen who were members of the Mahasabha were incapable of defending and promoting Hindu interests. He wanted the Mahasabha to send its own representatives to the various legislatures. But leaders like Lajpat Rai were not prepared for a complete break with the Congress. Finally, a compromise was arrived at. According to it, the Hindu Mahasabha was to oppose those candidates of the Congress who were considered to be hostile to the Hindus and support others. The group led by Bhai Permanand felt that this compromise was a victory for Lajpat Rai. So the struggle between the two groups continued.

In 1928, Lajpat Rai and Malaviya supported the steps taken by Gandhi and other Congress leaders to promote Hindu-Muslim unity. They supported the "All Parties Unity Conference" of the same year. These leaders also shared the anti-imperialist sentiments of the Congress leadership, and inspired by them, the Hindu Mahasabha resolved to boycott the Simon Commission. But Bhai Permanand defied this resolution and announced that he and the Punjab Hindu Mahasabha would co-operate with the Simon Commission. This was not only a step against the Congress, which was seeking Hindu-Muslim unity, but one towards co-operating with the Imperial Power in India against which the Congress was fighting. Within the Mahasabha the followers of Bhai Parmanand became increasingly influential and this led to the resignation of Congress leaders like Lajpat Rai and Malaviya from the Hindu Mahasabha. Bhai Parmanand and his followers maintained that those who left the Mahasabha were 'deserters'. These developments virtually terminated the indirect control the Congress leaders exercised over the Mahasabha. The break between the two parties and the Hindu Mahasabha's assertion of its independence was complete when Bhai Parmanand was elected President of the organization.

The Hindu Mahasabha did not have many achievements to its credit in this period. Apart from making an attempt to establish its identity as a separate organization, the Mahasabha was engaged in conducting a campaign against the introduction of separate electorates. But it failed miserably and separate electorates were introduced by the Government. And the Mahasabha never boycotted the elections on this ground. That

many of their candidates were defeated in the various elections
held in this period is entirely another matter. It only indicates
that when the politically conscious people in India under the
leadership of Gandhi and the Congress, were in an anti-imperialist mood, the spokesmen of a party, which was prepared to co-
operate with the British Government could not get much popular
support.

Other activities of the Hindu Mahasabha in this period were
connected with the *Sanghathan* and *Shuddhi.* The word
Sanghathan meant organization. The Sabha leaders used it to
express their desire to promote solidarity among the Hindus
and to consolidate all the Hindus under one flag.

A prominent leader of the Hindu Mahasabha explained the
meaning of the word, *Shudddi* in the following words : "The
word 'Shuddhi' is understood still by many people to mean a
movement for conversion to Hinduism of any of those who were
once Hindus but were subsequently converted to another faith.
It implies the readmission to the Hindu fold, also of those who
were never originally Hindus, but seek for the first time into that
fold". In actual practice, however, the *Shuddhi* movement was
aimed at those Hindus who were converted to Islam. Commenting
on the significance of the *Shuddhi* movement, V.D. Savarkar
observed : "In a country like India where a religious unit
tends invariably to grow into a cultural and national unity,
Shuddhi movement ceases to be merely theological or dogmatic
one but assumes the wider significance of a political movement."

The Shuddhi, however, received a setback following the
murder of Swami Shraddhanand in 1926.

A New Philosophy and a New Ideology

The year 1933 is a turning point in the history of the Hindu
Mahasabha. Under the leadership of Bhai Parmanand, who
was elected President in that year, the Mahasabha deplored the
action of the Congress party in the legislative assembly in not
voting against the resolution accepting the Communal Award.

V.D. Savarkar became the President of the Hindu Mahasabha in 1937. He continued to occupy that important position
in the organization continuously for many years. Unlike most
other leaders of the organization, Savarkar had a great reputation as a patriot who was prepared to take any risks and make

any sacrifice for the freedom of the country. He was once sentenced to imprisonment for fiftyfour years for having waged war against His Majesty's Government. He was sent to Andamans where he remained for fourteen years. Later, he was brought to India and interned in this country for another fourteen years. He was released only on 10 May 1937. In V.D. Savarkar the Hindu Mahasabha, for the first time, had an aggressive and dynamic leader. He was accredited to be the author of new philosophy and new ideology of Hindu Mahasabha. Very soon it became obvious that in his capacity as the leader of the Hindu Mahasabha Savarkar's dynamism and energy could be directed only against the Muslims and the Congress Party and not against the foreign rulers of the country. In many of his utterances he urged a total boycott of the Congress by the Hindus and called for the formation of a Hindu National Front. Addressing the twenty-first session of the Hindu Mahasabha held at Calcutta in 1939, he explained the meaning of the term "Hindu" in the following words :

> Every person is a Hindu who regards this Bharat Bhumi, this land from the Indus to the Seas, as his Fatherland and Holyland—i.e. the land of the origin of his religion— the cradle of his faith. The followers, therefore, of Vedicism, Sanatanism, Jainism, Buddhism, Lingaitism, Sikhism, the Arya Samaj, the Brahmo Samaj, the Dev Samaj, the Prarthana Samaj and such other religions of Indian origin are Hindus and constitute Hindu people as a whole.

It is significant that the list excludes Christians and Muslims and may of his other utterances make it clear that he considered the Muslims to be aliens. Under his leadership the Mahasabha gave slogans : "Hinduize all politics and militarize Hinduism". The Sabha urged the Government to throw open the armed forces of the country to the Hindus and to impart military training in all educational institutions so that a Hindu National Militia could be raised.

V.D. Savarkar was the first and perhaps the only theoretician of Hindu Mahasabha. Developing a new ideology and giving a new meaning to such words as "Hinduism", "Hindutva" and "Hindudom" he observed :

In expounding the ideology of the Hindu movement, it is absolutely necessary to have a correct grasp of the meaning attached to these three terms. From the word 'Hindu' has been coined the word 'Hinduism' in English. It means the school or system of religions the Hindus follow. The second word 'Hindutva' is far more comprehensive and refers not only to the religious aspect of the Hindu people as the word 'Hinduism' does but comprehends even their cultural, linguistic, social and political aspects as well. It is more or less akin to 'Hindu polity' and its nearly exact translation would be Hinduness. The third word 'Hindudom' means the Hindu people spoken of collectively. It is a collective name for the Hindu world just as Islam denotes the Muslim world or Christendom the Christian world.

V.D. Savarkar continuously attacked Congress ideology which according to him was initiated by the wrong assumptions that the territorial unity was the only factor that constituted a Nation. He maintained that only those nations had persisted in maintaining their National unity which has developed racial, linguistic, cultural and such other organic affinities in addition to their territorial unity. According to him the military defeat of Poland and Czechoslovakia at the beginning of the Second World War, was a stern warning against any efforts "to frame heterogeneous peoples into such hotch-potch Nations, based only on the shifting sands of the conception of Territorial Nationality, not cemented by any cultural, racial or historical affinities. The Hindu Mahasabha leader believed that the Hindus have these common affinities. He declared : "We, Hindus, in spite of thousand and one differences within our fold are bound by such religious, cultural, historical, racial, linguistic and other affinities in common as to stand out as a definitely homogeneous people as soon as we are placed in contrast with any other non-Hindu people-say the English or Japanese or even the Indian Muslims." He ridiculed those who contended that the Indian Muslims would identify themselves with the rest of the people of India and merge into one Indian nation. He said :

Some well-meaning but simple-minded Hindus assure themselves with the thought and hope against hope that in

as much as the majority of Indian Muslims also are in fact
allied to us by race and language and in case had not gone
over to the Muslim world in living memory of this very
generation, they could easily be persuaded to acknowledge
this homogeneity and even blood relation with the Hindus
and merge themselves into a common National being if
but we only remind them of these affinities and appeal to
them in thier name.   These innocent souls are really to be
pitied as if the Muslims do not know it all.   The fact is
that the Muslims know of these affinities all but too well :
the only difference to be taken into account being that
while the Hindus love these affinities which bind a Hindu
to a Hindu and to dwell on them with pride, the Muslims
hate the very mention of them and are trying to eradicate
the very memory to it all...Their religious and theoretic
traditions join hands in impressing upon their minds that
Hindustan is not and cannot be a Dar-ul-Islam, their
country which they may love until and unless the
Hindus—the Kafirs—are either converted to a man to
Islam or are reduced to helotage paying the Zisia to some
would be Muslim sovereignty over the land.

The post-war events showed that Savarkar's comments on
Poland and Czechoslovakia were completely off the mark ; but
events leading to the partition of India and those following it
pointed out to the strength of Savarkar's argument relating to
the political attitude of a large number of Muslims in the country. Of course, he was not prepared to accept the fact that the
Hindus were partly to be blamed for this attitude of Muslims.

These and many other speeches of the Hindu Mahasabha
leaders explain the new ideology of the organization. The
constitution of the Mahasabha, which was accepted by its annual session in 1938, stated :

The aim of the Hindu Mahasabha is the protection and
promotion of all that contributes to the advancement, strength and glory of the Hindu Rashtra—Hindu race, Hindu
culture and Hindu polity—and as a means to that end, the
attainment of Poorna Swaraj—that is absolute political independence for Hindus by all proper and legitimate means.
The objects of the Hindu Mahasabha are : (a) to organise

and consolidate all sections of Hindu society into one
organic whole; (b) to protect and promote Hindu interests
whenever and wherever necessary; (c) to remove untouchability and generally to ameliorate and improve the condition of the so called depressed classes among the Hindus ;
(d) to revive and promote the glorious ideals of Hindu wo-
manhood ; (e) to promote cow-protection ; (f) to improve
the physique of the Hindus and promote martial spirit
amongst them by establishing military schools and organizing volunteer corps ; (g) to reclaim all those who have left
the Hindu fold and welcome others into the Hindu fold.
These aims and objectives make the Hindu Mahasabha
clearly a communal organization. The fact that the Hindus, were
whose interests they wanted to champion, unlike the Muslims,
not a minority but the majority community in India, does not
make the organization less communal than Muslim League
and other political bodies which were the champions of the
minorities.

No New Programme

The aggressive and dynamic nature of the idology of the
Hindu Mahasabha was not reflected in the political programme
of the Mahasabha and the political activities of its members. The
programme was negative in character. It was directed against
Muslim League and the Indian National Congress, which, in the
opinion of the Sabha leaders, was appeasing the Muslim communalists. The Hindu Mahasabha and its spokesmen also criti-
cised British Government's action in providing communa
representation in the legislature and the services. Many other
steps taken by the Government to satisfy demands of the Muslim League were targets of the attack of the Sabha leaders. But
the Hindu Mahasabha as an organization and its members as
individuals did not lead any militant campaign against the authorities. They were not prepared to defy the government and
pay the price for any such defiance. In the native states of
India in which the princes were Hindus, they even glorified the
ruler and their autocratic administration. The following resolution passed at the Nagpur session of the Hindu Mahasabha

.reflected the view of the peoples of the native states for their political rights.

The Hindu Mahasabha declares that the Congress policy of coercion and interference in the internal administration of the Indian states, under the plausible slogans of responsible government, is not genuine, in as much as the Congress activities in the matter are restricted to and concentrated only in the Hindu states to the practical exclusion of the Muslim states.

On this matter, V.D. Savarkar declared :

That the campaign of the Congress in the Hindu states is anti-Hindu and mischievous. In view of this policy, the Mahasabha cannot be a party to the campaign which the Congress seeks to launch against the Hindu states alone on flimsy grounds and deprecates it as opportune, anti-Hindu and mischievous in as much as it deliberately overlooks the maladministration and the atrocious persecution to which the Hindus are subjected in Muslim states and dare not raise a finger against them. Referring to the Hindu princes, Bhai Parmanand said that the princes are the flesh of our flesh and the most essential part of our body politic.

Because the ruler of Hyderabad was a Muslim, the Hindu Mahasabha conducted a civil disobedience campaign against him. But lacking the spiritual stamina of the Congressmen and Mahatma Gandhi, who were prepared to makes sacrifices for a cause, the Sabha leaders inside Hyderabad and outside could not sustain a powerful movement against the repressive measures of the Nizam.

Although the political system in British India was, in many respects, more advanced than that of Nepal, the Mahasabha leaders were looking to the monarch of Nepal, who was heading an autocratic system for leadership. The book *Hindu Rashtra Darshan* notes : "Last year (1925) the proposal to offer Presidential chair of the Mahasabha to His Majesty, the King of Nepal, or to His Excellency the Prime Minister, was deliberately put forward from the Chair and was unanimously adopted at the special session of the Mahasabha at Belgaum." The lack of civil and political liberties and the absence of an efficient and incorruptible administration in the native states and in Nepal did not worry these Hindu leaders because they were satisfied with the fact that the rulers were Hindus.

One of the specific issues on which the Mahasabha took a stand was the national language. Its leaders stated that Sanskritized Hindi, with Devanagari script, should be the national language of India. Giving expression to this view, Savarkar observed during his presidential address to the Hindu Mahasabha in 1939 :

> The Sanskrit shall be our... sacred language and the 'Sanskrit Nisht' Hindi, the Hindi which is derived from Sanskrit and draws its nourishment from the latter, is our... our current National language... Besides being the richest and the most cultured of the ancient languages of the world, to us Hindus the Sanskrit is the holiest tongue of tongues.

Like so many Hindus of North Western India, many members of the Mahasabha did not know Hindi very well. But they supported the introduction of Sanskritized Hindi. Lajpat Rai was a typical case. He explained his position :

> The Hindi-Urdu controversy taught me my first lesson in Hindi nationalism. My mind took a turn at this time and there was no turning back thereafter. Early training and parental teachings should have enlisted my support on the side of Urdu ; that way lay personal gain to me, for I had spent years in the study of Persian and was fairly well acquainted with Urdu literature, whilst of Hindi I did not know even the alphabet. But as I became convinced that political solidarity demanded the spread of Hindi and Devanagari, I brushed aside all personal considerations and started propaganda for Hindi...

The Hindu Mahasabha leaders also maintained that the legislature of the country could be supreme and sovereign, and the Muslim members of legislative assemblies should not be allowed to veto legislations even when they are exclusively related to the personal laws of the Muslims.

The Mahasabha stood for joint electorates with no reservation of seats to any community. On the matter of communal representation, the eighth session of the Mahasabha held in

Calcutta in 1925, stated ;

> As it is essential to have one nation for peace and happiness and for the establishment and maintenance of Swarajya in the country ; and also as the opinion of the committee appointed at the special session of Belgaum to ascertain and formulate Hindu opinion on the subject of Hindu-Muslim problem is that communal representation in regard to national institutions and the services has been harmful and detrimental to create a united nation, Hindu Mahasabha strongly protests against the introduction of such a system ; also Mahasabha appeals to its non-Hindu brothers to give up such anti-national demands and help the Hindus in establishing a national solidarity and oneness.

It was against the federal system of government. According to the Hindu Mahasabha leaders, India needed a strong central power. While rejecting the Cabinet Mission's proposals of 1946, Ashutosh Lahiri, the General Secretary of the Hindu Mahasabha. said : "If the proposal is given effect to in its letter and spirit India will ultimately be broken to pieces."

Decline as a Political Force

These and other ideas of the Hindu Mahasabha and the political views of many of its leaders received considerable publicity in India. But as a political force it gradually declined. The elections to various legislative assemblies and local bodies exposed its weakness and owing to this declining influence of Hindu Mahasabha, as a political force, it is not surprising that during the final stages no negotiations between the British Government and the Indian leaders on the matter of the transfer of power and the partition of the country of Hindu Mahasabha was nowhere in the picture. Gandhi once said that there were two parties in India—the British Government and the Indian National Congress. Jinnah questioned the validity of the assertion of Gandhi and said that there was the Muslim League, The political events of India during 1936-1946 proved that Jinnah's claim was justified. Neither the British Government nor the Congress Party could ignore the League during this period. The correspondence between Gandhi and Nehru on the one hand

and Jinnah on the other and the various meetings Gandhi had
with the Muslim League leaders showed the anxiety of the Congress leaders to come to an agreement with League. Contrasted
with this was their attitude towards the Mahasabha. They
ignored it completely. The British Government also refused
to consider the Hindu Mahasabha as a political organization
which had some representative character.

What were the reasons of the failure of the Hindu
Mahasabha as a political organization ? There were many. One
of the most important was the fact that the Hindus were an
overwhelming majority in India. Unlike the Muslim masses,
their interests were not threatened in a political set-up where the
rule of the majority would prevail.

In some countries, some minorities like the Jews were a
privileged class. The majority were exclusive and were exploit-
ing the minority. In India the Muslims, who were in the
minority, were by no means the privileged class and the
Hindus, as a rule, did not feel that they were economically or in
any other manner exploited by the Muslims. There was nothing
defensive in Hindu communalism and its champions had no
social or economic base. Jawaharlal Nehru's following comment on the Mahasabha was substantially correct :

> Under cover of seeming nationalism the Mahasabha not
> only hides the rankest and narrowest communalism but
> also desires to preserve the vested interest of a group of
> big Hindu landlords and the princes. The policy of the
> Mahasabha as declared by its responsible leaders is one
> of co-operation with the foreign government so that their
> fawning to it and abasing themselves before it might
> result in a few crumbs coming in their way. This is
> betrayal of the freedom struggle, denial of every vestige of
> nationalism and suppression of every manly instinct in the
> Hindus. The Mahasabha showed its attachment to vested
> interests by openly condemning every form of socialism
> and social change.

This was another reason for their failure to become a mass
organization. Of course, some other communal organizations
did co-operate with the British Government and opposed the
freedom struggle led by the Congress. But none of them

opposed the movements for social change because they were representing the under-privileged sections of the people. Even in independent India, the Mahasabha opposed the introduction of such a legislation as the Hindu Code Bill which aimed at reorganising Hindu society on modern lines and provided for raising the status of women and making them equal to men as far as rights of property were concerned.

It is not surprising that few members of the low castes joined the members and none of them rose to the position of prominent leaders of the party. The Mahasabha represented the interests of those sections of the high caste Hindus who wanted the preservation of the *status quo*.

Even in the matter of support to the British Government and co-operating with it, there was a vast difference between the attitude of the Mahasabha and other communal organizations like the Muslim League. Neither the Scheduled Caste Federation nor the Muslim League gave the impression that they were prepared to work in accordance with the wishes of the British Government or that they were afraid of the struggle. As Gandhi's secretary notes :

> The anti-British slogan was still kept up by the Muslim League. Otherwise it would have lost standing with the Muslim masses. But care was taken not to get 'embroiled' with the British Power. The latter could very well afford to pay that price. The more strength the Muslim League could muster the more efficiently could it be used as a counterpoise to the Congress demand for independence. For all that there was not any love lost between the British Government and the League and neither fully trusted the other. Both understood it was a marriage of convenience.

The tragedy of the Hindu Mahasabha was that, while it was seeking the favours of the British authorities, it had nothing to offer to the Government. At least that was how the Government felt.

Nehru once observed : "The leaders of the Mahasabha mus realise that the inevitable consequence of this policy of their lining up with the enemies of Indian freedom and most reactionary elements in this country is for the rest of India, Hindu and non-Hindu, to face them squarely and oppose them and treat them as enemies of freedom and all we are striving for."

The majority of the politically conscious Hindus of India did treat the Hindu Mahasabha as the enemies of Indian freedom and social change. Their most important leader was Gandhi who led a militant, though non-violent, struggle for freedom. He used idioms and symbols which made a profound appeal to the Hindus. While opposing and criticizing Gandhi and his political methods, the Hindu Mahasabha was not having an encounter with a Westernised leader who was mechanically applying Western political concepts to the Indian situation. Gandhi knew the minds of the Hindus more than any leader India produced in this century. In the realm of thought and philosophy Hinduism preached highest level of tolerance and accepted the view that all religions are sacred. But the social behaviour of a large number of Hindus was based on many narrow and exclusive institutions like caste system, which, according to man orthodox Hindus, had a sanction in religion. Religious reformers like Vivekananda and political leaders like Gandhi inherited the best elements of Hindu religious thought and enriched it with their own contributions. The Hindu communalists did not fulfil this function. As many of them were orthodox people belonging to the highest castes, they could not also completely get away from the influence of traditional social institutions like caste. The impact of the west and the political and administrative institutions the British established in this country and the slow, but unquestionable, economic transformation the country was experiencing were undermining the foundations of such social institutions as the caste system. The Mahasabha leaders were clinging to such matters as the protection of cows and were hoping to derive strength from such institutions as the princely order without comprehending the rapid changes India was experiencing. In a struggle between the Congress, led by Gandhi, and the Mahasabha, which was led by the orthodox Hindus, for the capture of the position of the most importan political party, the defeat of Mahasabha was, therefore, inevitable.

In some parts of the country like the Punjab and Bengal, where Muslims were a majority, the Hindu Mahasabha had some vitality, because it was championing the cause of the minority and was resisting the real or alleged oppression of the majority community. In the Maharashtra area of the Bombay Presidency and the Central Provinces also, the Hindu Mahasabha could take some roots because, for historical reasons, the politics of these parts of India were coloured by Hindu revivalism and some antagonism between the Hindus and the Muslims. But in other parts of India, the Mahasabha made practically no mark. Even in these states, when politics was dominated by the anti-imperialist mood of the people consequent on the political campaign led by Gandhi, the Mahasabha retreated completely into the background.

However, one must not ignore the Mahasabha completely. As a lobbying force in favour of Hindu communalism and as a counterweight against Muslim communalism, the Mahasabha was effective in a limited manner on some occasions. Moreover, the ideas that the Mahasabha leaders spread during the nineteen-thirties and nineteen-forties continued to influence the political thinking of a significant section of the people of India even after 1947 when the Mahasabha declined as a political force almost to the extent of being a non-existent one.

In Independent India

As India's achievement of freedom in 1947 was accompanied by the partition of the country and Hindu-Muslim riots on a large scale, the climate was favourable to the strengthening of Hindu communalism. The difficulties the Government faced in suppressing the riots in north-Western and north-eastern parts of the country showed that at least in regard to the riots and the attack on the Muslims and looting their properties the Hindu communal forces were capable of displaying some strength. But the riots were the work of a well-organized minority who had, no doubt, in the abnormal conditions then prevailing in India, the passive support of a large number of other people. This passive support was withdrawn when normal conditions returned. When Gandhi was assassinated by a fanatical Hindu in 1948 the conditions became abnormal again—but, this time in reverse. In many parts of India, the Hindu Mahasabha leaders and offices were attacked with the assassination of Gandhi. Some leaders of Mahasabha like Dr. Khare were detained by the Government. After investigation the Government could not find any clear evidence of direct paricipation of the Mahasabha in the murder of Gandhi and the leaders were released. But Mahasabha became so unpopular in the country that, under S.P, Mookerji's leadership, it resolved to suspend political activity. In November 1949, Mookerji resigned from the Mahasabha working committee and in Decembar the Mahasabha voted to resume its political activity. The 1951-52 general elections—the first elections held in free India—again exposed Mahasabha's lack of popular support. It won only twenty seats in the state assemblies and only four seats for the parliament. But the legacy of the Mahasabha expressed itself through other organisations and the Hindu sectarian challenge it posed to the Indian democracy was once significant

Index